LIBRARY OF HEBREW BIBLE/ OLD TESTAMENT STUDIES

419

Formerly Journal for the Study of the Old Testament Supplement Series

To Church of the Nations

Linguistic Evidence for the Pre-exilic Date of the Yahwistic Source

Richard M. Wright

T & T CLARK INTERNATIONAL
A Continuum imprint
LONDON • NEW YORK

Copyright © Richard M. Wright, 2005
A Continuum imprint

Published by T&T Clark International
The Tower Building, 11 York Road, London SE1 7NX
15 East 26th Street, Suite 1703, New York, NY 10010

www.tandtclark.com

British Library Cataloguing-in-Publication Data
A catalogue record for this book is available from the British Library

ISBN 0 567 04121 2   (hardback)

Typeset by Data Standards Ltd, Frome, Somerset, BA11 1RE
Printed on acid-free paper in Great Britain
by Antony Rowe Ltd, Chippenham, Wiltshire

CONTENTS

ACKNOWLEDGEMENTS

I first express my gratitude to those persons and institutions who helped make possible the research and writing of the doctoral dissertation which this volume presents in published form: Cornell University's Graduate School, Department of Near Eastern Studies, and Freshmen Writing Program; the members of my doctoral committee which includes Profs. Gary Rendsburg, David Owen, and Martin Bernal; other faculty and staff including Profs. Ross Brann, Leslie Pierce, David Powers, Dr Munther Younes, and Mrs Phyllis Emdee.

I also express my deep appreciation to individuals and communities who encouraged and supported my doctoral studies both while I was at Cornell University and later when I was also pursuing a seminary education in Richmond, Virginia: Ithaca Baptist Church, Ithaca, New York; East Highland Park Baptist Church, Richmond, Virginia; Pope's Creek Baptist Church, Montross, Virginia; the Department of Health, Recreation, and Physical Education at Virginia Commonwealth University; the Baptist Theological Seminary at Richmond; and Union Theological Seminary, Richmond, Virginia.

I am also grateful to those who have encouraged me to maintain my involvement in biblical scholarship despite the often stressful demands of vocational ministry: Drs Samuel Balentine, William Brown, B. Keith Putt, Daniel Holcomb, John Pizer and Carey Froelich; Rev. Jeff Day; my ministerial colleagues at University Baptist Church, Baton Rouge, Louisiana; and perhaps most of all my friend Prof. Christian Brady, Tulane University, New Orleans, Louisiana. This volume is dedicated to Church of the Nations, Baton Rouge, Louisiana of which it has been my blessing and privilege to serve as pastor these past five years. It is a Christian community for all nations, languages, cultures, and traditions in which the eschatological vision of Revelation 7.9 breaks through imperfectly but powerfully into the present. And challenges understandings of the Christian movement that at times are too small, too parochial, and too bourgeois. "Then is now".

Others have provided invaluable help in obtaining some of the resources necessary for this volume and the doctoral dissertation upon which it is based: Prof. Ian Young; the reference librarians and interlibrary loan staff at Olin Library, Cornell University; Merton

Library, Union Theological Seminary, Richmond, Virginia; and New Orleans Baptist Theological Seminary, New Orleans, Louisiana.

My deep love and appreciation I express to my immediate and extended families for their support and encouragement. I am most grateful for the patient support of my wife Armetta and my daughters Mary Keziah and Anna McKay. I thank my God every time I think of them (Ephesians 1.3).

ABBREVIATIONS

Bibliographical

AB	Anchor Bible
ABD	David Noel Freedman (ed.), *The Anchor Bible Dictionary* (New York: Doubleday, 1992)
AnOr	Analectia Orientalia
AOS	American Oriental Series
ATANT	Abhandlungen zur Theologie des Alten und Neuen Testaments
BA	*Biblical Archeologist*
BASOR	*Bulletin of the American Schools of Oriental Research*
BDB	Francis Brown, S.R. Driver and Charles A. Briggs, *A Hebrew and English Lexicon of the Old Testament* (Oxford: Clarendon Press, 1907)
BHS	*Biblia Hebraica Stuttgartensia*
BibOr	Biblica et orientalia
BKAT	Biblische Kommentar: Altes Testament
BSO(A)S	*Bulletin of the School of Oriental (and African) Studies*
BWANT	Beiträge zur Wissenschaft vom Alten und Neuen Testament
BZAW	Beihefte zur *ZAW*
CAD	Ignance I. Gelb *et al.* (eds.), *The Assyrian Dictionary of the Oriental Institute of the University of Chicago* (Chicago: Oriental Institute, 1964)
CBQ	*Catholic Biblical Quarterly*
CBQMS	*Catholic Biblical Quarterly*, Monograph Series
DISO	Charles-F. Jean and Jacob Hoftijzer (eds.), *Dictionnaire des inscriptions sémitiques de l'ouest* (Leiden: E.J. Brill, 1965)
DJD	Discoveries in the Judean Desert
EncJud	*Encyclopaedia Judaica*
GKB	Gesenius, Wilhelm, E. Kautzsch and Gotthelf Bergsträsser, *Hebräische Grammatik* (Hildesheim: G. Olms, 28th edn, 1962)
GKC	*Genenius' Hebrew Grammar* (ed. E. Kautzsch, revised and trans. A.E. Cowley; Oxford: Clarendon Press, 1910)
HALAT	Ludwig Koehler *et al.* (eds.), *Hebräisches und ara-*

	mäisches Lexikon zum Alten Testament (5 vols.; Leiden: E.J. Brill, 1967–1995)
HAR	*Hebrew Annual Review*
HDHL	*Historical Dictionary of the Hebrew Language*
HDSS	Elisha Qimron *The Hebrew of the Dead Sea Scrolls* (HSS; Atlanta, GA: Scholars Press, 1986)
HSM	Harvard Semitic Monographs
HTR	*Harvard Theological Review*
HUCA	*Hebrew Union College Annual*
ICC	International Critical Commentary
IEJ	*Israel Exploration Journal*
Int	*Interpretation*
JANESCU	*Journal of the Ancient Near Eastern Society of Columbia University*
JAOS	*Journal of the American Oriental Society*
JBL	*Journal of Biblical Literature*
JCS	*Journal of Cuneiform Studies*
JETS	*Journal of the Evangelical Theological Society*
JNSL	*Journal of Northwest Semitic Languages*
JQR	*Jewish Quarterly Review*
JSOT	*Journal for the Study of the Old Testament*
JSOTSup	*Journal for the Study of the Old Testament*, Supplement Series
JSS	*Journal of Semitic Studies*
KAI	H. Donner and W. Röllig, *Kanaanäische und aramäische Inschriften* (3 vols., Wiesbaden: Harrassowitz, 1962–1964)
KB	Ludwig Koehler and Walter Baumgartner (eds.), *Lexicon in Veteris Testamenti libros* (Leiden: E.J. Brill, 1953)
Leš	*Lešonénu*
NICOT	New International Commentary on the Old Testament
OTL	Old Testament Library
RB	*Revue Biblique*
RTP	*Revue de théologie et de philosophie*
SBL	Society of Biblical Literature
SBLDS	SBL Dissertation Series
SBLMS	SBL Monograph Series
SBLSBS	SBL Sources for Biblical Study
SBLSP	SBL Seminar Papers
SJOT	*Scandinavian Journal of the Old Testament*
ThWAT	G.J. Botterweck and H. Ringgren (eds.), *Theologisches Wörterbuch zum Alten Testament* (Stuttgart: W. Kohlhammer, 1970–)

UT	Cyrus H. Gordon, *Ugaritic Textbook* (Analecta orientalia, 38; Rome: Pontifical Biblical Institute Press, 1965)
VT	*Vetus Testamentum*
VTSup	*Vetus Testamentum*, Supplements
WTJ	*Westminster Theological Journal*
ZAW	*Zeitschrift für die alttestamentliche Wissenschaft*

Other

11QT	Temple Scroll (11Q 19–20)
ABH	Archaic Biblical Hebrew
AH	Amoraic Hebrew
BA	Biblical Aramaic
CD	Damascus Covenant
DH	Deuteronomistic History
GN	geographic name
IH	Israelian Hebrew
K	Ketib
LBH	Late Biblical Hebrew
LXX	Septuagint
M.	Mishnah
MH	Mishnaic Hebrew
MT	Masoretic Text
Q	Qere
QH	Qumran Hebrew
SBH	Standard Biblical Hebrew
T.	Tosefta
Tg.	Targum
Tg. Onq.	Targum Onqelos
Tg. Yer. I	Targum Yerushalmi I (= Targum Pseudo-Jonathan)

Chapter 1

INTRODUCTION

In the historical-critical analysis of the Hebrew Bible, the so-called 'Yahwist' source (commonly abbreviated 'J') usually is regarded as the oldest of the four major sources of the Pentateuch.[1] During the early years of critical research on the Pentateuch, the so-called 'Priestly' source (commonly abbreviated 'P'), not 'J', was regarded as the oldest, until K. Graf and A. Keunen postulated that 'P' was in fact the latest source of the Pentateuch.[2] J. Wellhausen employed this discovery in his reconstruction of the history of the Pentateuch, in which he argued that 'J' is the earliest major source of the Pentateuch.[3] His schema of the sources, traditionally JEDP, was subsequently adopted by the vast majority of biblical scholars.[4] Wellhausen however did not attempt to date 'J' precisely, choosing only to attribute it to Israel's monarchic period. Wellhausen's successors continued to elucidate the identity of the author(s) or redactor(s) of 'J' as the earliest theologian and historian of the

1.   J. Wellhausen, *Die Composition des Hexateuchs und der historischen Bücher des Alten Testaments* (Berlin: W. de Gruyter, 1899); J. Wellhausen, *Prologomena to the History of Ancient Israel* (Edinburgh: A. and C. Black, 1885; repr., New York: Meridian Books, 1957); S.R. Driver, *An Introduction to the Literature of the Old Testament* (New York: Meridian Books, 1957; repr.), pp. 123–24; O. Eissfeldt, *The Old Testament: An Introduction*, (trans. P. Ackroyd; New York: Harper and Row, 1965), pp. 164–67; G. von Rad, *The Problem of the Hexateuch and Other Essays*, (trans. E.W. Trueman Dicken; London: SCM Press, 1966; rev. edn), p. 69; M. Noth, *A History of Pentateuchal Traditions*, (trans. B. Anderson; repr., Chico, CA: Scholars Press, 1981; Edgewood Cliffs, NJ: Prentice-Hall, 1972), especially pp. 42–51, 229–59 (page citations are to the reprint edition). Useful surveys of the historical-critical study of the Hebrew Bible may be found in R.K. Harrison, *Introduction to the Old Testament* (Grand Rapids, MI: Eerdmans, 1969), pp. 11–82; and J. Blenkinsopp, *The Pentateuch* (New York: Doubleday, 1993), pp. 1–25.
2.   H.-J. Kraus, *Geschichte der historisch-kiritischen Erforschung des Alten Testaments* (Neukirchen Vluyn: Neukirchener Verlag, 1969), pp. 222–29; J. Blenkinsopp, *The Pentateuch*, pp. 7–8.
3.   Wellhausen, *Die Composition des Hexateuchs*; Wellhausen, *Prologomena to the History of Ancient Israel*.
4.   See the concise survey of scholarship regarding the 'J' source in A. de Pury, 'Yahwist ("J") source', *ABD*, VI (New York: Doubleday, 1992), pp. 1012–20. This is not to imply that most biblical scholars accept Wellhausen's schema exactly as he formulated it, only that they accept the basic framework and approximate dates.

Pentateuch. Individuals such as G. von Rad and M. Noth attributed 'J' to the 10th century,[5] most likely during the so-called 'Solomonic enlightenment'. Von Rad's and Noth's approximate date for 'J', based on Wellhausen's original framework, has been accepted by most biblical scholars.[6]

Since the 1960's this traditional understanding of the date and origins of 'J' has been subjected to strong criticism. L. Perlitt and H. Schmid argued that the traditional 'J' (and 'E') source(s) are largely products of the Deuteronomic school, and thus should be dated to the late pre-exilic period (but not the exilic or post-exilic periods).[7] As early as 1939, J. Morgenstern proposed a post-exilic date for the 'J' material in Genesis 1–11.[8] L. Alonso-Schökel and G. Mendenhall later argued for the post-exilic date of Genesis 2–3 on lexicographic and thematic grounds.[9] But the case for a post-exilic 'J' has been argued most strongly by the 'Toronto school', led by F. Winnett and his students. C. de Catanzaro and N. Wagner attempted to demonstrate a post-exilic date for Genesis 1–11 and Genesis 12–26, respectively.[10] Winnett presented his argument for a post-exilic 'J' strand throughout Genesis in his presidential address to the Society of Biblical Literature in 1965.[11] A broader perspective was taken by M. Rose and J. van Seters, both of whom concluded that 'J' was composed later than DtrG (= basic core of Deuteronomy) as a 'prologue' to the

5.   Von Rad, *The Problem of the Hexateuch and Other Essays*, p. 69; Noth, *A History of Pentateuchal Traditions*, p. 230.

6.   See de Pury, 'Yahwist ("J") Source', pp. 1014–16; Blenkinsopp, *The Pentateuch*, pp. 19–20.

7.   L. Perlitt, *Bundestheologie im Alten Testament* (Neukirchen-Vluyn: Neukirchener Verlag, 1969); H. Schmid, *Der sogenannte Jahwist* (Zürich: Theologischer Verlag, 1976).

8.   J. Morgenstern, 'The Mythological Background of Psalm 82', *HUCA* 14 (1939), pp. 93–94.

9.   L. Alonso-Schökel, 'Motivos sapienciales y de alianza en Gn 2–3', *Biblica* 43 (1962), pp. 295–316; G. Mendenhall, 'The Shady Side of Wisdom: The Date and Purpose of Genesis 3', in Bream et al. (ed.), *A Light Unto My Path. Studies in Honor of Jacob M. Myers*, (Philadelphia: Temple University Press, 1974), pp. 319–34.

10.   C.J. de Catanzaro, 'A Literary Analysis of Genesis 1–11' (unpublished doctoral dissertation, University of Toronto, 1957); N.E. Wagner, 'A Literary Analysis of Genesis 12–36' (unpublished doctoral dissertation, University of Toronto, 1965); N.E. Wagner, 'Abraham and David?' in Wevers and Redford (eds.), *Studies on the Ancient Palestinian World*, (Toronto: University of Toronto, 1972), pp. 117–40.

11.   F. Winnett, 'Re-examining the Foundations', *JBL* 84 (1965), pp.1–19; F. Winnett, 'The Arabian Geneaologies in the Book of Genesis', in *Translating and Understanding the Old Testament: Essays in Honor of Herbert Gordon May*, Frank and Reed (eds.), (Nashville, TN: Abingdon Press, 1970), pp. 171–96.

Deuteronomic history during the Persian period.[12] Van Seters' more recent work situates 'J' against the background of the (mainly Greek) historiographic efforts of the exilic period.[13] The Joseph Story (Genesis 37–50), which von Rad viewed as a literary masterpiece by the 10th century Yahwist, was considered by scholars such as D. Redford and A. Meinhold to be a 'postexilic Jewish diaspora novel'.[14] Other biblical scholars, using similar or different methods of analysis, have also dated 'J' to the exilic or post-exilic periods.[15]

Although scholars have formulated their arguments for a late pre-exilic, exilic, or post-exilic date for 'J' on historical-critical and literary-critical grounds, they have not yet advanced a comprehensive linguistic argument.[16] That is, they have not yet compared the linguistic characteristics of 'J' to current scholarly understanding of the historical development of Biblical Hebrew (BH). Most scholars now recognize that the language of the Hebrew Bible can be divided into three main chronological stages: Archaic Biblical Hebrew (ABH), represented by some poetic passages in the Pentateuch and the Former Prophets; Standard Biblical Hebrew (SBH), represented by the majority of biblical prose; and Late Biblical Hebrew (LBH), characteristic of Chronicles and other indisputably late,

12. M. Rose, *Deuteronomist und Jahwist, Berührungspunkten beider Literawerke*, (ATANT, 67; Zürich: Theologischer Verlag, 1981); M. Rose, 'La croissance du corpus historiographique de la Bible - une proposition', *RTP* 118 (1986), pp. 217–26; J. van Seters, *Abraham in History and Tradition* (New Haven, CT: Yale University Press, 1975); J. van Seters, 'The Yahwist as Historian', (SBLSP, 25; Atlanta: Scholars Press, 1986), pp. 37–55. Note N. Sarna, review of J. van Seters *Abraham in History and Tradition, BARev* 3 (1977), pp. 5–9. See also J. van Seters, *In Search of History: Historiography in the Ancient World and the Origins of Biblical History* (New Haven, CT: Yale University, 1983); and Z. Zevit, 'Clio, I Presume', review of J. van Seters, *In Search of History, BASOR* 260 (1985), pp. 71–82.

13. J. van Seters, *Prologue to History: The Yahwist as Historian in Genesis* (Louisville, KY: Westminster/John Knox Press, 1992), especially pp. 1–22. See R. Boling, review of J. van Seters, *Prologue to History, Int* 48 (1994), pp. 289–91.

14. De Pury, 'Yahwist ("J") Source', p. 1017. See D. Redford, *A Study of the Biblical Story of Joseph*, (VTSup, 20; Leiden: E.J. Brill, 1970); A. Meinhold, 'Die Gattung der Josephsgeschichte und des Estherbuches: Diasporanovelle', *ZAW* 88 (1975/76), pp. 306–24.

15. T. Thompson, *The Historicity of the Patriarchal Narratives* (Berlin: W. de Gruyter, 1974); H. Vorländer, *Die Ensteheungszeit des jehowistischen Geschichtswerkes* (Frankfurt: Peter Lang, 1978). See Blenkinsopp, *The Penateuch*, pp. 19–26.

16. An exception is Redford who made some attempts to identify late (post-exilic) lexical or grammatical features in the Joseph Story: Redford, *A Study of the Biblical Story of Joseph*, pp. 54–65, 187–253. The problem with those expressions that Redford identified as late is that Redford did not (a) establish a contrast between the alleged late expression and an earlier expression of equivalent meaning, and (b) did not check to see if the alleged late expression is attested in post-biblical sources. See the methodology proposed below, pp. 6–8.

post-exilic works.[17] The purpose of the present study is to analyze the language of the so-called 'J' source in the light of what is known about the historical development of Biblical Hebrew. The results, it is hoped, will indicate the linguistic background against which 'J' was composed.

It should be noted that I am not convinced personally of the existence of a 'J' source. The narrative portions of the Pentateuch exhibit greater literary unity than the Documentary Hypothesis would seem to permit.[18] Nevertheless, it is still a useful exercise to analyze those passages which most scholars attribute to 'J' to ascertain their linguistic character, and to determine whether or not the alleged 'J' source exhibits features of Late Biblical Hebrew.[19]

Such a linguistic analysis of the 'J' source is predicated upon the realization that Biblical Hebrew developed over time.[20] The language of the Hebrew Bible displays remarkable linguistic unity considering that the biblical texts span a time interval of at least 1000 years (by conservative estimates).[21] The general stability of the language has been explained by

17.   See R.Y. Kutscher, *A History of the Hebrew Language*, (ed. Raphael Kutscher; Jerusalem: Magnes, 1982), pp. 12, 77–85. For the purposes of this study it is preferable to employ the more traditional label 'Late Biblical Hebrew' rather than 'Late Classical Hebrew', as S. Ólaffson proposes; see idem., 'Late Biblical Hebrew: Fact or Fiction?', in Zapera (ed.) *Intertestamental Essays in Honour of Józof Tadeusz Milik*, (Krakow: Enigma Press, 1992): p. 135, n. 2. Granted, not all post-exilic Hebrew is biblical, but no examples of post-exilic Hebrew which are not found in the Hebrew Bible will be considered.

18.   On the literary unity of the Pentateuch and how this creates problems for the Documentary Hypothesis, see G. Rendsburg, *The Redaction of Genesis* (Winona Lake, IN: Eisenbrauns, 1986); R. Alter, *The Art of Biblical Narrative* (New York: Basic Books, 1981); R. Alter, *The World of Biblical Literature* (New York: Basic Books, 1992).

19.   Thus I continue the use of the siglum 'J' – in quotation marks to indicate my doubts concerning its actual existence - for what is called the Yahwist source. Note similar comments by G.A. Rendsburg, 'Late Biblical Hebrew and the Date of "P"', *JANESCU* 12 (1980), p. 78, n. 58.

20.   For a concise summary of the theoretical foundations for the diachronic linguistic analysis of Biblical Hebrew, see R. Bergey, 'The Book of Esther - Its Place in the Linguistic Milieu of Post-Exilic Biblical Hebrew Prose: A Study in Late Biblical Hebrew' (unpublished doctoral dissertation, Dropsie College for Hebrew and Cognate Learning, 1983), pp. 1–11. See also M. Rooker, 'The Diachronic Study of Biblical Hebrew', *JNSL* 14 (1988), pp. 199–214; M. Rooker, 'Ezekiel and the Typology of Biblical Hebre', *HAR* 12 (1990), pp. 133–37. A similar phenomenon can be observed in Akkadian and Egyptian literature. Differences between recensions of the Epic of Gilgamesh sometimes reflect chronological changes which occurred in the Akkadian dialect(s); J. Tigay, *The Evolution of the Gilgamesh Epic* (Philadelphia: University of Pennsylvania Press, 1982), pp. 65–71. See also the efforts of S. Israelit-Groll to describe some of the diachronic changes which can be discerned in ancient Egyptian inscriptions; Israelit-Groll, 'Diachronic Grammar as a Means of Dating Undated Texts', in Groll (ed.), *Egyptological Studies*, (*Scripta Hierosolymitana*, 28; Jerusalem: Magnes Press, 1982), pp. 10–104.

21.   See W. Chomsky, *Hebrew: The Eternal Language* (Philadelphia: Jewish Publication Society, 1957), pp. 30–31;

the preserving influence of a common (religious) literature.[22] But despite the general uniformity of Biblical Hebrew, it nevertheless displays signs of diachronic development. Standard descriptions of Hebrew grammar recognize at least two major stages of linguistic development: pre-exilic and post-exilic Biblical Hebrew. As noted in GKC:

> There is [in Biblical Hebrew] a certain progress from an earlier to a later stage. Two periods, though with some reservations, may be distinguished: the *first*, down to the end of the Babylonian exile; the *second*, after the exile (emphasis in original).[23]

Though as noted above, it is more proper to speak of three periods: Archaic, Standard, and Late Biblical Hebrew (abbreviated ABH, SBH, and LBH, respectively).

Since standard treatments of Hebrew grammar present SBH in the main, specialized studies have been devoted to describing LBH. Early attempts in this direction include the studies of M. Löhr on the language of Lamentations,[24] A. Kropat on the syntax of Chronicles,[25] and H. Striedl on the syntax and style of Esther.[26] Driver, in his classic work *An Introduction to the Literature of the Old Testament*, listed distinctive features of the language of several late books of the Hebrew Bible, labeling many of them as 'late'.[27] In the past few decades, there have been many more studies devoted to analyzing Biblical Hebrew diachronically, with an attempt to identify and describe features of Late Biblical Hebrew. The most important and prolific of these scholars has been Avi Hurvitz, with others following in his footsteps.[28]

22. Chomsky, *Hebrew*, p. 30; Bergey, 'The Book of Esther', p. 11.

23. E. Kautsch (ed.), *Genesius' Hebrew Grammar*, (trans. A.E. Cowley; Oxford: Clarendon Press, 1910), pp. 12, §2l. See also [Wilhelm Gesenius-]Gotthelf Bergsträsser, *Hebräische Grammatik*, I (Leipzig: Hinrichs, 1918; repr., Hildesheim: George Olms, 1962; 29th edn), pp. 11–12, §2h-i; P. Joüon, and T. Muraoka, *A Grammar of Biblical Hebrew*, I (Subsidia Biblica, 14; Rome: Pontifical Biblical Institute, 1993), pp. 10–11, §3a-b.

24. M. Löhr, 'Der Sprachegebrauch des Buches des Klagelieder', *ZAW* 14 (1894), pp.31–50.

25. A. Kropat, *Die Syntax des Autors der Chronik*, (BZAW, 16; Gießen: Alfred Töpelman, 1909).

26. H. Striedl, 'Untersuchungen zur Syntax und Stilistik des hebräischen Buches Esther', *ZAW* 55 (1937), pp.73–108.

27. Driver, *Introduction to the Old Testament*, pp. 473–75, 484–85, 506–08, 535–40, 53.

28. See the following by Avi Hurvitz (I list here only the most important ones; additional articles are cited during the course of this study): *Beyn Lashon le-Lashon* (The Transition Period in Biblical Hebrew) (Jerusalem: Bialik, 1972) (Hebrew); idem., 'The Evidence of Language in Dating the Priestly Code', *RB* 81 (1974), pp. 24–56; idem., *A Linguistic Study of the Relationship between the Priestly Source and the Book of Ezekiel*, (Cahiers de la Revue Biblique, 20; Paris: Gabalda, 1982). See also Kutscher, *A History of the Hebrew Language*; R. Polzin, *Late Biblical Hebrew: Toward an Historical Typology of Biblical Hebrew Prose*, (HSM, 12; Missoula, MT: Scholars Press, 1976); Bergey, 'The Book of Esther'; R. Bergey,

One of the problems of the earlier studies is they did not always employ a reliable methodology for identifying features of LBH. Hurvitz, by contrast, established sound criteria for dating features of LBH, and, therefore, for dating biblical texts,[29] and it is his method which this study will use in order to search for possible examples of Late Biblical Hebrew in the so-called 'J' source.

Hurvitz' criteria are as follows. First, the linguistic feature in question must occur exclusively or predominantly in biblical books which are indisputably post-exilic in date; this is known as 'linguistic distribution'.[30] This criterion is the first indication that a given linguistic item is potentially a feature of LBH, and it ensures that the item is present in post-exilic Biblical Hebrew. If the linguistic item occurs sporadically in biblical books which are widely considered to be pre-exilic, this does not automatically disqualify the item from consideration. For example, the long waw-conversive וָאֶקְטְלָה form occurs predominately, but not exclusively, in post-exilic books; several examples in pre-exilic texts do occur.[31] But it is the preference of post-exilic Biblical Hebrew for the long waw-conversive וָאֶקְטְלָה as opposed to the shorter וָאֶקְטֹל that makes the וָאֶקְטְלָה form a characteristic of LBH.

Second, there must be expressions in earlier biblical books which express the same meaning as the linguistic item in question, and which are employed in similar or identical contexts; this is known as 'linguistic contrast'.[32] That is to say, one must demonstrate that the linguistic item which is potentially late is equivalent to and used in place of an earlier expression. This second criterion ensures that the linguistic item in

---

'Late Linguistic Features in Esther', *JQR* 75 (1984), pp. 66–78; idem., 'Post-exilic Features in Esther: A Diachronic Approach', *JETS* 31 (1988), pp. 161–68; Rooker, 'Ezekiel and the Typology of Biblical Hebrew', pp. 133–55; M. Rooker, *Biblical Hebrew in Transition: The Language of the Book of Ezekiel*, (JSOTSup, 90; Sheffield: JSOT Press, 1990); A. Hill, 'The Book of Malachi: Its Place in Post-exilic Chronology Linguistically Reconsidered', (unpublished doctoral dissertation, University of Michigan, 1981); idem., 'Dating Second Zechariah: A Linguistic Reexamination', *HAR* 6 (1982), pp.105–34. For a recent survey, see A. Sáenz-Badillos, *A History of the Hebrew Language*, (trans. John Elwolde; Cambridge: Cambridge University, 1993), pp. 112–29.

29. A. Hurvitz, 'Linguistic Criteria for Dating Problematic Biblical Texts', *Hebrew Abstracts* 14 (1973), pp. 74–79.

30. Hurvitz, *Beyn Lashon le-Lashon*, pp. 20–26; Hurvitz, 'Linguistic Criteria for Dating Problematic Biblical Texts', p. 76. See also Bergey, 'The Book of Esther', p. 17, who lists this criterion second.

31. For discussion, see below, pp. 22–26.

32. Hurvitz, *Beyn Lashon le-Lashon*, pp. 15–20; Hurvitz, 'Linguistic Criteria for Dating Problematic Biblical Texts', p. 30. See also Bergey, 'The Book of Esther', p. 17, who lists this as the first criterion. I have, with Hurvitz, listed linguistic distribution as the first criterion for determining the late nature of a linguistic item. One would not look for linguistic contrast until the criterion of linguistic distribution were first fulfilled.

question is not merely an expression that earlier books simply had no opportunity to employ. If the earlier expression continues to appear alongside its later equivalent in post-exilic literature, this does not automatically disqualify the late expression from consideration. For example, the LBH lexeme מלכות 'kingdom' occurs almost exclusively in post-exilic books; it is semantically equivalent to the earlier expression ממלכה 'kingdom' and is used in similar contexts.[33] The occasional appearance of SBH ממלכה alongside LBH מלכות in post-exilic books does not disqualify מלכות as a feature of LBH.[34]

Third, the linguistic item in question must appear in post-exilic sources other than the Hebrew Bible, such as Ben Sira, Qumran Hebrew (the Dead Sea Scrolls), Tannaitic Hebrew (see below, pp. 16–17), and Biblical Aramaic.[35] This third criterion ensures that the late expression is not a peculiarity of the biblical writer's style, and that the late expression reflects

33. For discussion, see Bergey, 'The Book of Esther', pp. 31–34; Hurvitz, *Beyn Lashon le-Lashon*, 79–88; Driver, *Introduction to the Old Testament*, p. 536; Polzin, *Late Biblical Hebrew*, p. 142; Kutscher, *A History of the Hebrew Language*, p. 81.

34. See A. Even-Shoshan, *A New Concordance of the Old Testament* (Jerusalem, Kiryat Sefer, 1990), pp. 673, 674–75. This last point should be self-evident: the emergence of a new expression in any language does not require an earlier, equivalent expression to disappear altogether. Consider the persistence of English *Mrs.* despite the presence of the late 20th century alternative *Ms.*

35. Hurvitz, 'Linguistic Criteria for Dating Problematic Biblical Texts', p. 76. See also A. Hurvitz, 'Observations on the Language of the Third Apocryphal Psalm from Qumrân', *Revue de Qumran* 5 (1965), pp.225–32; E.Y. Kutscher, *The Language and Linguistic Background of the Isaiah Scroll (1QIs^a)*, (Studies on the Texts of the Desert of Judah, 6; Leiden: E.J. Brill, 1974); E.Y. Kutscher, 'Hebrew Language, Mishnaic Hebrew', *EncJud*, XVI (Jerusalem: Keter, 1972), cols. 1590–1607; R. Gordis, 'Studies in the Relationship of Biblical and Rabbinic Hebrew', *Louis Ginzberg Jubilee Volume* (New York: American Academy for Jewish Research, 1945), pp. 173–99; C. Rabin, 'The Historical Background of Qumran Hebrew', (*Scripta Hierosolymitana*, 4; 1958), pp.144–161; M. Segal, 'Mishnaic Hebrew and its Relation to Biblical Hebrew and to Aramaic', *JQR* 20 (1908), pp.647–737.

Although Aramaic is not Hebrew, it is still important for determining whether or not an item is late. First, since both Aramaic and Hebrew were used by the post-exilic Jewish community, features of Biblical Aramaic may parallel features of Late Biblical Hebrew. Second, since Aramaic exerted greater influence on Hebrew during the post-exilic period, we can look to Aramaic as a possible source for developments which characterize LBH. Third, we can look even to post-biblical Aramaic for features which parallel characteristics of LBH, even though the parallel features in Aramaic are later than the biblical texts. With each discovery of an ancient Aramaic text, more of Middle Aramaic and Late Aramaic is revealed to have ancient antecedents; features of post-biblical Aramaic which parallel developments in LBH may still reflect the overall linguistic situation during the post-exilic period; see G.A. Rendsburg, *Linguistic Evidence for the Northern Origin of Selected Psalms*, (SBLMS, 43; Atlanta, GA: Scholars Press, 1990), p. 6, n. 25, and reference. For a recent critique of this aspect of Hurvitz' methodology, see Ian Young, 'Late Biblical Hebrew and Hebrew Inscription', in Ian Young (ed.), *Biblical Hebrew: Studies in Chronology and Typology* (London: T. & T. Clark, 2003), pp. 279–80.

the actual linguistic situation of the post-exilic period. That is, the development or emergence of the late expression is reflected in other post-exilic literature. For example, the LBH expression כל עו(ו)למים occurs only once in the Hebrew Bible, Ps. 145.13.[36] We can determine that this expression is not an idiosyncrasy of the psalmist because it appears frequently in extra-biblical sources, including the Dead Sea Scrolls and rabbinic literature.

Whereas the first three criteria establish whether a particular linguistic item is late, a fourth criterion is required to determine whether a particular biblical text is late. A biblical text must not be considered late on linguistic grounds unless it contains a concentration of several expressions which are characteristic of LBH.[37] One or two such late expressions are insufficient, as their presence may be explained by something other than the lateness of the text. Some texts–such as those which describe explicitly events which are set in the post-exilic period–are clearly late irrespective of linguistic features.

The above method for determining the lateness of particular expressions requires a working hypothesis as to which books of the Hebrew Bible are pre-exilic, exilic, or post-exilic in date. It is unnecessary for the purposes of this study to provide an exact date for each book because it is the general distinction between pre-exilic and post-exilic books which is of immediate concern. Granted, scholars are seldom in unanimous agreement as to the approximate date of most biblical books. Furthermore, they often date different sections of a given book to different periods. Nevertheless, for the purposes of this study it is possible to outline a working hypothesis as to which general period each biblical book belongs: pre-exilic, exilic, or post-exilic. When specific chapters or sections within a given book cause particular problems for dating, special note will be made.

Several studies on the Pentateuch have shown that the work is pre-exilic. G.A. Rendsburg has published literary analyses which demonstrate that Genesis is a compositional unity, and can be dated to the early pre-exilic period.[38] M. Haran, Y. Kaufmann, J. Milgrom, and Z. Zevit have argued persuasively for the pre-exilic background of the Priestly ('P')

---

36. For discussion, see below, pp. 68–71.

37. Hurvitz, 'Linguistic Criteria for Dating Problematic Biblical Texts', pp. 76–77. See also Bergey, 'The Book of Esther', p. 19.

38. Rendsburg, *The Redaction of Genesis*; G.A. Rendsburg, 'David and His Circle in Genesis XXXVIII', *VT* 36 (1986), pp. 438–46; G.A. Rendsburg, 'Biblical Literature as Politics: The Case of Genesis', in A. Berlin (ed.), *Religion and Politics in the Ancient Near East*, (Bethesda, MD: University Press of Maryland, 1996), pp. 47–70.

source.[39] M. Weinfeld dated Deuteronomy and the Deuteronomic source ('D') to the 7th century BCE[40] Studies of the language of the Pentateuch support the above conclusions.[41] A. Hurvitz demonstrated that the 'P' source contains no LBH elements, but always uses SBH lexemes and formulae in preference to their post-exilic equivalents.[42] His analysis has been confirmed by other scholars.[43] Those who do not agree with a pre-exilic date for the entire Pentateuch may disregard any evidence which they attribute to a post-exilic source or redactor.[44] Clearly this study cannot treat 'J' as pre-exilic for the purpose of determining LBH expressions, since it is the date of 'J' that is in question.

The date of Joshua-Kings depends heavily upon scholarly theories about the composition and date of the Deuteronomic History (DH).[45] A brief survey of scholarly opinion reveals a broad consensus that a first version of the DH was compiled in the late pre-exilic period, with a final

---

39. See M. Haran, *Temples and Temple-Service in Ancient Israel: An Inquiry into the Character of Cult Phenomena and the Historical Setting of the Priestly School* (Oxford: Clarendon Press, 1978); Y. Kaufmann, *The Religion of Israel: From its Beginnings to the Babylonian Exile*, (trans. M. Greenberg; Chicago: Chicago University Press, 1960; rev. edn); J. Milgrom, *Studies in Levitical Terminology* (Berkeley: University of California, 1970). See also the discussion and references in M. Weinfeld, 'Pentateuch', *EncJud*, XII (Jerusalem: Keter, 1972), cols. 232–61; Z. Zevit, 'Converging Lines of Evidence Bearing on the Date of P', pp. 481–493.

40. M. Weinfeld, *Deuteronomy and the Deuteronomic School* (Oxford: Clarendon Press, 1972). See also discussion and references in M. Weinfeld, 'Deuteronomy, Book of', *ABD*, II (New York: Doubleday, 1992), pp. 168–183.

41. See especially the study of A. Guenther, 'A Diachronic Study of Biblical Hebrew Prose Syntax: An Analysis of the Verbal Clause in Jeremiah 37–45 and Esther 1–10', (Unpublished doctoral dissertation, University of Toronto, 1977).

42. Hurvitz, *A Linguistic Study of the Relationship between the Priestly Source and the Book of Ezekiel*; A. Hurvitz, 'The Usage of *šēš* and *bûs* in the Bible and its Implications for the Date of P', *HTR* 60 (1967), pp. 117–21.

43. See Polzin, *Late Biblical Hebrew*; Rendsburg, 'Late Biblical Hebrew and the Date of "P"', pp. 65–80; Zevit, 'Converging Lines of Evidence Bearing on the Date of P', pp. 481–511; M. Rooker, *Biblical Hebrew in Transition: The Language of the Book of Ezekiel*; Rooker, 'Ezekiel and the Typology of Biblical Hebrew', pp. 133–55. Although Polzin found that P is later than the rest of the Pentateuch, he nevertheless concluded that P is earlier than LBH, and therefore pre-exilic. Note that much of Rooker's work is a reformulation of Hurvitz' analysis. See also J. Milgrom, review of *A Linguistic Study of the Relationship between the Priestly Source and the Book of Ezekiel*, by A. Hurvitz, *CBQ* 46 (1984), pp. 118–19. For more critical appraisals of Hurvitz' work, see J. Becker, review of A. Hurvitz, *A Linguistic Study of the Relationship between the Priestly Source and the Book of Ezekiel*, *Biblica* 64 (1983), pp. 583–86; G. Davies, review of A. Hurvitz, *A Linguistic Study of the Relationship between the Priestly Source and the Book of Ezekiel*, *VT* 37 (1987), pp. 117–18.

44. See Bergey, 'The Book of Esther', p. 20.

45. See the discussion in S. McKenzie, 'Deuteronomistic History', *ABD*, II (New York: Doubleday, 1992), pp. 160–68.

redaction being completed during the exile.[46] Recent scholarship has argued for successive revisions of the DH during the pre-exilic monarchic period, maintaining the antiquity of much of its material.[47] This study will treat Joshua-Kings as pre-exilic (with the exception of the last 2 chapters of 2 Kings, which are exilic).[48]

The primary sources for post-exilic BH are: Chronicles,[49]

46. For the classic formulation of the DH hypothesis, see M. Noth, *The Deuteronomistic History*, (JSOTSup, 15; Sheffield, England: JSOT Press, 1981). For revisions of Noth's initial work, see R. Nicholson, *Deuteronomy and Tradition* (Philadelphia: Fortress Press, 1967); Weinfeld, *Deuteronomy and the Deuteronomic School*. For Joshua, see discussion and references in R. Boling, 'Joshua, Book of', *ABD*, III (New York: Doubleday, 1992), pp. 1002–15. For Judges, see Boling, *Judges*, (AB; Garden City, NY: Doubleday, 1985); Boling, 'Judges, Book of', *ABD*, III (New York: Doubleday, 1992), pp. 1107–27. For 1–2 Samuel, see J. Flanagan, 'Samuel, Book of 1–2', *ABD*, V (New York: Doubleday, 1992), pp. 957–65; for Kings, see S. Holloway, 'Kings, Book of 1–2', *ABD*, IV (New York: Doubleday, 1992), pp. 69–83. Features of Israelian Hebrew often appear in portions of the DH which deal with the northern kingdom, which argues strongly that these portions are drawn from authentic sources composed before ca. 722 BCE and the fall of the northern kingdom. On Israelian Hebrew, see Rendsburg, *Linguistic Evidence for the Northern Origin of Selected Psalms*, pp. 1–17; and now idem., *Israelian Hebrew in The Book of Kings* (Occasional Publications of the Department of Near Eastern Studies and the Program of Jewish Studies, Cornell University, 5; Bethesda, Maryland: CDL Press, 2002), especially pp. 17–26.

47. See F. Cross, *Canaanite Myth and Hebrew Epic* (Cambridge, MA: Harvard University Press, 1973), pp. 274–90; A. Campbell, *Of Prophets and Kings*, (CBQMS, 17; Washington, DC: Catholic Biblical Association of America, 1986); and especially K. McCarter, *1 Samuel*, (AB; Garden City, NY: Doubleday, 1980), pp. 12–30. Note also the work of Smend, who argued for an exilic date for the first and second redactions of DH (DtrG and DtrN, respectively); R. Smend, 'Das Gesetz und die Völker. Ein Beitrag zur deuteronomistischen Redaktionsgeschichte', in Wolff (ed.), *Probleme biblischer Theologie*, (Festschrift G. von Rad; Munich: Chron. Kaiser Verlag, 1971), pp. 494–509.

48. For a strong challenge to the traditional (late) pre-exilic date of Samuel Kings from a text-critical perspective, see Robert Rezetko, 'Dating Biblical Hebrew: Evidence from Samuel-Kings and Chronicles', in Ian Young (ed.), *Biblical Hebrew: Studies in Chronology and Typology* (London: T. & T. Clark, 2003), pp. 215–50; but also Z. Zevit, review of Ian Young (ed.), *Biblical Hebrew: Studies in Chronology and Typology* (http://www.bookreviews.org/pdf/4084_3967.pdf), pp. 8–9.

49. Earlier scholarship dated Chronicles to the Greek period (after 333 BCE); see E. Curtis and A. Madsen, *A Critical and Exegetical Commentary on the Books of Chronicles*, (ICC; Edinburgh: T. & T. Clark, 1910), Noting the apparent lack of Hellenistic-Greek influence, most scholars date Chronicles to c. 400 BCE at the latest; much of its material was first composed as early as 515 BCE during the early Persian period. See R. Klein, 'Chronicles, Book of 1–2', *ABD*, I (New York: Doubleday, 1992), pp. 992–1002; F. Cross, 'A Reconstruction of the Judean Restoration', *JBL* 94 (1975), pp. 4–18; S. McKenzie, *The Chronicler's Use of the Deuteronomistic History*, (HSM; Cambridge, MA: Harvard University, 1985); but also Rezetko, 'Dating Biblical Hebrew: Evidence from Samuel-Kings and Chronicles', pp. 215–50.

Ezra, Nehemiah,[50] Daniel,[51] Esther,[52] and Qohelet (Ecclesiastes).[53] To
this list can be added: Isaiah 56–66 (Third Isaiah),[54]

50. Scholars suggest a range of dates for Ezra-Nehemiah, ranging from 400–300 BCE See
L. Batten, *An Exegetical and Critical Commentary on the Books of Ezra and Nehemiah*, (ICC;
Edinburgh: T. & T. Clark, 1913), pp. 2–3; S. Japhet, 'Sheshbazzar und [*sic*] Zerubbabel -
Against the Background of the Historical and Religious Tendencies of Ezra-Nehemiah',
ZAW 95 (1982), pp. 66–98; H. Williamson, *Ezra, Nehemiah*, (Word Biblical Commentary,
16; Waco, TX: Word Books, 1985), p. xxxvi; J. Meyers, *Ezra, Nehemiah*, (AB; Garden City,
NY: Doubleday, 1965), pp. lxviii-lxxi; R. Klein, 'Ezra-Nehemiah, Books of', *ABD*, II (New
York: Doubleday, 1992), pp. 731–42.
51. There is a consensus that chapters 1–6 of Daniel were composed before the
Maccabean period, but after the division of the Alexandrian empire (3rd century BCE), and
that chapter 7–12 belong to the period of Antiochus IV (c. 160–140 BCE, with some placing
them earlier, 186–184 BCE). See J. Montgomery, *A Critical and Exegetical Commentary on the
Book of Daniel*, (ICC; Edinburgh: T. & T. Clark, 1927), pp. 96–99; L. Hartman and
Alexander di Lella, *The Book of Daniel*, (AB; Garden City, NY: Doubleday, 1978), pp. 9–18;
J. Collins, 'Daniel, Book of', *ABD*, II (New York: Doubleday, 1992), pp. 29–37.
52. L. Paton argued that Esther was composed at least later than 169 BCE (Antiochus IV);
Paton, *A Critical and Exegetical Commentary on the Book of Esther*, (ICC; Edinburgh: T. &
T. Clark, 1908), pp. 60–63. C. Moore preferred to push the date of Esther back into the late
Persian-early Hellenistic period; C. Moore, *Esther*, (AB; Garden City, NY: Doubleday,
1971), pp. lvii-lx. See also S. Berg, *The Book of Esther: Motifs, Themes, and Structures*,
(SBLDS, 44; Missoula, MT: Scholars Press, 1979), pp. 170–171; C. Moore, 'Esther, Book of',
ABD, II (New York: Doubleday, 1992), pp. 633–43.
53. Bergey excluded Qohelet from his list of primary LBH sources because it is
predominately poetic; Bergey, 'The Book of Esther', p. 21. Scholars generally date Qohelet to
the late post-exilic period, some as late as 200–195 BCE See G. Barton, *A Critical and
Exegetical Commentary on the Book of Ecclesiastes*, (ICC; Edinburgh: T. & T. Clark, 1908),
pp. 58–63; R. Scott, *Proverbs. Ecclesiastes*, (AB; Garden City, NY: Doubleday, 1965), pp.
196–98; J. Crenshaw, 'Ecclesiastes, Book of', *ABD*, II (New York: Doubleday, 1992), pp.
271–80. Note however C. Moore, who along with other wishes to push back the date of
Qohelet at least to the late Persian period; Moore, *Esther*, (AB; Garden City, NY:
Doubleday, 1971), pp. lvii-lx. See most recently C.L. Seow, 'Linguistic Evidence and the
Dating of Qohelet', *JBL* 115 (1996), pp.643–66. Seow confirmed that the 'language of the
book of Qohelet clearly belongs to the postexilic period'; Seow, ibid., 665. See also idem.,
Ecclesiastes (AB; New York: Doubleday, 1997), pp. 11–21, especially pp. 11–16. The late
character of Qohelet's language was challenged by D. Fredericks in *Qoheleth's Language: Re-
evaluating its Nature and Date*, (Ancient Near Eastern Texts and Studies, 3; Lewiston, NY:
Edwin Mellen, 1988). But see critique by A. Hurvitz, review of D. Fredericks, *Qoheleth's
Language, Hebrew Studies* 31 (1990), pp.144–52.
54. Most scholars date the so-called Third Isaiah (chapters 56–66) to the early post-exilic
period. See C. Seitz, 'Isaiah, Book of (Third Isaiah)', *ABD*, III (New York: Doubleday,
1992), pp. 501–07; B. Duhm, *Die Theologie der Propheten als Grundlage für die innere
Entwicklungsgeschichte der israelitischen Religion* (Bonn: Adolph Marcus, 1875), pp. 275–
301; K. Elliger, *Die Einheit des Tritojesaiah (Jesaia 56–66)* (Stuttgart: W. Kohlhammer,
1928), pp. 1–5; C. Westermann, *Isaiah 40–66*, (OTL; Philadelphia: Westminster Press, 1969),
pp. 295–308. Note that Seitz calls into question the distinction between Second and Third
Isaiah, while maintaining that Second–Third Isaiah is post-exilic.

Jonah,[55] Haggai,[56] Zechariah,[57] and Malachi.[58] The book of Ezekiel is widely accepted as exilic.[59] Jeremiah poses a special problem, since it spans both the late pre-exilic and early exilic periods.[60] This study will treat it alongside Ezekiel as exilic, although its late pre-exilic status will not be ignored.

55. J. Sasson was uncertain of the date of Jonah, but observed that most evidence places it in the post-exilic period; Sasson, *Jonah* (AB; Garden City, NY: Doubleday, 1990), pp. 20–28. See also J. Magonet, 'Jonah, Book of', *ABD*, III (New York: Doubleday, 1992), pp. 936–42; L. Allen, *The Books of Joel, Obadiah, Jonah, and Micah*, (NICOT; Grand Rapids, MI: Eerdmans, 1976), pp. 185–91; H. Wolff, *Dodekapropheten 3. Obadja und Jona*, (BKAT XIV/3; Neukirchen-Vluyn: Neukirchener Verlag, 1977), pp. 54–56; H.G.T. Mitchell, J.M.O. Smith, and J.A. Bewer, *A Critical and Exegetical Commentary on Haggai, Zechariah, Malachi and Jonah*, (ICC; Edinburgh: T. & T. Clark, 1912), pp. 12–13.

56. Scholars date Haggai close to the events which it describes, 520–516 BCE See C. Meyers and E. Meyers, 'Haggai, Book of', *ABD*, III (New York: Doubleday, 1992), pp. 20–23; Mitchell, Smith. and Bewer, *A Critical and Exegetical Commentary on Haggai, Zechariah, Malachi and Jonah*, pp. 3–30; Verhoef, *The Books of Haggai and Malachi*, (NICOT; Grand Rapids, MI: Eerdmans, 1987), pp. 9–13.

57. Few biblical books have generated as much discussion concerning their date of composition as has Zechariah. Nearly all scholars distinguish at least two major divisions within the book: Zechariah 1–8, considered with Haggai as a single unit, and also dating to 520–516 BCE; and Zechariah 9–14, regarding which there is little consensus as to composition or date. Most are willing to date chapters 12–14 at least as late as the Persian period, although others see certain sections (particularly chapter 9) as containing some pre-exilic material. See D. Peterson, 'Zechariah, Book of', *ABD*, VI (New York: Doubleday, 1992), vol. 6, pp. 1061–1068; B. Stade, 'Deuterosacharja: Eine kritische Studie', *ZAW* 2 (1882), pp.308–309; B. Otzen, *Studien über Deuterosacharja*, (Acta Theologica Danica, 6; Copenhagen: Prostant apud Munksgaard, 1964), pp. 11–34, 124–25; P. Hanson, *The Dawn of Apocalyptic* (Philadelphia: Fortress Press, 1975), pp. 280–401, especially 286. For good summaries of the history of scholarship, see P. Lamarches, *Zacharies IX-XIV. Structure Lettéraire et Messianisme* (Paris: Gabalda, 1961), pp. 20–23; D. Petersen, *Zechariah 9–14 and Malachi. A Commentary*, (OTL; Lousiville, KY: Westminster/John Knox Press, 1990), pp. 3–6; A. Hill, 'Dating Second Zechariah: A Linguistic Reexamination', *HAR* 6 (1982), pp.105–34.

58. Most date Malachi to the period between the rededication of the temple and the beginning of Ezra's reforms (c. 516–458 BCE). See Mitchell, Smith, and Bewer, *A Critical and Exegetical Commentary on Haggai, Zechariah, Malachi and Jonah*, pp. 5–9; A. Hill, 'Malachi, Book of', *ABD*, IV (New York: Doubleday, 1992), pp. 478–85; A. Hill, 'Dating the Book of Malachi: A Linguistic Reexamination', in Meyers and O'Connor (eds.), *The Word of the Lord Shall Go Forth*, (Winona Lake, IN: Eisenbrauns, 1983), pp. 77–89. An exception is Verhoef, who places Malachi between Nehemiah's two visits to Jerusalem (c. 433 BCE); *The Books of Haggai and Malachi*, pp. 156–60.

59. The book of Ezekiel was composed close to the dates which are provided within the book, 593–571 BCE See G. Fohrer, 'Die Glossen im Buche Ezekiel', *ZAW* 63 (1950), pp. 33–53; C. Howie, *The Date and Composition of Ezekiel*, (SBLMS, 4; Philadelphia: Scholars Press, 1950); W. Zimmerli, *Ezekiel*, I (Hermeneia; Philadelphia: Fortress, 1979), pp. 593–71; M. Greenberg, *Ezekiel 1–20* (AB; Garden City, NY: Doubleday, 1983), pp. 12–17; L. Boadt, 'Ezekiel, Book of', *ABD*, II (New York: Doubleday, 1992), pp. 711–722.

60. See J. Bright, *Jeremiah*, (AB; Garden City, NY: Doubleday, 1965); J. Lundbom, 'Jeremiah, Book of', *ABD*, II (New York: Doubleday, 1992), pp. 706–721.

Some books are of highly uncertain date: Ruth,[61] Joel,[62] Job,[63] Proverbs,[64] Song of Songs,[65] and Lamentations.[66] Hurvitz has shown that several of the Psalms contain sufficient LBH elements to be described as post-exilic: Psalms 103, 117, 119, 124, 125, 144, 145, and the doxologies of Psalms 41, 72, and 106.[67] Several other Psalms containing LBH elements Hurvitz was unwilling to call late.[68] Books which have not specifically been discussed (such as the pre-exilic prophets) will be treated as early.

This study will follow certain guidelines in approaching the biblical evidence. First, it will make use of the unemended Masoretic Text (MT) of

61. Earlier scholarship dated Ruth to the exilic or post-exilic periods. More recent studies date the book to the 10th–7th centuries BCE See E.F. Campbell, *Ruth*, (AB; Garden City, NY: Doubleday, 1975); P. Trible, 'Ruth, Book of', *ABD*, V (New York: Doubleday, 1992), pp. 842–47. On the apparent lateness of certain verses, see for example, A. Hurvitz, 'Ruth 2.7 – "A Midrashic Gloss"?' *ZAW* 95 (1983), pp.121–23; concerning Ruth 4.7, see Hurvitz, 'Sheliphat ha-Na'al', *Shnaton* 1 (1975), pp. 45–49 (English summary on pp. xiii-xiv).

62. The book has traditionally been regarded as pre-exilic, but more recent scholarship argues for a post-exilic date of composition. See H. Wolff, *Joel and Amos*, Hermeneia (Philadelphia: Fortress Press, 1977), pp. 4–6; G.W. Ahlström, *Joel and the Temple Cult of Jerusalem*, (VTSup, 21; Leiden: E.J. Brill, 1971), pp. 111–29; T. Hiebert, 'Joel, Book of', *ABD*, III (New York: Doubleday, 1992), pp. 873–80.

63. The date of composition for Job is difficult to determine, partly because of the highly composite nature of the book. M. Pope commented on the 'equivocal and inconclusive' nature of the evidence, but nevertheless suggested the 7th century for the date of the Dialogue; M. Pope, *Job* (AB; Garden City, NY: Doubleday, 1973), p. xl. A. Hurvitz convincingly showed that the prose portions contain several features of LBH and are thus post-exilic; Hurvitz, 'The Date of the Prose-Tale of Job Linguistically Reconsidered', *HTR* 67 (1974), pp. 17–34. The remainder of the book is of uncertain date, but most likely post-exilic, so Pope, ibid.; J. Crenshaw, 'Job, Book of', *ABD*, III (New York: Doubleday, 1992), pp. 863–64.

64. The date of Proverbs is uncertain, but on the basis of internal and comparitive evidence, most of its material is pre-exilic, so Scott, *Proverbs, Ecclesiastes*, pp. xxv-xl; J. Crenshaw, 'Proverbs, Book of', *ABD*, V (New York: Doubleday, 1992), pp. 514–15.

65. Little consensus exists on the date of the Song of Songs. Scholars who see the work as composite hold some material is as early as 960 BCE, some as late as 200 BCE Linguistic studies date the final composition of the book to the late Persian-early Greek period; M. Pope, *Song of Songs* (AB; Garden City, NY: Doubleday, 1977), 22–33; R. Murphy, 'Song of Songs, Book of', *ABD*, III (New York: Doubleday, 1992), pp. 150–55.

66. Lamentations is widely held to have been written shortly after the events which it describes, 587–538 BCE See D. Hillers, *Lamentations*, (AB; Garden City, NY: Doubleday, 1972), pp. xviii-xix; D. Hillers, 'Lamentations, Book of', *ABD*, IV (New York: Doubleday, 1992), p.138; Ackroyd, review of D. Hillers, *Lamentations*, *Int* 27 (1973), pp. 223–26. Few have accepted the argument of W. Rudolph that chapter 1 belongs to 597 BCE; Rudolph, 'Der Text der Klagelieder', *ZAW* 56 (1938), pp. 101–22.

67. Hurvitz, *Beyn Lashon le-Lashon*, pp. 67–173.

68. Psalms 19, 28, 33, 40, 63, 75, 104, 106, 107, 109, 111, 112, 113, 126, 137, 143, 146, 147, and 148. See Hurvitz, *Beyn Lashon le-Lashon*, pp. 173–76. E. Qimron also has attempted to identify LBH features in the Psalms: Qimron, 'Li-lshon Bayit Sheni be-Sefer Tehillim', *Bet Mikra* 73 (1978), pp. 139–50.

the Hebrew Bible.[69] This is not because the MT contains no errors or because widely held principles of textual criticism are faulty, but because a linguistic investigation must base itself upon actual rather than reconstructed texts which may or may not have existed. Furthermore, it is not always certain whether a textual difficulty represents a corruption or a lack of information on our part.[70] Nor is it always certain whether we can accurately restore the original text. Second, this study will include both *ketib* (K) and *qere* (Q) readings in its analysis. Q readings are not corrections of corrupt K readings, but are often part of the textual tradition,[71] and at the very least they represent Masoretic tradition for reciting the text.[72] Third, the analysis herein will not distinguish between prose and poetry. Hurvitz' analysis of LBH in the book of Psalms demonstrated that late poetry, as well as late prose, reflects changes in

---

69. Hurvitz, *A Linguistic Study of the Relationship between the Priestly Source and the Book of Ezekiel*, p. 19; Hurvitz, 'Linguistic Criteria For Dating Problematic Biblical Texts', p. 74.

70. Two brief examples should suffice to demonstrate this point. First, the Hebrew verbs וממהר in Gen. 41.32, ומפלא in Judg. 13.19, ומסרפו in Amos 6.10, and ומאת in Ruth 4.5 resisted understanding until the discovery of the Ebla (Tell Mardikh) tablets. We now understand that the -מֹן prefix in these forms is conjunctive *waw* and *mem* enclitic, analogous to Eblaite *ù-ma*; G.A. Rendsburg, 'Eblaite *Ù-MA* and Hebrew *WM-*', in Gordon and Rendsburg (eds.), *Eblaitica*, I (Winona Lake, IN: Eisenbrauns, 1987), pp. 33–41.

Second, the MT of Prov. 26.23 contains the curious expression כסף סיגים 'silver of dross'. After the discovery of the Ugaritic texts from Ras Shamra, H.L. Ginsberg was able to emend כְּסֶף סִיגִים to the more plausible (?סם)כְּסַפְסָגִ 'as glaze [covers the pottery]' on the basis of Ugaritic *spsg* 'glaze' (related to Hittite *zapzaga* 'glaze'). Although this examples requires minor emendation of the text, it still demonstrates how new discoveries can elucidate problematic texts. See C. Gordon, *UT*, III (AnOr, 38; Rome: Pontifical Biblical Institute), p. 451, §1792; H.L. Ginsberg, 'The North-Canaanite Myth of Anat and Aqht', *BASOR* 98 (1945), p. 21; idem., 'Ugaritic Studies and the Bible', *BA* 8 (1945), pp. 57–58; W.F. Albright, 'A New Hebrew Word for "Glaze" in Proverbs 26.23', *BASOR* 98 (1945), pp. 24–25.

71. H.M. Orlinsky, 'The Origin of the Ketib-Qere System: A New Approach', (VTSup, 7; 1960), pp. 184–92. Basing his views on key passages in rabbinic literature, Orlinsky determined that three scrolls (copies) of the Hebrew Bible were on file in the Temple Court. *Ketib-qere* readings reflect variations between the three texts: the reading of the majority became the *qere* reading, the reading of the minority became the *ketib* reading.

72. J. Barr, 'A New Look at Kethibh-Qere', *Remembering All the Way...* (Oudtestamentlischer Studien, 21; 1981), pp. 19–37. Barr strongly critiqued the position of Orlinsky (ibid.), arguing that the *ketib-qere* (KQ) system was not as mechanical as Orlinsky maintained. Barr discerned at least five classes of (KQ) readings. In general, Q readings (1) represented how the text was to be recited, regardless of how it was written; and (2) often brought the K reading into line with more current spelling convention.

post-exilic Hebrew;[73] therefore poetry as well as prose can be used to determine late expressions.[74] Finally, this study will use the text of the Hebrew Bible from the Leningrad Codex B 19^A (L) as published in *Biblia Hebraica Stuttgartensia* (*BHS*).[75]

Although it is no longer correct to describe Qumran Hebrew as a stage between Late Biblical Hebrew and Tannaitic Hebrew, it still is important for elucidating the character of LBH. Recent scholarship has pointed out that several features of LBH which appear in QH are absent from TH.[76] Likewise, there are other features of LBH that are well attested in TH that do not appear in the Dead Sea Scrolls. Therefore QH cannot have been simply a transitional stage between LBH and TH, but rather was its own late form of the Hebrew language.[77] The language of the Dead Sea Scrolls nevertheless helps us identify those characteristics of the Biblical Hebrew that developed during the post-exilic period and continued in QH. C. Rabin noted, 'Many traits connecting the style of the Scrolls specifically with the post-exilic books of the Bible show that there was a continuous tradition'.[78] The texts from Qumran date between 150 BCE and

73. Hurvitz, *Beyn Lashon le-Lashon*, pp. 56–61.

74. See discussion in Bergey, 'The Book of Esther', pp. 19–20. On the distinctive characteristics of BH poetry, see Joüon-Muraoka, *A Grammar of Biblical Hebrew*, pp. 11–12, §3d; p. 365, §112l; pp. 506–08, §137f; G. Bergsträsser, *Hebräische Grammatik*, I, p. 12, §2l; F. Cross and D. Freedman, *Studies in Ancient Yahwistic Poetry*, (SBLDS, 21; Missoula, MT: Scholars Press, 1975), pp. 27–35.

75. *Biblia Hebraica Stuttgartensia*, (ed. K. Elliger and W. Rudolph; Stuttgart: Deutsche Bibelgesellschaft, 1967/1977). Although the Aleppo Codex is older and more reliable, it lacks most of the Pentateuch and all of the 'J' material.

76. See in particular E. Qimron, 'Observations on the History of Early Hebrew (1000 BCE–200 CE) in the Light of the Dead Sea Documents', in Dimant and Rappaport (eds.), *The Dead Sea Scrolls: Forty Years of Research*, (Leiden: E.J. Brill, 1992), pp. 349–61; S. Morag, 'Qumran Hebrew: Some Typological Observations', *VT* 38 (1988), pp. 148–64.

77. Note Qimron's apt summary: 'We suggest that the information in the early sources does not reflect a single language as it developed and changed over time, but rather different types of Hebrew at different stages of development. All attempts to fit the surviving fragments of early Hebrew into a single historical sequence are misguided and misleading'; idem., 'Observations on the History of Early Hebrew', p. 360. This would appear to refute the chronological schema employed in this study, but Qimron added: 'However, since similar processes often occurred in different Hebrew dialects, the contrast between classical BH and Palestinian MH can help to delineate those same processes elsewhere'. I would add that QH can help to delineate the development from SBH to LBH.

78. Rabin, 'The Historical Background of Qumran Hebrew', p. 149. Hence Rabin was incorrect when he added, 'The development during the latter part of the Second Temple period thus took the perfectly natural course of gradual transition towards later forms of the language'; ibid., p. 158. See also Kutscher, 'Hebrew Language', col. 1584; Bergey, 'The Book of Esther', pp. 21–22.

50 CE[79] Some of the texts from nearby Murabba'at and Naḥal Ḥever date to the 2nd century CE

Several useful publications provide valuable access to the DSS materials. The most important of these is the series published under the title *DJD*. This study will refer also to several other critical studies of DSS texts which have been published separately.[80] Photographs of all DSS texts and text fragments are accessible in microfiche form in the collection *Dead Sea Scrolls on Microfiche*.[81]

A second source which helps determine the features of LBH is Mishnaic Hebrew. Current scholarship recognizes two main types of Mishnaic Hebrew: Tannaitic Hebrew and Amoraic Hebrew.[82] The first is the language of the *tannaim*, that is, the Hebrew of the Mishnah, the Tosefta, the halakhic Midrashim, and the *baraitot* in the two Talmuds.[83] These writings date to a time when MH was still spoken, through ca. 220 CE. The second main type of Hebrew is the language of the *amoraim*, that is, the Hebrew of the Palestinian Talmud, the aggadic Midrashim, and of the Babylonian Talmud.[84] These writings date to the third through fifth centuries CE, when MH was no longer a living language. Because TH represents MH when it was still a living language, it is a more trustworthy basis than AH for the linguistic study of LBH, and this study will refer to it frequently.

One of the problems with using TH in a linguistic study is that the printed editions are unreliable. Kutscher wrote:

> It can be shown that during the Middle Ages the copyists, and later the printers, tried to harmonize MH with BH because they considered departures from BH in MH as mistakes. This 'correcting' tendency led to a complete distortion of the linguistic structure of MH.[85]

---

79. J. Collins, 'Dead Sea Scrolls', *ABD*, II (New York: Doubleday, 1992), pp. 85–101, especially 86; F.M. Cross, *The Ancient Library of Qumran* (Garden City, NY: Doubleday, 1961).

80. Kutscher, *The Language and Linguistic Background of the Isaiah Scroll (1QIsa)*; C. Newsom, *Songs of the Sabbath Sacrifice: A Critical Edition*, (HSM, 27; Atlanta, GA: Scholars Press, 1985); B. Kittel, *The Hymns of Qumran*, (SBLDS, 50; Missoula, MT: Scholars Press, 1981).

81. Emmanuel Tov, ed., *Dead Sea Scrolls on Microfiche* (Leiden: E.J. Brill, 1993), fiche.

82. See discussion in E. Kutscher, 'Hebrew Language, Mishnaic Hebrew', cols. 1590–93. See also references in Bergey, 'The Book of Esther', pp. 23–25.

83. Thus we can further distinguish a Palestinian (TH[1]) and a Babylonian form (TH[2]) of Tannaitic Hebrew; E. Kutscher, 'Hebrew Language, Mishnaic Hebrew', col. 1591; E.Y. Kutscher, *Hebrew and Aramaic Studies*, (ed. Z. Ben-Hayyim et al.; Jerusalem: Magnes Press, 1977, pp. קט-נט (Hebrew).

84. As is the case with TH, we can distinguish a Palestinian (AH[1]) and a Babylonian (AH[2]) form of Amoraic Hebrew. See references above, p. 16, n. 82.

85. E.Y. Kutscher, 'Hebrew Language, Mishnaic Hebrew', col. 1593.

Thus, printed editions of the Mishnah from the seventeenth century onwards minimized the differences between MH and BH.[86] In several studies Kutscher was able to identify several good manuscripts of TH[1] which avoid harmonization with BH: the Kaufmann MS of the Mishnah,[87] the Parma MS of the Mishnah, the Cambridge MS published by W. Lowe, and fragments from the Cairo Genizah. Reliable manuscripts of TH[2] include the Sifra MS and certain Mishnah fragments from the Cairo Genizah.[88]

This study will also employ Aramaic sources to help determine characteristics of LBH.[89] These will include the Biblical Aramaic portions of the Hebrew Bible,[90] Aramaic texts from Qumran,[91] and Targumic Aramaic. The close relationship between Hebrew and Aramaic during the post-exilic period is well established:[92] although Aramaic elements do occur sporadically in pre-exilic biblical texts,[93] following the Babylonian

---

86. C. Rabin, 'Hebrew', in *Current Trends in Linguistics*, VI (ed. T Sebeok; The Hague: Moulton, 1970), p. 321. Note that M. Segal, *Grammar of Mishnaic Hebrew*, relies heavily upon printed editions of the Mishnah and thus should be used with caution.

87. Georg Beer (ed.), *Faksimile-Ausgabe des Mishnacodex Kaufmann A. 50* (The Hague: Nijhoff, 1929).

88. See Kutscher, 'Hebrew Language, Mishnaic Hebrew', col. 1594; Kutscher, *Hebrew and Aramaic Studies* (ed. Z. Ben-Hayyim et.al.; Jerusalem: Magnes Press, 1977), pp. עה-חה (Hebrew).

89. See Hurvitz, 'Linguistic Criteria for Dating Problematic Biblical Texts', p. 76; Hurvitz, *A Linguistic Study of the Relationship between the Priestly Source and the Book of Ezekiel*, p. 158. Driver frequently referred to Aramaic in his efforts to identify features of LBH; Driver, *Introduction to the Old Testament*, pp. 474–75, 484–85, 506–08, 535–40, 547.

90. Jer. 10.11; Ezra 4.8–6.18; 7.12–26; Dan. 2.4–7.28. See F. Rosenthal, *A Grammar of Biblical Aramaic*, (Wiesbaden: Otto Harrassowitz, 1995; 6th edn).

91. Chiefly the Genesis Apocryphon (1QGenAp); see N. Avigad and Y. Yadin, *A Genesis Apocryphon: A Scroll from the Wilderness of Judea* (Jerusalem: Magnes Press, 1956); J. Fitzmeyer, *The Genesis Apocryphon of Qumran Cave I: A Commentary* (BibOr, 18; Rome: Pontifical Biblical Institute, 1966).

92. Note in particular the assessment of J. Naveh and J. Greenfield: 'For those [Israelites] who returned after Cyrus' edict and for the groups which returned later, Hebrew was no longer a mother tongue; they were surely Aramaic speakers. This, together with Aramaic's official status throughout the Achemenid realm, strongly influenced the linguistic situation in the land... Yet Hebrew, to judge from the sources available to us, remained as both a literary and a spoken language in Judah and perhaps in other parts of the country too'; 'Hebrew and Aramaic in the Persian Period', in Davies and Finkelstein (eds.), *Cambridge History of Judaism*, I, *Introduction: the Persian Period* (Cambridge: Cambridge University Press, 1984), p. 119.

93. See especially Hurvitz, 'The Chronological Significance of "Aramaisms"', *IEJ* 18 (1968), pp.234–40; and recently Hurvitz, 'Hebrew and Aramaic in the Biblical Period: The Problem of "Aramaisms" in Linguistic Research of the Hebrew Bible', in Ian Young (ed.), *Biblical Hebrew: Studies in Chronology and Typology* (JSOTSup, 369; London: T. & T. Clark, 2003), pp. 24–37.

exile Aramaic began to exert greater influence on the Hebrew language. Thus many developments in post-exilic Hebrew are paralleled in post-exilic Aramaic. This study will make note of instances in which the Targumim render a SBH expression with the Aramaic equivalent of the corresponding LBH idiom.[94]

Further evidence bearing on the character of Hebrew throughout antiquity comes from inscriptional remains.[95] Particularly important are the Gezer calendar (ca. 10th century BCE),[96] the Samaria ostraca (8th century BCE),[97] the Siloam tunnel inscription (ca. 700 BCE),[98] the Siloam tomb inscription (ca. 700 BCE),[99] the Lachish and the Arad letters (early

94. For Pentateuchal passages, reference will be made most often to the earliest Targumic version of the Pentateuch, Targum Onqelos, which dates to the 1st or early 2nd centuries CE Occasional reference will be made to Targum Pseudo-Jonathan (also known as Targum Yerushalmi I), which, although it was not completed until the 7th-8th centuries CE, does contain a pre-Mishnah stratum; P. Alexander, 'Targum, Targumim', *ABD*, VI (New York: Doubleday, 1992), pp. 321–22, and references.

95. See H. Donner and W. Röllig, *KAI*, I, *Texte*, pp. 34–36, §§182–200 (Wiesbaden: Otto Harrassowitz, 1966); J. Gibson, *Textbook of Syrian Semitic Inscriptions*, I, *Hebrew and Moabite Inscriptions* (Oxford: Clarendon Press, 1971), pp. 1–53; D. Pardee, *Handbook of Ancient Hebrew Letters* (SBLSBS, 15; Chico, CA: Scholars Press, 1982); J. Lindenberger, *Ancient Aramaic and Hebrew Letters*, (SBL Writings from the Ancient World Series, 4; Atlanta, GA: Scholars Press, 1994), pp. 99–116.

96. Gibson, *Textbook of Syrian Semitic Inscriptions*, I, pp. 1–4; Donner and Röllig, *KAI*, II, *Kommentar*, pp. 181–82, §182; G. Davies, *Ancient Hebrew Inscriptions* (Cambridge: Cambridge University Press, 1991), p. 85, §10.001.

97. Gibson, *Textbook of Syrian Semitic Inscriptions*, I, pp. 5–20; Donner and Röllig, *KAI*, II, pp. 183–186, §§183–188; Davies, *Ancient Hebrew Inscriptions*, pp. 39–65, §3. See discussion in I. Young, *Diversity in Pre-Exilic Hebrew* (Tübingen: J.C.B. Mohr, 1993), pp. 114–15. The Samaria ostraca reflect the Northern (Israelian) dialect of Hebrew during the pre-exilic period and are linguistically distinct from the other inscriptions mentioned here. See in particular G.A. Rendsburg, 'Morphological Evidence for Regional Dialects in Ancient Hebrew', in W. Bodine, *Linguistics and Biblical Hebrew* (Winona Lake, IN: Eisenbrauns, 1992), pp. 65–88; Rendsburg, 'The Strata of Biblical Hebrew', *JNSL* 17 (1991), pp. 81–99.

98. Gibson, *Textbook of Syrian Semitic Inscriptions*, I, pp. 21–23; Donner and Röllig, *KAI*, I, pp. 189–188, §§189; Davies, *Ancient Hebrew Inscriptions*, p. 68, §4.116. See discussion in Young, *Diversity in Pre-Exilic Hebrew*, pp. 104–07.

99. Gibson, *Textbook of Syrian Semitic Inscriptions*, vol. 1, pp. 23–24; Donner and Röllig, *KAI*, vol. 2, p. 189, §191; Davies, *Ancient Hebrew Inscriptions*, p. 73, §4.401. See discussion in Young, *Diversity in Pre-exilic Hebrew*, pp. 107–08.

6th century),[100] and the recently discovered silver plaques from Ketef Hinnom in Jerusalem (late 7th century BCE).[101]

The extent of the 'J' source that would be subject to linguistic analysis was determined by which verses of the Pentateuch were attributed to 'J' by all of the following scholars: J. Carpenter and G. Harford-Battersby,[102] S.R. Driver,[103] M. Noth,[104] G. von Rad,[105] and O. Eissfeldt.[106] These scholars were chosen for three principal reasons. First, they all held an important place in the history of biblical scholarship. Second, they all published lists ascribing verses of the Pentateuch to the different major sources.[107] Third, most of these scholars – Carpenter and Harford-Battersby, Driver, Noth, and Eissfeldt – are cited in previous analyses of LBH by Polzin and Hurvitz.[108] Thus I hope to maintain a degree of consistency with the work of these other scholars. The following verses are considered 'J' by all of the aforementioned scholars:

100. Gibson, *Textbook of Syrian Semitic Inscriptions*, I, pp. 32–54; Donner and Röllig, *KAI*, II, pp. 189–99, §§192–199 (*KAI* does not contain the Arad inscriptions); Davies, *Ancient Hebrew Inscriptions*, pp. 1–38, §§1–2; H. Torczyner, *Lachish*, I, *Lachish Letters* (London: Oxford University Press, 1938); Y. Aharoni, *Arad Inscriptions* (Jerusalem: Israel Exploration Society, 1981). *Contra* Polzin (*Late Biblical Hebrew*, p. 4), the language of the Lachish and Arad letters is SBH. See Hurvitz, *Beyn Lashon le-Lashon*, pp. 177–79; Hurvitz, *Linguistic Study*, p. 162, n. 20; Rabin, 'Hebrew and Aramaic in the First Century', pp. 1012–13; Young, *Diversity in Pre-Exilic Hebrew*, p. 110.

101. Davies, *Ancient Hebrew Inscriptions*, p. 72, §§4.301–4.302; G. Barkay, 'The Priestly Benediction on Silver Plaques From Ketef Hinnom in Jerusalem', *Tel Aviv* 19 (1992), pp.139–92, especially 174.

102. J. Carpenter and G. Harford-Battersby, *The Hexateuch According to the Revised Version*, I (London: Longmans, Green, and Co., 1900), especially pp. 272–78.

103. Driver, *Introduction to the Old Testament*, pp. 14–69.

104. Noth, *A History of Pentateuchal Origins*, pp. 261–76.

105. G. von Rad, *Genesis: A Commentary*, (Philadelphia, PA: Westminster Press, 1972; rev. edn). Note that Von Rad delineated 'J' only for the book of Genesis.

106. Eissfeldt, *The Old Testament: An Introduction*, pp. 188–204. Note that Eissfeldt further distinguished an 'L' ('Lay') source within 'J'. Since his 'L' source is essentially a subset of what other scholars call 'J', 'L' verses were treated as 'J' for the purpose of this study.

107. Although biblical scholarship is replete with references to the major Pentateuchal sources, there are remarkably few examples of lists which specify which verses belong to each source. See also W. Harrelson, *Interpreting the Old Testament* (New York: Holt, Rinehart and Winston, 1964), pp. 487–92; B. Anderson, *Understanding the Old Testament*, (Englewood Cliffs, NJ: Prentice Hall, Inc., 1966; 2nd edn), pp. 170–71; A. Campbell and M. O'Brien, *Sources of the Pentateuch: Texts, Introductions, Annotations* (Minneapolis, MN: Fortress Press, 1993), pp. 91–160. The source outlines provided in these works are based explicitly on the work of M. Noth, and were not included.

108. See Polzin, *Late Biblical Hebrew*, 85, p. 117; Hurvitz, *A Linguistic Study of the Relationship between the Priestly Source and the Book of Ezekiel*, especially pp. 7–21, 143–70.

Genesis
2.4b-25
3.1–24
4.1–24
6.1–8
7.1–5, 7–10, 12, 17b, 22
8.2b-3a, 6, 8–12, 13b, 20–22
9.18–27
10.8–19, 21, 25–30
11.1–9, 28–30
12.1–4a, 6–8
13.7–11a, 13–18
16.1b-2, 4–8, 11–14
18.1–33
19.1–28, 30–35
21.7
22.20–24
24.1–6, 8–9, 11, 18, 21–67
25.1–5, 11b, 21–25a, 26a, 28
26.1–3a, 6–14, 16–17, 19–33
27.1a, 2, 4b, 5b-7a, 15, 18b-20, 24–27, 29–30, 31b-34
28.13–16, 19a
29.2–14, 26, 30
30.27, 31a, 34–38a, 39–43
31.3, 46, 48
32.3–7a, 22a, 23b, 24–29, 31–32
34.2b-3, 5, 7, 11, 19, 26, 30–31
35.21–22a
37.12–13a, 14b, 18b, 21, 25b-27, 28b
38.1–30
39.1–5, 6b, 7b-23
40.1
43.1–13, 15–23a, 24–34
44.1–34
45.4, 28
46.28–34
47.1–4, 6b, 13–26, 29–31
50.1–10a, 14
Exodus
3.7–8, 16–18
4.1–9, 19–20a, 22–26, 29, 30b-31
5.3, 5–23
6.1
7.14, 16–17a, 18, 25–29

8.4–11a, 16–28
9.13–18, 23b, 24b
10.1–7, 13b, 14b-19, 28–29
11.4–8
12.29–30
13.21–22
14.5b, 6, 19b, 20b, 24a, 25b, 30
15.22–25a
17.2b
19.20–22, 24–25

As one can see, the number of verses which are universally accepted as 'J' is quite small. Verses which are considered 'J' by some but not all of the above scholars will be treated in a separate chapter (including, of course, sections from the book of Numbers).

The following discussion is presented as follows: chapter 2 will analyze 'J' with respect to morphological traits of LBH; chapter 3 will analyze 'J' with respect to syntactic features of LBH; chapter 4 will discuss expressions which are characteristic of LBH; chapter 5 will treat 'J' with respect to lexical characteristics of LBH; chapter 6 will discuss the issue of Persian loan-words in the Hebrew Bible and in 'J'; chapter 7 will treat those verses which are not universally accepted as 'J' (see above); and chapter 8 will summarize the results of the research.

Chapter 2

MORPHOLOGY

Several characteristic features of LBH are morphological in nature, that is, morphemes or morphological traits which are either nonexistent or unproductive in pre-exilic texts. Several such morphological features of LBH which can be compared to 'J' are discussed in this chapter:

	Late Biblical Hebrew	*Standard Biblical Hebrew*
1)	וָאֶקְטְלָה	וָאֶקְטֹל
2)	־ותיהם	־ותם
3)	חיה	חי
4)	קים	הקים
5)	שתיה	שתות, שתה

1. וָאֶקְטְלָה

The *waw*-consecutive (or *wayyiqtōl*) in BH is normally understood as the imperfect (or 'prefixed') form of the verb preceded by a strong *waw*.[1] As Joüon-Muraoka stated:

> With the Waw inversive the verb form undergoes two changes in accordance with phonetic laws: 1) the final vowel reflects earlier shortening as in the jussive; 2) the stress recedes, and as a consequence, the post-stress vowel becomes short. These changes may occur only if the first syllable is open, and the last closed, and the first vowel is qameṣ, ṣere or ṣiriq. ... Sometimes one observes the first change, sometimes the second, and sometimes neither.

Thus the *waw*-consecutive traditionally has been understood as a strong *waw* added to the imperfect form of the verb, which then undergoes

---

1. The 'strong *waw*' is 'a Waw which has vowel *a* that adds some force (like that of the definite article and that of the interrogative pronoun) to the following consonant, which, as a consequence, is doubled'; Joüon-Muraoka, *Grammar of Biblical Hebrew*, p. 139, §47a. Hence the alternation between יִקְטֹל and *waw*-conversive וַיִּקְטֹל. I find the morpho-phonemic explanation of Joüon-Muraoka preferable to that of C.H. Gordon and G.D. Young. See Gordon, *UT*, II, pp. 110–11, §12.9; and G.D. Young, 'The Origin of the Waw Conversive', *JNES* 12 (1953), pp. 248–52. For the contrary view, see Joüon-Muraoka, *Grammar of Biblical Hebrew*, p. 140, §79a and references; see also E. Revell, 'Stress and the Waw "Consecutive" in Biblical Hebrew', *JAOS* 104 (1984), pp. 437–44.

certain changes, as described above.[2] Recent research in the development of the Hebrew verbal systems would indicate that the prefix conjugation of ancient Hebrew had two tenses, each with three modes:[3]

	Indicative		Injunctive
Preterite	*yaqṭul*	Jussive	*yaqṭul*
Imperfect	*yaqṭulu*	Volitive	*yaqṭula*
Energic	*yaqṭulun(n)a*	Energic	*yaqṭulun(n)a*

The *waw*-consecutive,[4] then, is based on the ancient Hebrew preterite, introduced by the strong *waw*.[5] The lack of an original final short vowel in both the jussive and the preterite goes far in explaining the vocalic and morphological differences between the indicative imperfect and both the jussive and the *waw*-consecutive.[6]

The Hebrew cohortative נֶ/אֶקְטְלָה is now understood to derive from the ancient Hebrew volitive,[7] and it should not be compared to the Arabic second energic.[8] In Hebrew the use of the cohortative is limited to the 1st person.[9] Moreover, because the ancient Hebrew volitive (later cohortative) was distinct from the preterite (later part of the *waw*-consecutive, as above), the *waw*-consecutive normally does not appear with the attached cohortative form. In other words, for the first person, Hebrew normally displays וָאֶקְטֹל but not וָאֶקְטְלָה.[10]

2. See also S.R. Driver, *A Treatise on the Use of the Tenses in Hebrew* (Oxford: Clarendon Press, 1892), pp. 50–53, §§44–47; and GKC, pp. 129–32, §48.

3. A. Rainey, 'The Ancient Hebrew Prefix Conjugation in the Light of Amarnah Canaanite', *Hebrew Studies* 27 (1986), pp. 4–16.

4. Rainey commented, 'Because of its [the *waw*-consecutive's] function in the narration of sequential actions, I propose to call this conjugation pattern the preterite continuative. The term *waw consersive* is obsolete.... The term *waw consecutive* is appropriate' (emphasis in original); 'The Ancient Hebrew Prefix Conjugation', p. 6. I have declined to adopt the term *waw*-consecutive because that term is already reserved for the simple *waw* plus the imperfect.

5. Revell, 'Stress and the *Waw* "Consecutive" in Biblical Hebrew', p. 443.

6. Rainey, 'The Ancient Hebrew Prefix Conjugation', p. 5; and R. Goerwitz, 'The Accentuation of the Hebrew Jussive and Preterite', *JAOS* 112 (1992), pp. 198–203.

7. See Joüon-Muraoka, *Grammar of Biblical Hebrew*, who compares the Hebrew cohortative to the Arabic subjunctive, as in *fa'akula*; *Grammar of Biblical Hebrew*, §116b, p. 382, n. 1. See also Rainey, 'The Ancient Hebrew Prefix Conjugation', pp. 8–10.

8. *Contra* W. LaSor, *Handbook of Biblical Hebrew*, II (Grand Rapids, MI: Eerdmans, 1979), p. 97, §27.53; and GKC, pp. 129–30, §48b.

9. GKC, §48b, p. 129.

10. This section will not, for the most part, deal with the problem of final weak verbs, for which the cohortative form is morphologically identical with the imperfect; note Rainey, 'The Ancient Hebrew Prefix Conjugation', p. 9; but there are exceptions, discussed in E. Revell, 'First Person Imperfect Forms with *Waw* Consecutive', *VT* 38 (1988), pp. 419–26. Nor will it treat the problem of apocapated versus non-apocapated forms when attached to *waw*-conversive, since different morphological and analogical processes are involved for final weak verbs; see E. Qimron, 'Consecutive and Conjunctive Imperfect: the Form of the Imperfect with *Waw* in Biblical Hebrew', *JQR* 77 (1986–87), pp. 149–61.

A long *waw*-consecutive וָאֶקְטְלָה occurs in the Bible with the same meaning as וָאֶקְטֹל.[11] This long *waw*-consecutive occurs 94 times for the 1st person singular in the Bible. It occurs rarely in pre-exilic and exilic texts: Gen. 32.6; Josh. 24.8; Judg. 6.9, 6.10, 10.12; 1 Sam. 2.28, 28.15;[12] 2 Sam. 4.10, 7.9, 12.8, 22.24; Ps 3.6, 7.5, 69.12, 69.21, 73.16;[13] Jer. 11.18; Ezek. 3.3, 9.8, 16.1. It occurs predominantly in post-exilic texts, however: Zech. 11.13; Ps. 119.55, 119.59, 119.106, 119.131, 119.147, 119.158; Job 19.20, 29.17; Ezra 7.28, 8.15, 8.16, 8.17, 8.24, 8.25, 8.26, 8.28, 9.3, 9.5, 9.6; Neh. 1.4, 2.1, 2.6, 2.9, 2.13, 5.7, 5.8, 5.13, 6.3, 6.11, 6.12, 7.5, 12.31, 13.7, 13.8, 13.9, 13.10, 13.11, 13.13, 13.17, 13.19, 13.21, 13.22; Dan. 8.13, 8.15, 8.17, 9.3, 9.4, 10.16, 10.19, 12.8.[14]

Although the *waw*-consecutive appears several times in pre-exilic and exilic texts, the normal *waw*-consecutive וָאֶקְטֹל pattern is more common. The ratio of normal to long *waw*-consecutive forms in early texts is 11:1 in Joshua, 10:3 in Judges, 9:2 in 1 Samuel, 39:1 in Jeremiah, and 57:3 in Ezekiel. Note, however, the unusual preponderance of וָאֶקְטְלָה forms in 2 Samuel, where the ratio is 4:4.[15] Certain late books and texts, however, display a strong preference for the וָאֶקְטְלָה pattern. The ratio of normal to long *waw*-consecutive verbs is 0:6 in Psalm 119, 0:11 in Ezra, 3:23 in Nehemiah, 1:8 in Daniel, and 0:4 in prose sections of Job. Note, however, the ratio of 5:1 in Zechariah, which displays a preference for the unlengthened form. The above evidence suggests that the long *waw*-consecutive was used in the pre-exilic and exilic periods, but became the predominant form of the 1cs *waw*-consecutive only in the post-exilic period. (Although, it must be noted, not all post-exilic books made use of the late form.)

When the *waw*-consecutive is understood as a strong *waw* preceding the preterite (which is morphologically identical with the jussive) or, in the case of the long *waw*-consecutive, the cohortative, that the shift from וְאֶקְטֹל to וְאֶקְטְלָה can be understood. The modal distinction between the indicative אֶקְטֹל and אֶקְטְלָה broke down in late Hebrew. Bergsträsser commented:

---

11. See Bergsträsser, *Hebräische Grammatik*, II, p. 23, §5f. This section will focus on the 1st person singular rather than the 1st person plural forms וַנִּקְטֹל and וַנִּקְטְלָה. The long *waw*-consecutive of the 1st person plural occurs only 5 times in the Hebrew Bible: Gen. 41.11, 43.21; Ps. 90.10; Ezra 8.23, 8.31. There are not sufficient examples of וַנִּקְטְלָה to establish whether it is significantly more common in post-exilic than pre-exilic texts.

12. *BHS* notes, '2 Mss. no ה-.'

13. *BHS* notes that several manuscripts read וָאֶחֶשְׁבָה instead of וָאֲחַשְּׁבָה.

14. Concerning the absence of וָאֶקְטְלָה in Chronicles, see comments by Rezetko, 'Dating Biblical Hebrew', pp. 227–28.

15. The use of only the long *waw*-conversive in 2 Samuel might be a coincidence, or it might reflect intrusions of dialectal or colloquial forms in classical Hebrew; see Rendsburg, 'The Strata of Biblical Hebrew', pp. 81–99.

Cohortative and jussive are also to be found more often than what is commonly measured in the sense of a simple statement... For more recent poetry (also Dan.) this can be recognized as an authentic linguistic practice. This more recent poetry has partially lost the sense for mood differentiations as it has for tense differences.[16]

Kutscher also observed that Ezra, Nehemiah, and Daniel contain examples of אקטלה and ואקטלה which are 'not necessarily cohortative'.[17] Just as the meaning and the use of the cohortative began to merge with that of the indicative, so the meaning and use of the long *waw*-consecutive began to merge with and sometimes supplant that of the normal *waw*-consecutive.

The lateness of the long *waw*-consecutive is confirmed by its predominance at Qumran. There the normal *waw*-consecutive occurs but once, besides which the only form of the *waw*-consecutive (or conjunctive) in the 1st person singular is ואקטלה, which occurs 31 times.[18] Qimron added, 'The consistency of this feature in DSS Hebrew implies that it reflects the spoken language. It cannot have been either borrowed or invented.'[19] If the use of ואקטלה reflects spoken Hebrew, this may help explain the occasional appearance of the form in pre-exilic and exilic texts.[20] In addition, the Isaiah scroll from Qumran frequently uses a long *waw*-consecutive to render a ואקטל form in the MT.[21]

As for other post-biblical evidence, the Samaritan Pentateuch, like QH, employs אקטלה for the past tense.[22] The long *waw*-consecutive does not appear in rabbinic Hebrew most likely because TH (MH) is colloquial, and the *waw*-consecutive was a literary form.[23]

Since the frequent use of the long *waw*-consecutive instead of וָאֶקְטֹל is characteristic of LBH, it is noteworthy that 'J' never employs the form וָאֶקְטְלָה. The ratio of normal to long *waw*-consecutive forms in the 1st

---

16. Bergsträsser, *Hebräische Grammatik*, II, p. 50, §10l.

17. Kutscher, *The Language and Linguistic Background of the Isaiah Scroll (1QIsa)*, p. 327.

18. E. Qimron, *HDSS*, pp. 44, §310.122. See also M. Smith, *The Origins and Development of the Waw-consecutive*, (HSM, 39; Atlanta: Scholars Press, 1991).

19. Qimron, 'The History of Early Hebrew', p. 355.

20. For further evidence of spoken Hebrew (as against the classical, literary form of the language) in the Bible, see G.A. Rendsburg, *Diglossia in Ancient Hebrew*, (AOS, 72; New Haven, CT: American Oriental Society, 1990).

21. Kutscher, *The Language and Linguistic Background of the Isaiah Scoll (1QIsa)*, 326. Kutscher added: 'On the other hand, the first part of the [Isaiah] Scr. is parallel in this respect to Chronicles, where the [long] usage is not found, and whose author evinces a tendency to delete it even where his sources have it'; ibid., p. 327. This helps explain why ואקטלה never occurs in Chronicles (see above, pp. 24–25).

22. Qimron, *HDSS*, p. 44, n. 5.

23. See, for example, Qimron, 'Observations on the History of Early Hebrew', pp. 349–61.

person singular is 23:0 in 'J'. Note the following examples of וָאֶקְטֹל in 'J' source texts:[24]

Gen. 3.10	וָאִירָא...וָאֵחָבֵא
Gen. 3.12	וָאֹכֵל
Gen. 3.13	וָאֹכֵל
Gen. 24.39	וָאֹמַר
Gen. 24.42	וָאָבֹא
Gen. 24.45	וָאֹמַר
Gen. 24.47	וָאֶשְׁאַל
Gen. 24.48	וָאֶקֹּד...וָאֶשְׁתַּחֲוֶה...וָאֲבָרֵךְ
Gen. 27.33	וָאֹכַל
Gen. 32.5	וָאֵחַר
Gen. 39.14	וָאֶקְרָא
Gen. 39.15	וָאֶקְרָא
Gen. 39.18	וָאֶקְרָא
Gen. 44.28	וָאֹמַר
Exod. 3.8	וָאֵרֵד
Exod. 3.17	וָאֹמַר
Exod. 4.23	וָאֹמַר

'J''s consistent preference for וָאֶקְטֹל against וָאֶקְטְלָה agrees with early Hebrew usage.

2. וֹ'תִיהֶם

There are two possible forms that the 3rd person masculine plural suffix can take when attached to a feminine plural noun ending in *-ôt* וֹת-: *-ām* ־ָם or *-êhem* ־ֵיהֶם.[25] For example, compare בְּמֹשְׁבֹתָם (Numb. 31.10) and מוֹשְׁבוֹתֵיהֶם (Ezek. 6.14). This situation is true even when the pronominal suffix is added to masculine plural nouns which take the feminine plural ending *-ôt* וֹת-. For example, compare אֲבֹתָם (Exod. 4.5) and אֲבֹתֵיהֶם (Neh. 9.2). Although there is no discernable difference in meaning between the shorter and longer endings, they are not free variants. The following chart lists how often the endings *-ôtām* ־וֹתָם and *-ôtêhem* ־וֹתֵיהֶם occur throughout the Hebrew Bible and the ratio between the two:[26]

24. Although this section does not focus on *waw*-consecutive forms for the 1st person plural, note the following examples of the normal *waw*-consecutive (1cp) in 'J' source texts: וַנֹּאמֶר (Gen. 44.20); וַנֹּאמֶר (Gen. 44.22); וַנַּגֶּד (Gen. 44.24).

25. GKC, p. 259, §91n; Joüon-Muraoka, *Grammar of Biblical Hebrew*, p. 288, §94g. For a fuller discussion, see Hurvitz, *A Linguistic Study of the Relationship between the Priestly Source and the Book of Ezekiel*, pp. 24–27.

26. See also the convenient chart in A. Cohen, 'Makotkha', *Bet Mikra* 61 (1975), pp. 303–305.

	‫וֹתם‬	‫וֹתיהם‬	ratioio of short to long forms
Genesis–Deuteronomy[27]	231[28]	8	1:0.04
Joshua–Kings	79	14	1:0.18
Jeremiah	15	19	1:1.27
Exilic books[29]	28	9	1:0.32
Post-exilic books[30]	50	67	1:1.34

The above numbers suggest that there is a gradual process in which the extended ending begins to replace the shorter ending. The shorter ending ‫וֹתם‬ dominates in pre-exilic texts, the extended form ‫וֹתיהם‬ being rare in comparison. Only in later books of the Bible does the extended form ‫וֹתיהם‬ occur more frequently, eventually becoming more common than the shorter ending in the post-exilic period.[31] Some words – ‫תולדות‬, ‫ארצות, דורות, צבאות, נפשות, גלגלות, שמות‬ ‫סבלות‬ – occur only with the short ending, even in exilic and post-exilic texts.[32] But other words display strongly the trend in which the extended ending replaced the short ending in the post-exilic period, such as ‫אבות‬:[33]

	‫אבותם‬	‫אבותיהם‬
Genesis–Deuteronomy (excluding 'J')	42	0
Joshua–Kings	21	1 (1 Kings 14.15)
Jeremiah	10	3
Exilic books	9	25
Post-exilic books	9	25

27. Verses ascribed to the 'J' source are not included in these totals.

28. This high figure is distorted by the fact that certain chapters of the Pentateuch, due to their subject matter, contain unusually high numbers of words ending in ‫וֹתם‬. The book of Numbers alone contains 93 such examples because of the frequent repetition of the phrase ‫לבני... תולדתם למשפחתם לבית אבתם‬. Even if we exclude Numbers from this chart, that leaves 138 examples of the short ending and 8 of the long, a ratio of 1:0.06

29. As noted in the Introduction, exilic books include Isaiah 40–55, Ezekiel, and Lamentations.

30. As noted in the Introduction, post-exilic books include Isaiah 56–66, Jonah, Haggai, Zechariah, Malachi, late Psalms, prose portions of Job, Qohelet, Esther, Daniel, Ezra, Nehemiah, and Chronicles.

31. Both GKC and Joüon-Muraoka observe that ‫וֹתם‬ is older than ‫וֹתיהם‬, and that the former is more common in earlier books; GKC, p. 259, §91n; Joüon-Muraoka, p. 288, §94g.

32. F. Böttcher noted 56 nouns that appear only with ‫וֹתם‬. He found another 35 only with ‫וֹתיהם‬, many of which occur only in exilic or post-exilic texts. But 22 nouns appear with both the short and extended endings, although most of these nouns usually take the short ending (one exception is ‫בנותיהם‬, which occurs 20 times as opposed to ‫בנותם‬, which occurs but once in Gen. 34.21); Böttcher, *Ausführliches Lehrbuch des hebräischen Sprache*, II (ed. F. Mühlau; Leipzig: Johann Ambrosius Barth, 1868), p. 42.

33. Another good example is ‫מושבות‬, which Hurvitz discussed in *A Linguistic Study of the Relationship between the Priestly Source and the Book of Ezekiel*, pp. 24–27.

This contrast can be more clearly seen in the following examples:[34]

Exod. 36.34	וְאֶת־טַבְּעֹתָם עָשָׂה זָהָב
(Samaritan Pentateuch:	...טבעתיהם)
2 Sam. 22.46	וְיַחְגְּרוּ מִמִּסְגְּרֹתָם
(Compare Ps 18.46:	...ממסגרותיהם)
1 Kgs 8.34	אֶל־הָאֲדָמָה אֲשֶׁר נָתַתָּ לַאֲבוֹתָם
(Compare 2 Chr 6.25:	...לאבתיהם)
Isa. 59.8	וְאֵין מִשְׁפָּט בְּמַעְגְּלוֹתָם)
(Compare 1QIsaª:[35]	במעגלותיהמה)

Hurvitz explained well the distinction between the short and long endings:

> The short form *mōsᵉbhōthām*–whose plurality is indicated only in the noun base (וֹת) but not by the attached possessive suffix (ם‾) - is forced out by a more 'transparent' form, in which the possessive pronoun also acquires its own morpheme of plurality (יהֶם‾). The extended new form *mōsᵉbhōthēyhem* is tautological, since the morpheme *-ōth* is sufficient indication of a plural word... Such redundant employment of two plural morphemes usually stems from attempts, perhaps even unconscious, to emphasize the *meaning* (plural sense), which is liable to be felt insufficient on account of the *form* (plural ending) (emphasis in original).[36]

Two factors may have influenced this shift from ם‾ to ותיהם‾ in Biblical Hebrew: the influence of the Aramaic third person plural suffix הם‾, and internal analogy with the regular Hebrew masculine plural suffix יהֶם‾.[37] Although the extended ending ותיהם‾ does occur sporadically in early texts, it is the intensification of its use in exilic and post-exilic texts which characterizes LBH.

The late character of ותיהם‾ can be seen in post-biblical literature. In

---

34. Cited in Hurvitz, *A Linguistic Study of the Relationship between the Priestly Source and the Book of Ezekiel*, p. 26.

35. Kutscher, *The Language and Linguistic Background of the Isaiah Scroll (1QIsa)*, p. 451.

36. Hurvitz, *A Linguistic Study of the Relationship between the Priestly Source and the Book of Ezekiel*, p. 25.

37. Hurvitz, *A Linguistic Study of the Relationship between the Priestly Source and the Book of Ezekiel*, p. 25; Kutscher, *The Language and Linguistic Background of the Isaiah Scroll (1QIsa)*, p. 445: 'process of analogy'. Further evidence that internal analogy played a significant role is the alternation between the forms עמיהם-עם and תחתיהם-תחת:

	עמם	עמיהם	תחת	תחתיהם
Pentateuch (excluding J)	20	2	4	1
Joshua–Kings	16	0	0	1
Post-exilic texts	2	17	0	2

Post-exilic texts show a marked preference for the longer forms עמיהם and תחתיהם. See BDB, 767a, s.v. עם; 1065a, s.v. תחת; KB, 771a, s.v. עם; 1026a, s.v. תחת. Concerning the בם and בהם see Rezetko, 'Dating Biblical Hebrew', pp. 226–27.

Tannaitic literature, the long form ‎וֹתֵיהֶ/ם‎ occurs far more regularly than the shorter ending ‎וֹתָ/ם‎.[38] For example, ‎אֲבוֹתֵיהֶם/ן‎ occurs 16 times, compared to ‎אֲבוֹתָם/ן‎ which occurs 6 times; ‎אִמּוֹתֵיהֶם/ן‎ occurs 4 times, and only once do we find ‎אִמּוֹתָם/ן‎ in TH.[39] Bar-Asher noted that short forms in TH should probably be understood as the result of biblicizing tendencies among the Tannaim:

> One gets the impression that the occurrences of ‎אֲבוֹתָן‎ (e.g., 'Avot 2.2, Niddah 4.2 [2x]) and ‎אִמּוֹתָן‎ (T. Soṭah 6.4 according to MS Vienna; in MS Erfurt we find ‎אֵם‎ in the singular) are due to the literary influence of the Bible. That is to say, it is 'borrowed', to use Hannemann's term, and is not due to the copying of the texts by later generations... Rather, it is through the work of the Tannaitic authors themselves that we may understand the form ‎זְכוּת אֲבוֹתָן‎ in Mishnah 'Avot, which is a tractate with a clear literary relationship to the writings of the Bible.[40]

The evidence from Qumran is more ambiguous. Biblical texts from Qumran prefer the longer form;[41] for example, the Isaiah scroll from Qumran (1QIsaᵃ) twice replaces MT ‎וֹתָם‎ with ‎וֹתֵיהֵמָה‎ (Isa. 59.8, 66.4).[42] But elsewhere the form ‎ם‎ (or ‎מָה‎) is preferred over ‎יהֶם‎ (or ‎יהֵמָה‎).[43] Nevertheless, the evidence of TH and the biblical texts from Qumran still allow us to conclude that in post-biblical literature, ‎וֹתֵיהֶם‎ (or ‎וֹתֵיהֵמָה‎ in QH) began to replace SBH ‎וֹתָם‎ in similar contexts.

The longer ending ‎וֹתֵיהֶם‎ which predominates in LBH is absent from texts attributed to 'J.' Instead, we find two examples in which 'J' employs the preferred SBH ending ‎וֹתָם‎:[44]

Gen. 44.13	וַיִּקְרְעוּ שִׂמְלֹתָם
Exod. 5.5	וְהִשְׁבַּתֶּם אֹתָם מִסִּבְלֹתָם

If 'J' were composed during after the Exile as some maintain, we might expect at least one of these examples to display the longer form ‎וֹתֵיהֶם‎,

38. Hurvitz, *A Linguistic Study of the Relationship between the Priestly Source and the Book of Ezekiel*, p. 25, n. 9. This feature is not specifically discussed in M.H. Segal, *Grammar of Mishnaic Hebrew* (Oxford: Clarendon Press, 1927).

39. M. Bar-Asher, 'The Study of Mishnaic Hebrew Grammar - Achievements, Problems, and Goals', in M. Bar-Asher (ed.), *Proceedings of the Ninth World Congress of Jewish Studies: Panel Sessions: Hebrew and Aramaic*, (Jerusalem: World Union of Jewish Studies, 1985), pp. 3–37 (in Hebrew). I would like to thank Steven Fassberg of Hebrew University for this reference, which was passed on to me by Gary Rendsburg of Cornell University.

40. Bar-Asher, 'The Study of Mishnaic Hebrew Grammar', p. 11.

41. Qimron, *HDSS*, p. 63, n. 81.

42. Kutscher, *The Language and Linguistic Background of the Isaiah Scoll (1QIsa)*, p. 445.

43. Qimron, *HDSS*, p. 63. But twice in 11QT ‎לְדוֹרֹתָמָה‎ is corrected to ‎לְדוֹרֹתֵיהֵמָה‎ (TS 21.9, 27.5); Qimron, ibid., p. 63, n. 80.

44. Note also that 'J' displays the SBH form ‎עִמָּם‎ at Gen. 18.16 and 29.9. LBH ‎עִמָּהֶם‎ is absent from 'J' source verses.

but such is not the case. 'J' employs morphology which is consistent with the pre-exilic period.

3. חיה

The verb חיה 'live' occurs frequently throughout the MT.[45] The normal form of the 3ms perfect of חיה is חַי.[46] Regarding this form, Hurvitz commented:

> Contrary to the standard inflection of final ה verbs, in which the third radical of the 3rd m.s. appears in the perfect as הָ֫ (*e.g.*, בָּנָה), the root חיה loses both its final vowel and ה. In the paradigm of *hyh*, one finds the 3rd m.s. as חַי - a form modelled after the pattern of the ע״ע verb (*e.g.*, תַּם).[47]

The form חַי occurs frequently in pre-exilic texts:

Deut. 4.42[48]　　　　　ונס אל־אחת מן־הערים האל וחי

And in exilic and post-exilic texts:

Ezek. 20.11, 13, 21[49]　　　אשר יעשה אתם האדם וחי בהם
Neh. 6.11　　　　　　　　אשר־יבוא אל־ההיכל וחי

However, 3ms perfect חיה, which reflects the standard inflection of ל״ה (IIIy) verbs, occurs several times in exilic and post-exilic texts:

---

45. For a fuller discussion see Hurvitz, *A Linguistic Study of the Relationship between the Priestly Source and the Book of Ezekiel*, pp. 46–48; and Bergey, 'The Book of Esther', pp. 35–36.

46. See BDB, חיה, p. 510b; KB, p. 292b; *HALAT*, p. 296b. For the cognate חיא in BA, see BDB, p. 1092b; and KB, חיה, p. 1092a.

47. Hurvitz, *A Linguistic Study of the Relationship between the Priestly Source and the Book of Ezekiel*, p. 47. Also cited in Bergey, 'The Book of Esther', p. 35. The 3ms perfect forms for חיה are discussed also in GKC, p. 218, §76i; and in Joüon-Muraoka, *Grammar of Biblical Hebrew*, pp. 210–211, §79s.

48. Also Gen. 5.5, 11.12, 11.14, 25.7; Lev. 18.5, 25.35; Deut. 5.21, 19.4, 19.5; 1 Sam. 20.31; 2 Sam. 12.22.

49. Also Jer. 21.9(K), 38.2(K); Ezek. 18.13, 18.24, 47.9. Note that Ezek. 20.11, 13, 21 = Lev. 18.5.

50. Also Jer. 21.9(Q), 38.2(Q); Ezek. 33.11. Baruch Levine argued that the unusual appearance of both SBH חי and LBH חיה in Ezekiel 18 threatens this understanding of חי as early and חיה as late (see below), especially given his argument that 'P' is literarily dependent upon Ezekiel (personal communication, March 21, 1994). First, this is not the only instance in the Bible where the same passage (sometimes the same verse) employs two different forms of the same word: consider, as but one example, the famous case of the alternation between Aramaic ארקא and ארעא in Jer. 10.11; see R. Ratner, 'Morphological Variation in Biblical Hebrew Rhetoric', *Maarav* 8 (1992): pp. 143–159. Second, note Hurvitz' comment:

Ezek. 18.23 et passim[50]   הלוא בשובו מדרכיו וחיה

Esth. 4.11 et passim[51]   מאשר יושיט־לו המלך...וחיה

The form חַי occurs in pre- and post-exilic Hebrew, but חיה occurs only in late texts.

The lateness of the form חיה is confirmed by its frequent appearance in post-biblical Hebrew.[52] It occurs in Qumran Hebrew. Note the following example:

CD 3.16   אמתו וחפצי רצונו אשר האדם וחיה בהם פתח לפניהם
(Compare Lev. 18.5   אשר יעשה אתם האדם וחי בהם
and Neh. 9.29   (אשר־יעשה אדם וחיה בהם

It is also well attested in rabbinic literature:

T. Shabbat 15.8   המתינו לו ומלווהו וחיה
Seder 'Olam Rabbah 1   נמחא נח חיה אחר הפלגה אשר שנים

The above evidence clearly indicates that חיה reflects a secondary development which took place in exilic period Hebrew, in which חַי became חיה through analogy with regular IIIy verbs.[53]

It is therefore significant that the 3ms perfect of חיה is חַי in 'J'. Note the following example:

Gen. 3.22   פן ישלח ידו...ואכל וחי לעלם

The form of the 3ms perfect of חיה in 'J' conforms to the classical usage, and is further evidence of the pre-exilic linguistic character of 'J'.

It is interesting to note that while using the formula 'statutes and ordinances, by whose observance a man shall live' and referring to the law of interest - both of which are mentioned in the Pentateuch - Ez. employs strictly the classical model [חי] as found in Lev. However, when its statements have no direct parallel in the Pentateuch, its author apparently feels himself less bound by classical usage. This may suggest that Ez. here is not only later than P *linguistically*, but also dependent on P *literarily* (emphasis in original).

See Hurvitz, *A Linguistic Study of the Relationship between the Priestly Source and the Book of Ezekiel*, p. 48

51. Also Neh. 9.29; Qoh. 6.6.

52. James H. Charlesworth, and R.E. Whitaker, *Graphic Concordance to the Dead Sea Scrolls* (Tübingen: J.C.B. Mohr, 1991), p. 192; see also Academy of the Hebrew Language, *Historical Dictionary of the Hebrew Language* (Jerusalem: Academy of the Hebrew Language, 1988; microfiche), plate 8340 (Hebrew).

53. Thus Hurvitz, *A Linguistic Study of the Relationship between the Priestly Source and the Book of Ezekiel*, p. 47.

4. קִים

The Piel of the hollow verb קוּם appears 10 times in exilic and post-exilic texts. Note the following:

Ezek. 13.6	וַיְחַלּוּ לְקַיֵּם דָּבָר
Ps. 119.28	קַיְּמֵנִי כִּדְבָרֶךָ
Ps. 119.106	נִשְׁבַּעְתִּי וָאֲקַיֵּמָה
Esth. 9.21	לְקַיֵּם עֲלֵיהֶם
Esth. 9.27	קִיְּמוּ וְקִבְּלוּ (Q) הַיְּהוּדִים עֲלֵיהֶם
Esth. 9.29	לְקַיֵּם אֵת אִגֶּרֶת הַפּוּרִים
Esth. 9.31	לְקַיֵּם אֶת־יְמֵי הַפֻּרִים הָאֵלֶּה בִּזְמַנֵּיהֶם
	כַּאֲשֶׁר קִיַּם עֲלֵיהֶם
Esth. 9.32	קִיַּם דִּבְרֵי הַפֻּרִים
Ruth 4.7[54]	לְקַיֵּם כָּל־דָּבָר

As can be seen in the above examples, the Piel of קוּם is used in the sense of 'fulfill (a word or promise), establish (a thing), confirm (a word), or impose (something on someone).'[55] The Aramaic equivalent of this expression, the Pael of קוּם, occurs once in Daniel:[56]

Dan. 6.8	אִתְיָעַטוּ...לְקַיָּמָה קְיָם מַלְכָּא

The Hiphil of קוּם is used with the same meaning in early texts of the Bible. Compare the use of הֵקִים with the similar use of קִים in late texts:[57]

2 Kgs 23.24	לְמַעַן הָקִים אֶת־דִּבְרֵי הַתּוֹרָה הַכְּתֻבִים עַל־הַסֵּפֶר
(Compare Ezek. 13.6:	לְקַיֵּם דָּבָר)
1 Kgs 2.4	לְמַעַן יָקִים יְהוָה אֶת־דְּבָרוֹ
(Compare Esth. 9.32:	קִיַּם דִּבְרֵי הַפֻּרִים)

The above evidence suggests that SBH employed the Hiphil of קוּם to mean 'carry out, give effect to (an oath, covenant, vow, word, plan, or command of man)',[58] and this was replaced in late texts by the Piel of קוּם.

The lateness of the form קִים is confirmed by its frequency in post-biblical Hebrew and Aramaic. Although the Hiphil of קוּם is prevalent at Qumran, קִים occurs once:

CD 12.20	וַאֲמָנָה אֲשֶׁר קִיְּמוּ בְּאֶרֶץ דַּמֶּשֶׂק וְהוּא בְּרִית הַחֲדָשָׁה

---

54. On the late dating of this verse only (not the entire book of Ruth), see A. Hurvitz, 'Shelifat ha-Na'al', pp. 44–49; and Hurvitz, *Beyn Lashon le-Lashon*, p. 140, n. 189.

55. See BDB, p. 878b; and KB, p. 832b, which calls קִים 'late.' See especially *HALAT*, 1016b: 'spät, aram. Einfluss.'

56. See BDB, p. 1110b: 'set up, establish as ordinance'; and KB, p. 1118b.

57. Examples from Bergey, 'The Book of Esther', p. 41.

58. BDB, p. 879a; KB, p. 832b; *HALAT*, p. 1017a.

In rabbinic writings, the Hiphil of קוּם has almost completely disappeared, having been replaced by the Piel. Note the following examples:[59]

M. Baba Batra 9.7	מתה וקיימו את דבריה
M. Shavu'ot 3.6	לקיים את המצוה ולא קיים כטור
M. 'Eduyyot 1.3	וקיימו את דבריהן
(Compare 1 Sam. 15.11:	(ואת־דברי לא הקים
T. Makkot 5.11	קיימו את מצות

The widespread use of the Piel of קוּם in both LBH and post-biblical Hebrew and Aramaic reflects a larger morphological development. Hurvitz explained:

> Furthermore, these forms constitute part of a general process manifested during this [late] period–apparently under the influence of Aramaic–in which the second radical of the Hollow Verb group (in *Pi'ēl, Pu'al, Hithpa'āl*) is modified into a consonant.[60]

It is not only the use of קִים in late and post-biblical texts which demonstrates that it is a late replacement for SBH הקִים: it is also the morphological development of hollow verbs in the post-exilic and post-biblical periods which demonstrate the lateness of קִים.[61]

The 'J' source, however, only employs the Hiphil of קוּם and never LBH קים:

Gen. 26.3	והקמתי את־השבעה אשר נשבעתי לאברהם
(Compare M. Shavu'ot 3.6:	(נשבע...לקיים ולא קיים

That 'J' employs הקִים instead of קִים reflects SBH usage.

Besides the contrast between LBH קִים and SBH הקִים, we can observe how LBH קים (and the Pael of קוּם in Aramaic) replaces other early expressions such as חיה, מלא, נצב, עמד, and the Qal of קוּם.[62] Note these examples where the early expression is used with דבר, in the sense of 'fulfill or establish (a word or matter)':[63]

1 Kgs 2.27	למלא את דבר יהוה
(Compare Tg. Jon.:	(לקיימא ית פתמא דיוי
Deut. 19.15	על פי שני עדים יקום בדר

---

59. *HDSS*, plates 16051–16060.

60. Hurvitz, *A Linguistic Study of the Relationship between the Priestly Source and the Book of Ezekiel*, p. 34. For the morphological distinction between the Hiphil and the Piel of hollow verbs, see also GKC, p. 197, §72m; and Joüon-Muraoka, *Grammar of Biblical Hebrew*, p. 215, §80h: 'The examples [of piel of *ayin-waw* verbs], rather rare and late, appear to be loans from Aramaic.'

61. See Hurvitz, *A Linguistic Study of the Relationship between the Priestly Source and the Book of Ezekiel*, pp. 34.

62. For a fuller discussion, see Hurvitz, *Beyn Lashon le-Lashon*, pp. 139–142.

63. See *HDHL*, plates 16051–16060; and Hurvitz, *Beyn Lashon le-Lashon*, pp. 141–142.

(Compare Tg. Onq.: ...יתקיים פתגמא

and M. Soṭah 6.3 עדות הַאַחרונה...אינו דין שלא תיתקיים

and M. Baba Batra 8.5 המחלק נכסין על פיו...דבריו קיימין)

Note also several instances where post-biblical Aramaic קים is employed
to render Hebrew הציב 'set up, establish', העמיד 'raise up', שבע 'swear
(an oath)', and חיה 'to live':

Deut. 32.8	יצב גבלת עמים
(Compare Tg. Onq.:	קיים תחומא עממיא)
Exod. 9.16	בעבור זאת העמדתיך
(Compare Tg. Onq.:	בדיל דא קיימתך)
2 Sam. 15.21	ויאמר חי יהוה וחי אדני
(Compare Tg. Jon.:	ואמר קיים הוא יוי וחיי דבוני)
Deut. 6.13	את יהוה אלהיך תירא...ובשמו תשבע
(Compare Tg. Onq.:	ובשמיה תקיים...
and M. Shavu'ot	נשבע...לקיים ולא קיים)

Although many of the early expressions continued to appear in post-exilic
and post-biblical Hebrew, it is important to note that LBH קים came to
be used in expressions of similar meaning.

Significantly, 'J' not only never displays LBH קים, but in several
instances uses expressions in which the verb is later replaced, in post-exilic
and post-biblical texts, by the Piel of קום. Note the following:

Gen. 3.22	פן...וחי לעלם
(Compare Tg. Yer.	...)הוי חי וקיים עד לעלמין)[64]
Gen. 26.3	והקמתי את־השבה אשר נשבעתי לאברהם
(Compare Tg. Onq.	ואקיים ית קירא דקיימית לאברהם
and Tg. Yer. I.	ואקיים ית קירא דקיימית לאברהם
and M. Shavu'ot 3.6	נשבע...לקיים ולא קיים)
Gen. 47.25	ויאמרו החיתנו
(Compare Tg. Onq. and Yer. I	ואמרו קיימתנא)
Exod. 9.16	בעבור זאת העמדתיך
(Compare Tg. Onq.	וברם בדיל דא קיימתך)

Wherever 'J' could have used a later expression with קים, it consistently
displays the classical usage. The absence of LBH קים is further evidence
of the early background of 'J'.

---

64. Although in this example the Targum added something not present in the MT,
nevertheless the Aramaic equivalent of LBH קים was employed to render fully the expression
וחי in Gen. 3.22. Compare to the Targumic renditions of החיתנו in Gen. 47.25, below.

5. שְׁתִיָּה

The term שְׁתִיָּה for the act of drinking appears but once in the Bible,[65] in the post-exilic book of Esther:[66]

Esth. 1.8 וְהַשְּׁתִיָּה כַדָּת אֵין אֹנֵס

Elsewhere in the Bible, (1) the infinitive absolute שָׁתֹה or (2) the infinitive construct שְׁתוֹת are employed for the same purpose.[67] Note the following examples:

(1) 1 Sam. 1.9   אָרְחִי אָכְלָה בְשִׁלֹה וְאַחֲרֵי שָׁתֹה

Isa. 21.5   עָרֹךְ הַשֻּׁלְחָן...אָכוֹל שָׁתֹה

Hag. 1.6   שָׁתוֹ וְאֵין־לְשָׁכְרָה

(2) Numb. 33.14   וְלֹא־הָיָה שָׁם מַיִם לָעָם לִשְׁתּוֹת

Isa. 5.22   הוֹי גִּבּוֹרִים לִשְׁתּוֹת יָיִן

Jer. 2.18   לִשְׁתּוֹת מֵי שִׁחוֹר

Qoh. 8.15   לֶאֱכֹל וְלִשְׁתּוֹת

The late character of שְׁתִיָּה in Esther is confirmed by its frequent appearance in rabbinic literature.[68] Note the following illustrations:[69]

M. Ma'aser Sheni 1.7   כֹל שֶׁהוּא חוּץ לַאֲכִילָה וְלִשְׁתִיָּיה

(Compare Qoh 8.15.   (לֶאֱכֹל וְלִשְׁתּוֹת

M. Nedarim 8.7   אֶלָּא לְשֵׁם אֲכִילָה וּשְׁתִיָּיה

Sifre Deuteronomy 107   אֵין לִי אֶלָּא אֲכִילָה...שְׁתִיָּיה מַיִן

One should note the contrast between the use of אֲכִילָה and שְׁתִיָּיה in M. Ma'aser Sheni 1.7 and M. Nedarim 8.7 and the use of the infinitives construct אֱכֹל and שְׁתוֹת in Qoh 8.15 (and elsewhere, see above). The $q^e t \hat{\imath} l \bar{a}(h)$ noun pattern is itself characteristic of post-biblical Hebrew. Segal commented: 'The Fem. form $Q^e t \hat{\imath} l\_$ is exceedingly common in MH [TH] as a *nomen actionis* for the *Qal*, taking the place of the old BH construct infinitive.'[70] Although there are examples of the $q^e t \hat{\imath} l \bar{a}(h)$ in earlier books of the Bible, these occur primarily in Northern (or non-

---

65. BDB, p. 1059a; KB, p. 1015a; *HALAT*, p. 1539b.

66. For a fuller discussion, see Bergey, 'The Book of Esther', pp. 29–30. See also Paton, *Esther*, p. 63; and Driver, *An Introduction to the Literature of the Old Testament*, p. 455.

67. BDB, p. 1059a; KB, p. 1014b; *HALAT*, p. 1537b.

68. Hebrew שְׁתִיָּה is not attested at Qumran, which displays instead the participle for the same purpose; Bergey, 'The Book of Esther', p. 29.

69. See *HDHL*, plates 18343–18344; and Bergey, 'The Book of Esther', p. 30. The writing שְׁתִיָּיה in the below examples is present in *HDHL*, which bases its readings on MS Kaufmann.

70. Segal, *Grammar of Mishnaic Hebrew*, p. 103, §228.

Jerusalem) contexts.[71] Thus the appearance of שׁתיה in Esth 1.8 represents a development in post-exilic Hebrew, occurring alongside the SBH use of the infinitives (שׁתות/שׁתה).[72]

The 'J' source, on the other hand, never displays LBH שׁתיה, but employs instead only the SBH infinitive construct שׁתות. Note the following:

Gen. 24.19	עד־אם כלו לשתת
Gen. 24.22	כאשר כלו הגמלים לשתות
Gen. 30.38	תבאן הצאן לשתות
Exod. 7.18	ונלאו מצרים לשתות מים מן־היאר
Exod. 15.23	ולא יכלו לשתת מים ממרה
Exod. 17.1	ואין מים לשתת העם

'J''s preference for the infinitive construct שׁתות in contrast to LBH שׁתיה is further evidence that 'J' was composed before the post-exilic period.

71. 4 examples of the *qᵉtîla(h)* pattern occur in northern contexts: שׁתיקות (Judg. 5.16), אבילה (1 Kgs 19.8), and יגיעה (Qoh. 12.12). 2 other examples occur in contexts which do not appear to be northern. שׁגיאות (Ps. 19.13), שׁחיטה (2 Chron. 30.17). Although שׁחיטה in 2 Chron. 30.17 could reflect the post-exilic date of Chronicles, it should be noted that שׁחיטה (2 Chron. 30.17) occurs in a passage describing the pilgrimage of the northern tribes to Jerusalem. Although he did not mention the examples other than in Judg 5.16 and 1 Kgs 19.8, Segal's observation is worth repeating: 'The fact that in earlier BH [this form] occurs only in the Song of Deborah and in the story of Elijah may, perhaps, tend to show that it was originally a Northern dialectal form, which was received into the literary language only after it had established itself in the spoken language'; Segal, *Grammar of Mishnaic Hebrew*, p. 103, §228.

72. Examples such as ולשׁתות in Qoh. 8.15 testify to the persistence of the SBH forms in post-exilic Hebrew.

Chapter 3

SYNTAX

This chapter discusses syntactic constructions which are characteristic of
LBH and which can be compared to similar constructions in 'J' source
verses. These constructions include words or morphemes which are not
themselves considered late; it is the syntactic constructions in which these
words and morphemes appear which are considered features of LBH. For
example, the word כּוֹל is not late, but the syntagma כּוֹל X ו-X which is
representative of LBH. Items discussed in this chapter include:

	Late Biblical Hebrew	Standard Biblical Hebrew
1)	Decreased use of אֵת + suffix	Predominant use of אֵת + suffix
2)	Infinitive construct + כ/ב	Infinitive construct + כ/ב with ויהיה/ויהי
3)	בֵּין X ל-Y	בֵּין X וּבֵין Y
4)	כּוֹל X ב-X	X X, X ו X
5)	לוּלֵי...שֶׁ...אֵז/אֲזַי	לוּלֵא/לוּלֵי...כִּי
6)	לְמַעַן לֹא	לְבִלְתִּי, פֶּן

1. Decreased use of אֵת with pronominal suffix

There are two methods of expressing the pronominal direct object in
Biblical Hebrew: (a) utilizing אֵת with the pronominal suffix, or (b)
attaching the pronominal suffix directly to the verb.[1] Both forms of the

---

1. See GKC, pp. 154–55, §§57–58a; pp. 364–66, §§117e-m; Joüon-Muraoka, *Grammar of
Biblical Hebrew*, pp. 170–171, §61a; pp. 440–44, §§125a-e; BDB, pp. 84b-85b; KB, pp. 99a-
100a. Both GKC and Joüon-Muraoka specify the conditions under which אֵת with
pronominal suffix must be emploted instead of the verbal suffix. Joüon-Muraoka also notes
that not all pronominal suffixes attached to the verb indicate the accusative, that is, they are
not always equivalent in meaning to אֵת plus the suffix; *Grammar of Biblical Hebrew*, pp.
441–42, §125ba. For a fuller discussion, see Polzin, *Late Biblical Hebrew*, pp. 28–31; Bergey,
'The Book of Esther', pp. 85–89.

direct object occur throughout the Hebrew Bible. The following chart displays the number of occurences of אֵת plus pronominal suffix versus the verb with pronominal suffix in those books of the Bible which are predominantly prose:[2]

	(a) אֵת plus suffix	(b) Verb with suffix	Ratio of (a) to (b)
Genesis	136	189	1:1.39
Exodus	142	140	1:0.97
Leviticus	134	92	1:0.69
Numbers	124	88	1:0.71
Deuteronomy	78	292	1:3.74
Joshua	66	49	1:0.74
Judges	59	72	1:1.22
1–2 Samuel	75	215	1:2.87
1–2 Kings	65	175	1:2.69
Jeremiah (prose)	13	19	1:1.46
Ezekiel (prose)	16	9	1:0.56
Jonah	0	6	–
Haggai	2	3	1:1.5
Job (prose)	1	4	1:4
Esther	1	9	1:9
Daniel	0	49	–
Ezra	1	13	1:13
Nehemiah	5	27	1:5.4
1–2 Chronicles	34	152	1:4.47

Because it is difficult to discern trends in individual books, we can combine some of these results to see if any larger patterns exist:

2.   Because of the nature of Hebrew poetry, אֵת with suffix almost never occurs in books which are mostly poetic, and those books – with the exception of certain prose portions of later books – are not included in this analysis. That is not to preclude the possibility that a contrast can be seen between pre- and post-exilic poetic books; for example see Seow, 'Linguistic Evidence and the Dating of Qohelet', p. 662. In order to avoid the problems inherent in judging whether a suffix attached to an infinite or participle indicates the direct object, this analysis includes only the direct objects – אֵת plus suffix or verbal suffix – of finite verbs: imperfect, perfect, and imperative forms. Many of the references are provided in Bergey, 'The Book of Esther', pp. 85–87; Polzin, *Late Biblical Hebrew*, pp. 118, 119, nn. 14, 23, 32.

	(a) את plus suffix	(b) Verb with suffix	Ratio of (a) to (b)
Pentateuch (Genesis-Deuteronomy)	614	801	1:1.30
Joshua–Kings	298	511	1:1.71
Jeremiah (prose)	13	19	1:1.46
Ezekiel (prose)	16	9	1:0.56
Post-exilic prose	42	245	1:5.83

The results for 1 and 2 Chronicles deserve comment, since they do not take into account verses which are parallel with Samuel–Kings. If we consider only non-parallel verses, we find 14 examples of את plus suffix compared to 141 examples of the finite verb with pronominal suffix,[3] a ratio of 1:11.1. Note that the use of את with pronominal suffix is significantly lower in non-parallel verses. If we consider only non-parallel verses in 1 and 2 Chronicles in our totals for post-exilic prose, the results are 22 examples of את plus suffix, 234 of the finite verb with suffix, a ratio of 1:10.64. This is significantly higher than what we find in pre-exilic and even exilic prose.

The evidence suggests that although both forms occur throughout the Hebrew Bible, the use of את with suffix decreased in the post-exilic period.[4] This finding is confirmed by Polzin, who commented:

> The true situation is that in prose of the OT the verbal suffix quite substantially predominates over 'et with suffix *in all stages of BH*. It is more precise therefore to maintain that 'et with suffix almost always exhibits less density than verbal suffixes (except for P), but that the younger language in general shows a marked decrease in the already less frequent use of 'et with suffix.[5] (emphasis in original)

It is worth nothing that the prose portions of Jeremiah and Ezekiel conform to the use of את with suffix in early literature. Note that both forms occur side by side in narrative portions of the Hebrew Bible. It is not the use of את with suffix that indicates early usage or verbal suffixes that indicate late usage; it is the decreased use of את with pronominal

---

3. See Polzin, *Late Biblical Hebrew*, p. 77, n. 3.

4. Compare the results in this table with the results of Polzin, who analyzed a sampling of verses in JE in Exodus and Numbers, the Court History, and DTR (Deuteronomist); see *Late Biblical Hebrew*, p. 30; also pp. 91, 93, 94; and pp. 118, 119, nn. 14, 23, 32.

5. Polzin, *Late Biblical Hebrew*, p. 30. See also Kropat, *Die Syntax des Autors der Chronik*, pp. 35–36; Striedl, 'Syntax und Stylistik', p. 77; Rendsburg, 'Late Biblical Hebrew and the Dating of "P"', p. 66.

suffix – or the increased preference for finite verbs with attached pronominal suffix – that would appear to be a post-exilic trait.

Hebrew inscriptions of the late pre-exilic period provide examples of the two forms being discussed here. In the Lachish letters, there is one example of את plus suffix, and five examples of the verbal suffix.[6] At Arad we find one example of את plus suffix, and two examples of the verbal suffix.[7] And in the Yavneh Yam inscription there is one example of the verbal suffix.[8] Thus the ratio of את plus suffix to the verbal suffix in inscriptions from the 6th century BCE is 1:4.[9] This ratio differs from what we find in Jeremiah (late pre-exilic and exilic) and Ezekiel (exilic), and matches better what we find in post-exilic prose. Due to the limited nature of the epigraphic evidence – only 10 examples of either form – we should be careful about drawing too strong a conclusion.

Post-biblical evidence confirms the impression that the reduced use of את plus suffix is characteristic of post-exilic Hebrew. In Hebrew texts from Qumran there are 250 examples of finite verbs with pronominal suffixes, and 16 examples of finite verbs taking את plus suffix.[10] There are several instances in which we can contrast the use of a verbal suffix with the use of את plus suffix in a parallel biblical passage. Note the following:[11]

TS 53.21	הניאה
(Compare Numb. 30.6	(הניא אביה אתה
TS 62.16	ילמדוכה

---

6. Donner and Röllig, *KAI*, I, p. 30, 35; texts 193.7, 193.8, 193.12, 193.21; 194.6, 194.7. Harry Torczyner offered slightly different readings of some of these examples; Torczyner, *Lachish*, I, pp. 54–55, letter III.7, 8; see also Z. Zevit, *Matres Lectionis In Ancient Hebrew Epigraphs*, (American Schools of Oriental Research Monograph Series, 2; Cambridge, MA: American School of Oriental Research, 1980), p. 30. If Torczyner and Zevit are correct, then we have 3 clear examples of the verbal suffix in the Lachish inscriptions. Note also a second example (reconstructed) of את plus suffix in Torczyner, ibid., p. 153, letter XII.4.

7. Aharoni, *Arad Inscriptions*, pp. 34, 46, texts 17.6, 24.13; Y. Aharoni, 'Hebrew Ostraca from Tel Arad', *IEJ* 16 (1966), p. 6. There is a third example of את plus suffix (reconstructed) in Aharoni, *Arad Inscriptions*, p. 26, text 12.2.

8. Donner and Röllig, *KAI*, I, p. 35, text 200.14.

9. This ratio is uncertain because of alternative readings of the texts cited here. If we take into account these readings, the ratio could be as low as 1:1.5. Note also two examples of the verbal suffix in the Mesha inscription (Moabite); Donner and Röllig, *KAI*, I, p. 33, text 181.4, 181.11.

10. Qimron, *HDSS*, pp. 75–76, §400.08. On the examples of את with suffix, Qimron noted: 'In these few cases, there are generally special circumstances which explain the deviation from the DSS norm: 5 instances are linked to biblical passages; 3 occur with the form קְטַלְתָּם, which tends not to take pronominal suffixes in Hebrew; 4 occur with ל''ה verbs; 2 come in syntactical environments which demand the use of את. Only twice does the construction with את occur for no apparent reason'; ibid.

11. Examples are from Qimron, *HDSS*, p. 76, §400.08.

(Compare Deut. 20.18	ילמדו אתכם)
TS 64.3	והוציאוהו
(Compare Deut. 21.19	והוציאו אתו)
TS 66.2	וסקלום
(Compare Deut. 22.24	וסקלתם אתם)

We find a similar situation in Tannaitic Hebrew, where את plus suffix occurs with a finite verb only when required for syntactic or phonological reasons.[12]

How the 'J' source fits into this schema is unclear. In 'J' we find 35 instances of the את plus suffix in the following verses:

> Gen. 4.14, 4.15, 7.1, 8.9, 19.5, 19.8, 24.27, 24.56, 26.14, 26.27, 32.5, 34.2(2x), 34.30, 37.18(2x), 38.8, 38.10, 39.4, 39.9, 39.20, 43.18, 43.21, 45.11, 47.19, 47.21, 47.23, 47.26
> Exod. 3.16, 3.17, 5.5, 5.19, 8.10, 8.27, 9.15

And there are 92 examples of the finite verb plus pronominal suffix in the following verses:

> Gen. 3.11, 3.15, 3.17, 4.14, 6.7, 7.5, 11.9, 12.1, 12.2, 13.9(2x), 13.15, 13.17, 18.5, 18.19, 18.21, 19.5(2x), 19.19, 19.34, 24.3, 24.43, 24.45, 24.54, 24.56, 26.7, 26.24, 26.29, 27.4, 27.19, 27.25, 27.27, 27.29, 27.31, 27.34, 28.13, 28.15(2x), 30.40, 32.3, 32.27(2x), 34.30, 37.13, 37.14, 37.21, 37.27, 38.22, 38.23, 38.24, 38.26, 39.1, 43.9(2x), 43.29, 44.4, 44.20, 44.21, 44.28, 44.29, 47.6(2x), 47.21, 47.25, 47.30(2x), 50.5, 50.6
> Exod. 4.3, 4.23, 5.3, 5.22, 6.1(2x), 7.16(2x), 7.26, 8.16, 8.22, 9.13, 9.16, 10.3, 15.25

The ratio between 35 examples of את plus suffix to 92 examples of the finite verb with suffix is 1:2.80. Although this is higher than the overall ratio of 1:1.30 for the entire Pentateuch, it is lower than what we find in Deuteronomy, and significantly lower than the overall ratio of 1:5.83 – or 1:10.64 if we exclude parallel verses in 1–2 Chronicles – we find in post-exilic prose. With respect to the use of את plus suffix throughout the Hebrew Bible, 'J' resembles more closely the pre-exilic situation.

---

12.   In TH את plus suffix does occur frequently with the plural participle, but not with finite verbs; see H. Cohen, 'Ha-Shimush be-Kinuy ha-Musa' ha-Davuq le-'Umat ha-Shimush "'et + Kinuy" ('ot-) be-Lashon ha-Mishna', *Leš* 47 (1983), pp. 208–18 (Hebrew); Bergey, 'The Book of Esther', p. 88; Kutscher, 'Hebrew Language, DSS', *EncJud*, XVI, col. 1588; Segal, *Grammar of Mishnaic Hebrew*, pp. 95–96, §213; Polzin, *Late Biblical Hebrew*, p. 30.

2. *Infinitive Construct plus* כְּ/בְּ

The infinitive construct with בְּ or כְּ is used frequently in the Hebrew Bible as an introductory temporal clause.[13] Such a construction can occur with וַיְהִי or וְהָיָה before the infinitive. There is a marked preference for the introductory infinitive with בְּ/כְּ without preceding וְהָיָה/וַיְהִי in exilic and post-exilic books.[14] See the following chart:[15]

Introductory infinitive construct with:without preceding וְהָיָה/וַיְהִי

	With בְּ	With כְּ	With כְּ/בְּ
Ezekiel	2.29	3.0	5.29
Jonah	0.1	1.0	1.1
Esther	1.6	2.0	3.6
Daniel	1.4	0.1	1.5
Ezra	0.1	0.3	0.4
Nehemiah	–	2.1	2.1
1–2 Chronicles	3.7	8.7	11.14
Qohelet	0.1	–	0.1

Although the ratio between the syntagma with and without וְהָיָה/וַיְהִי is not consistent in all late books, overall late books display a strong preference for the construction without וְהָיָה/וַיְהִי. Even if we exclude the examples from Ezekiel,[16] the ratio is 18:32. Compare this to the situation we find in earlier books of the Hebrew Bible:[17]

---

13. See Waltke-O'Connor, *An Introduction to Biblical Hebrew Syntax*, pp. 604, §36.2.2b; and comment in GKC, pp. 347–48, §§114d-e: 'This use of the infinitive construction is especially frequent in connexion with or to express time-determination (in English resolved with a temporal clause)'; see also GKC, p. 327, §111g. There is a subtle distinction between the use of בְּ or כְּ with the infinitive construction in an introductory clause: בְּ indicates, properly speaking, the inclusion of an action *in* the time of another; כְּ indicates, strictly speaking, the correspondence of two actions in time: the time of one is *like* that of the other' (emphasis in original); Joüon-Muraoka, *Grammar of Biblical Hebrew*, pp. 625–626, §§166l-m. Although this distinction is important, it does not effect significantly the discussion below. Joüon-Muraoka added, 'We see that the two prepositions are virtually synonymous, yet distinct in ways explicable in terms of their basic meanings'; Joüon-Muraoka, *Grammar of Biblical Hebrew*, p. 625, §166l.

14. For a fuller discussion, see Polzin, *Late Biblical Hebrew*, pp. 45–46; Bergey, 'The Book of Esther', pp. 52–55; see also comments in Driver, *Introduction to the Literature of the Old Testament*, pp. 506, 538.

15. There are no examples in Isaiah 40–66, late Psalms, or prose (late) Job.

16. The especially wide ratio in Ezekiel between the infinitive construction with וַיְהִי/וְהָיָה and without could be considered a stylistic peculiarity of the writer(s) of the book.

17. The introductory infinitive construct is primarily a feature of narrative texts, hence no examples from pre-exilic prophetic books exist. Examples from 'J' source verses were excluded from this chart.

Introductory infinitive construct with:without preceding וְיִהִי/וְהָיָה

	With בְּ	With כְּ	With בְּ/כְּ
Genesis	6.0	1.0	7.0
Exodus	3.0	3.0	6.0
Leviticus	0.5	1.0	1.5
Numbers	3.6	–	3.6
Deuteronomy	3.4	5.0	8.4
Joshua	5.1	13.1	18.2
Judges	4.2	5.1	9.3
1–2 Samuel	9.1	9.3	18.4
1–2 Kings	7.2	33.0	40.2

Again, although the ratios are not consistent in all books, the overall situation is clear. Pre-exilic writings prefer the infinitive construct with וְהָיָה/וְיִהִי at a ratio of 3.98:1. Although both variations – the introductory infinitive construct plus כְּ/בְּ with וְהָיָה/וְיִהִי and without – occur throughout the Hebrew Bible, it is in late texts that the construction without וְהָיָה/וְיִהִי predominates.[18]

The diachronic contrast is clearer still if we compare specific phrases from parallel sources. Note the following examples:

1 Kgs 8.54	וַיְהִי כְּכַלּוֹת שְׁלֹמֹה לְהִתְפַּלֵּל
(Compare 2 Chron. 7.1	(וּכְכַלּוֹת שְׁלֹמֹה לְהִתְפַּלֵּל
2 Kgs 12.11	וַיְהִי כִּרְאוֹתָם כִּי־רַב הַכֶּסֶף
(Compare 2 Chron. 24.11	(וְכִרְאוֹתָם כִּי־רַב הַכֶּסֶף

Although for the most part parallel verses in Kings–Chronicles display identical wording, in the above two examples, the author(s) of Chronicles altered the wording in Kings and omitted וַיְהִי before the infinitive construct in accordance with the predominant post-exilic practice.

We can confirm that the introductory infinitive construct without וְיִהִי/וְהָיָה became the preferred usage in the later period by examining evidence from post-biblical Hebrew sources. The SBH construction with וְהָיָה/וְיִהִי is almost entirely absent from the Dead Sea Scrolls,[19] which instead

---

18.   These findings agree in the main with those of Bergey and Polzin; Bergey, 'The Book of Esther', pp. 52–54; Polzin, *Late Biblical Hebrew*, pp. 91, 93, 94, 96, 104–105, and 118, n. 17, 119, nn. 17, 35. The above totals differ slightly from those of Polzin because my analysis includes both parallel and non-parallel verses in Kings–Chronicles.

Polzin explained well that the decreased use of וְהָיָה/וְיִהִי before the infintive construct should not be considered the result of Aramaic influence; Polzin, *Late Biblical Hebrew*, pp. 57–58; responding to Kropat, *Die Syntax der Autors der Chronik*, pp. 19, 74.

19.   Qimron, *HDSS* pp. 72–73, §400.03.

display the introductory infinitive construct plus ־בְּ without preceding וְהָיָה/וַיְהִי,[20] as the following examples demonstrate:[21]

1QM 3.10	ובשובם מן המלחמה
1QM 4.6	ובלכתם המלחמה
1QM 10.2	בקרבכם למלחמה ועמד הכוהן ודבר אל העם
(Compare Deut 20.2	והיה כקרבכם אל המלחמה ונגש הכהן
	(ודבר אל העם
1QS 9.3	בהיות אלה בישראל
TS 32.12	בבואם לרשת בקודש
TS 33.15	ובכלותמה לקטיר

Although examples of the SBH construction with וְהָיָה/וַיְהִי do occur in the DSS,[22] these are only in biblical paraphrases.[23] The introductory infinitive construct plus ־בְּ/־כְּ with or without preceding וְהָיָה/וַיְהִי is altogether absent from TH.[24] The post-biblical evidence indicates that where the infinitive construct with ־בְּ/־כְּ persisted, the LBH construction without וְהָיָה/וַיְהִי was preferred. In TH, both the SBH and LBH constructions had disappeared completely.

Verses which all scholars attribute to the 'J' source employ almost exclusively the introductory infinitive construct with וְהָיָה/וַיְהִי. Note the following examples of the introductory infinitive construct (a) with ־בְּ and (b) with ־כְּ:

(a)	Gen 11.2	ויהי בנסעם מקדם
	Gen 35.22	ויהי בשכן ישראל בארץ ההוא
	Gen 38.28	ויהי בלדתה ויתן-יד
(b)	Gen 19.17	ויהי כהוציאם אתם החוצה
	Gen 24.30	ויהי כראת את-הנזם ואת-הצמדים על-ידי אחתו
	Gen 29.13	ויהי כשמע לבן את-שמע יעקב בן-אחתו
	Gen 39.10	ויהי כדברה אל-יוסף יום יום
	Gen 39.13	ויהי כראותה כי-עזב בגדו בידה
	Gen 39.15	ויהי כשמעו כי-הרימתי קולי
	Gen 39.18	ויהי כהרימי קולי
	Gen 39.19	ויהי כשמע אדניו את-דברי אשתו

---

20. 'Forms with *kaf* (וכקטלו etc. – temporal) do not occur. Accordingly, TS paraphrasing the Pentateuch, may have בְּ where the MT has כְּ: והיה בשבתו 56.20 (=בשתו והיה Dt 17.18), בבוא השמש 50.4 (the editor erroneously read השמש as in BH), cf. also בקרבכם M 10.2'; Qimron, *Hebrew of the Dead Sea Scrolls*, p. 72, n. 12.

21. See also 1QM 4.7; 4.8; 4.9; 4.11; 4.13; 7.12; 9.3; 9.7; 16.9; 1QS 1.18; 4.24; 5.7; 6.15; 6.16; 8.4. See Polzin, *Late Biblical Hebrew*, p. 46; Bergey, 'The Book of Esther', pp. 54–55.

22. See 1QS 2.12–13; TS 56.20; 61.14–15.

23. Qimron, *Hebrew of the Dead Sea Scrolls*, p. 72, §400.03.

24. Segal attributed the loss of this and other infinitival constructions in TH to 'natural decay'; *Grammar of Mishnaic Hebrew*, pp. 165–66, §344; see also Kutscher, 'Hebrew Language, Mishnaic Hebrew', col. 1602; Bergey, 'The Book of Esther', p. 54.

Gen 44.31   וְהָיָה כִּרְאוֹתוֹ כִּי־אֵין הַנַּעַר וָמֵת

There is a single example of the introductory infinite construct without
וְהָיָה/וַיְהִי in 'J'. Note the following:

Gen 27.34   כִּשְׁמֹעַ עֵשָׂו אֶת־דִּבְרֵי אָבִיו

Thus in 'J' we find 12 examples of the SBH syntagma, and but one
example of the LBH construction. This matches well with what was seen
in clearly pre-exilic texts, which for the most part employ וְהָיָה/וַיְהִי
before the infinitive construct. If the 'J' source were composed during the
Persian period, we would expect to see more than one instance of simply
כ/בְּ־ plus the introductory infinitive construct. With regard to the
infinitive construct, the examples from 'J' clearly reflect the linguistic
background of the pre-exilic period.

3. בֵּין X לְ Y

There are two basic phrases used in Biblical Hebrew to express 'between X
and Y,' (a) בֵּין X וּבֵין Y, and (b) בֵּין X לְ Y.[25] Both phrases occur
throughout the Hebrew Bible, but the latter construction (b) occurs
primarily in late books, 10 times in exilic and post-exilic texts:[26]

Ezek. 22.26	בֵּין־קֹדֶשׁ לְחֹל
Ezek. 42.20	בֵּין־הַקֹּדֶשׁ לְחֹל
Jonah 4.11	בֵּין־יְמִינוֹ לִשְׂמֹאלוֹ
Mal. 3.18 (2x)	בֵּין צַדִּיק לְרָשָׁע...בֵּין עֹבֵד אֱלֹהִים לַאֲשֶׁר לֹא עֲבָדוֹ
Dan. 11.45	בֵּין יַמִּים לְהַר־צְבִי־קֹדֶשׁ
2 Chron. 14.10	בֵּין רַב לְאֵין כֹּחַ
2 Chron. 19.10	בֵּין תּוֹרָה לְמִצְוָה לְחֻקִּים
Neh. 3.32	וּבֵין עֲלִיַּת הַפִּנָּה לְשַׁעַר הַצֹּאן

And once in a text of uncertain date, but probably post-exilic:

Joel 2.17   בֵּין הָאוּלָם וְלַמִּזְבֵּחַ יִבְכּוּ

---

25. For a fuller discussion, see Hurvitz, *A Linguistic Study of the Relationship between the
Priestly Source and the Book of Ezekiel*, pp. 113–15; G. Hannemann, 'Al Millat-ha-Yaḥas
"Beyn" ba-Mishna u-va-Mikra', *Leš* 40 (1975–1976), pp. 33–53 (Hebrew). This discussion
will not include 'between X and Y' phrases where either X or Y are pronouns (pronominal
suffixes), since in all such cases in the Hebrew Bible, the construction used is בֵּין X וּבֵין Y.
Similarly, when X and Y are the same word, בֵּין X לְ Y is preferred, although examples of
בֵּין X וּבֵין X do occur, as seen below.

26. See Even-Shoshan, *A New Concordance of the Old Testament*, p. 167; Hannemann,
'Al Millat-ha-Yaḥas "Beyn" ba-Mishna u-va-Mikra', pp. 43–44. Examples of the בֵּין X לְ Y
construction where X and Y are the same word include: Ezek. 16.8, 34.17, 33.22, 41.18; 2
Chron. 19.10.

This construction (b) Y-ל X בין occurs only 4 times in pre-exilic texts.[27] Note the following examples:

Lev. 20.25	בין־הבהמה הטהרה לטמאה
Numb. 26.56	בין רב למעט
Numb. 30.17 (2x)	בין איש לאשתו בין־אב לבתו

The alternative syntagma (a) occurs primarily in early books, 54 times in pre-exilic texts. See the following:[28]

Gen. 1.4[29]	בין האור ובין החשך
Exod. 18.16[30]	בין איש ובין רעהו
Lev. 10.10[31]	בין הקדש ובין החל
Numb. 17.13[32]	בין־המתים ובין החיים
Deut. 1.16[33]	בין־איש ובין־אחיו ובין גדו
Josh. 8.9[34]	בין בית־אל ובין העי
Judg. 4.17[35]	בין ובין מלך־חצור ובין בית חבר הקיני
1 Sam. 7.14[36]	בין ישראל ובין האמרי
2 Sam. 3.1[37]	בין בית שאול ובין בית דוד
1 Kgs 5.26[38]	בין חירם ובין שלמה
2 Kgs 11.17	בין יהוה ובין המלך ובין העם...ובין המלך ובין העם
Jer. 7.5	בין איש ובין רעהו

This construction (a) also occurs 11 times in exilic and post-exilic texts. Note the following illustrations:

Ezek. 8.3[39]	בין־הארץ ובין השמים
Zech. 5.9[40]	בין הארץ ובין השמים
1 Chron. 21.16	בין הארץ ובין השמים

---

27. There are 3 examples of this construction where X and Y are the same word: Gen. 1.6, Deut. 17.8 (2x).
28. This list does not include examples from undisputed 'J' source verses.
29. See also Gen. 1.7, 1.14, 1.18, 9.16, 13.3, 13.7.
30. See also Exod. 9.24, 14.2, 14.20, 16.1, 26.33, 30.18, 40.7, 40.30.
31. See also Lev. 27.33, 27.12, 27.14.
32. See also Numb. 21.13, 31.27, 35.24.
33. See also Deut. 1.1, 5.5.
34. See also Josh. 8.12, 18.1.
35. See also Judg. 4.5, 9.23, 11.27, 13.25, 16.31.
36. See also 1 Sam. 7.12, 17.1, 20.42.
37. See also 2 Sam. 18.9, 3.6, 21.7.
38. See also 1 Kgs 7.26, 14.30, 15.6, 15.7, 15.16, 15.19, 15.32, 22.1, 22.34.
39. See also Ezek. 8.16, 47.16, 48.22.
40. See also Zech. 11.14.

2 Chron. 4.17 (=1 Kgs 7.46) et passim[41]   בין סכות ובין צרדתה

The above evidence suggests that although both constructions occur throughout the Hebrew Bible, the use of בֵּין X וּבֵין Y began to decrease and give way to the more frequent use of בֵּין X לְ Y‾ in the exilic and post-exilic periods.

That the predominant use of בֵּין X לְ Y‾ as opposed to בֵּין X וּבֵין Y characterizes LBH is confirmed by observing the incidence of these two constructions in post-biblical literature. The classical expression בֵּין X וּבֵין Y is completely absent from Ben Sira and the Dead Sea Scrolls, where instead we find numerous examples of LBH בֵּין X לְ Y‾. Note the following illustrations:[42]

Ben Sira 42.4	בין רב למעט
Extracanonical Psalms 150	בין חשך לאור ובין טמא
	לטהור ובין צדק לשקר
1QH 7.12	ל?הבדיל בי בין צדיק לרשע?
4Q509 1	בין צדיק לרשע
CD 6.17	ולהבדרל בין הטמא ולהודיע בין הקודש לחול
TS 46.10	יהיה	מדביל בין מקדש הקודש לעיר

Although the classical expression does occur in Tannaitic literature, the LBH construction predominates in nonbiblical passages.[43] See the following examples:[44]

M. 'Avot 5.19	מה בין תלמידיו של אברהם לתלמידיו של בלעם
M. Berakhot 1.2	משיכירו בין תכלת ללבן
M. Megillah 1.9	אין בין כהן משמש לכהן שעבר אלא
M. Middot 3.1	להבדיל בין דמים העליונים לדמים התחתונים
M. Nedarim 5.5	מה בין כותב לנשיא לכותב להדיוט
M. 'Oholot 16.3	אם יש בין לזה
M. Zebaḥim 14.10	ומה בין במת יחיד לבמת ציבור

As Hannemann noted, 'The distribution of this model [בֵּין X לְ Y‾] indicates that is indeed this structure which expanded and penetrated into

---

41.   See also 2 Chron. 13.2 (=1 Kgs 15.6), 16.3 (= 1 Kgs 15.19), 18.33 (= 1 Kgs 22.34). Note that in 4 of the 5 examples of בֵּין X וּבֵין Y in Chronicles occur in parallel verses.

42.   See *HDHL*, plates 5496–5563. Qimron observed that only LBH בֵּין X לְ Y‾ occurs in the DSS; see Qimron, *Hebrew of the Dead Sea Scrolls*, p. 83, §400.17.

43.   Hannemann analyzed biblical and Tannaitic literature, and concluded that there is 'a continuing diachronic transition from the use of model A [בֵּין X וּבֵין Y] to the use of model B [בֵּין X לְ Y‾] – the origins of which are to be found in the classical phase of BH and its final development in late biblical literature'; Hannemann, 'Al Millat-ha-Yaḥas "Beyn" ba-Mishna u-va-Mikra', p. 44, as translated in Hurvitz, *A Linguistic Study of the Relationship between the Priestly Source and the Book of Ezekiel*, p.113.

44.   Examples are drawn from Hannemann, 'Al Millat-ha-Yaḥas "Beyn" ba-Mishna u-va-Mikra', p. 37. See also *HDHL*, plates 5496–5563.

the realm of model A [X וּבֵין Y בֵּין].'[45] In Ben Sira and Qumran Hebrew, the late expression displaced the classic construction completely. In Tannaitic Hebrew, the SBH expression continued to survive, particularly in passages dependent upon the Hebrew Bible.

In light of the above discussion, we note that verses attributed to the 'J' source never employ the LBH construction. Instead, we find 5 examples of only the classical expression. Note the following examples:

Gen 13.8	וּבֵין רֹעִי וּבֵין רֹעֶיךָ
Gen 16.14	הִנֵּה בֵין־קָדֵשׁ וּבֵין בָּרֶד
Gen 32.17	וְרֶוַח תָּשִׂימוּ בֵּין עֵדֶר וּבֵין עֵדֶר
Exod 8.19	בֵּין עַמִּי וּבֵין עַמֶּךָ
Exod 11.7	אֲשֶׁר יַפְלֶה יְהוָה בֵּין מִצְרַיִם וּבֵין יִשְׂרָאֵל

Since Y לְ X בֵּין occurs more freqeuntly than X וּבֵין Y בֵּין in exilic and post-exilic texts, if 'J' were composed later than the pre-exilic period we should expect to find at least some examples of the preferred LBH expression. That 'J' employs only the SBH construction X וּבֵין Y בֵּין reflects strongly the pre-exilic linguistic situation.

4. *X וְ X כֹּל*

The syntagma X וְ X כֹּל occurs 14 times in the Hebrew Bible.[46] It occurs 13 times in clearly post-exilic texts:

Ps. 145.13	בְּכָל דּוֹר וָדוֹר
Esth. 2.11	וּבְכָל יוֹם וָיוֹם
Esth. 3.14, 4.3, 8.13, 8.17	בְּכָל מְדִינָה וּמְדִינָה
Esth. 8.11, 8.17	כָל עִיר וָעִיר
Esth. 9.21, 9.27	בְּכָל שָׁנָה וְשָׁנָה
Esth. 9.28	בְּכוֹל דּוֹר וָדוֹר
2 Chron. 28.25	וּבְכָל עִיר וָעִיר
2 Chron. 32.28	לְכָל בְּהֵמָה וּבְהֵמָה

And once in a text of uncertain date, though probably pre-exilic:[47]

---

45. Hannemann, 'Al Millat-ha-Yaḥas "Beyn" ba-Mishna u-va-Mikra', p. 45.

46. Examples cited by Hurvitz, *Beyn Lashon le-Lashon*, p. 70; and Bergey, 'The Book of Esther', pp. 68–69.

47. Psalm 45 is one of the clearest examples of a northern text in the Hebrew Bible; see Rendsburg, *Linguistic Evidence for the Northern Origin of Selected Psalms*, pp. 45–50. Are we to conclude that the syntagma X וְ X כֹּל originated in IH, and appeared in the Judahite dialect of LBH only after the exile? See recently Richard Wright, 'Further Evidence for North Israelite Contributions to Late Biblical Hebrew', in Ian Young (ed.), *Biblical Hebrew: Studies in Chronology and Typology* (London: T. and T. Clark, 2003), pp. 136–38.

Ps. 45.18 בכל דר ודר

In each of these examples, the idea of totality is expressed by כל followed by a repeated singular noun joined by *waw*.[48] This construction does not occur, however, in earlier books of the Bible. Standard Biblical Hebrew employed either (a) an asyndetic construction in which a singular noun is repeated without an intervening *waw*, or (b) a syndetic construction in which the repeated singular noun is joined by *waw*. Contrary to Polzin,[49] there is no semantic distinction between the syndetic and asyndetic *quivis* constructions. Rendsburg called this a 'distinction without a difference.'[50] Nor was Polzin correct to argue that the syndetic construction is distinctively post-exilic, since syndetic constructions occur in early biblical (and extra-biblical) contexts, as Gevirtz showed.[51] Polzin was correct insofar that the asyndetic construction is more archaic. Rendsburg commented:

> I would conclude by positing the following chronological development. The asyndeta *dôr dôr*, *yôm yôm*, etc., were used first, as in the Ugaritic texts and commonly in the Pentateuch (as well as in Ps. 68). The syndeta *dôr wādôr*, *yôm wāyôm*, etc., developed next, gradually replacing the earlier formulation (but note that *yôm yôm* occurs still in Prov. 8.34).[52]

So although the asyndetic construction is indeed older, both it and the syndetic formulation are characteristic of SBH.[53]

In neither the syndetic nor asyndetic *quivis* constructions does SBH display the repeated singular noun with preceding כל:[54]

(a) Exod. 3.15 דור דור

---

48. See GKG, p. 395, §123c; BDB, p. 481b. See also Joüon-Muraoka, *Grammar of Biblical Hebrew*, p. 499, §135d: 'Certain ideas analogous to the idea of plurality are expressed by the repetition of the singular noun: the idea of *each, every*... With the addition of כל and Waw as in LBH, QH, and MH'. The repeated singular noun used to signify 'all, every' is also known as the *quivis* construction.

49. Polzin, *Late Biblical Hebrew*, pp. 49–51. See also Qimron, *Hebrew of the Dead Sea Scrolls*, p. 81, §400.14: 'This construction [X ו X]... is characteristic of texts from the Second Temple period.'

50. G.A. Rendsburg, 'Late Biblical Hebrew and the Date of "P"', p. 68.

51. S. Gevirtz, 'Of Syntax and Style in the "Late Biblical Hebrew" – "Old Canoanik" Connection', *JANESCU* 18 (1986), pp. 26–27.

52. Rendsburg, 'Late Biblical Hebrew and the Date of "P"', p. 69. See also Rendsburg, 'The Strata of Biblical Hebrew', pp. 82–83.

53. For recent applications of the syndetic versus asyndetic constructions to the books of Zechariah and Ezekiel, see Hill, 'Dating Second Zechariah: A Linguistic Reexamination', p. 121; and Rooker 'Ezekiel and the Typology of Biblical Hebrew', pp. 148–149. Note that their analyses depend upon Polzin's conclusions, and therefore should be reconsidered.

54. The lists below are not necessarily exhaustive.

	(Note Tg. Yer. I:	(לכל דר ודר
	Exod. 36.4 et passim[55]	איש איש
(b)	Deut. 32.7	שׁנת דור־ודור
	(Note Tg. Yer. I:	(דכל דר ודר
	Isa. 13.20 et passim[56]	דור ודור
	Ps. 33.11	לדר ודר
	Ps. 19.3	ולילה לְלילה
	Ps. 87.5	איש ואיש

These SBH formulations, without כל, continued to be used in exilic and post-exilic texts:[57]

(a)	Isa. 58.2	יום יום
	Ezek. 14.4, 14.7	איש איש·
(b)	Isa. 58.12 et passim[58]	דור־ודור
	Jer. 50.39[59]	עד־דור ודור
	Esth. 1.8	איש ואיש
	Esth. 1.22 et passim[60]	עם ועם

Although the syndetic and asyndetic formulations without preceding כל continued to be used in LBH, it is important to note that the construction with כל appears only in post-exilic texts (Ps 45.18 is the only exception, see above p. 49). Moreover, compare these instances in which a *quivis* construction appeared in a later text with preceding כל:[61]

Gen. 39.10	יום ויום
(Compare Esth. 2.11	(ובכל יום ויום
Exod. 17.16	מדור דור
(Compare Ps. 145.13	(בכל דור ודור
Deut. 14.22	שׁנה שׁנה
(Note Tg. Yer. I:	כל שׁתא ושׁתא
and Esth. 9.21	(בכל שׁנה ושׁנה
Josh. 21.42	עיר עיר
(Compare 2 Chron. 28.25	(ובכל עיר ועיר

---

55. See also Lev. 15.2, 17.3, 17.6, 17.8, 17.10, 17.13, 18.6, 20.2, 20.9, 22.4, 22.18, 24.15; Numb. 1.4, 4.19, 4.49, 5.12, 9.10.

56. See also Ps. 49.12, 77.9, 69.13, 85.6, 89.2, 89.5, 102.13; Isa. 34.10, 34.17.

57. Of uncertain date are Prov. 8.30, 34.

58. See also Isa. 60.15, 61.4; Ps. 119.90. Of uncertain date are Prov. 27.24 (Q לדור ודור); Ps. 106.31, 146.10.

59. And Lam. 5.19 (לדר ודור).

60. See also Esth. 3.12, 8.9; Neh. 13.24.

61. As cited in Bergey, 'The Book of Esther', p. 69.

The above examples indicate that the SBH constructions continued in post-exilic Hebrew. In post-exilic texts a more explicit form, with pleonastic כל, began to appear alongside the classical usages.

Additional evidence demonstrates that the LBH syntagma is characteristic of post-exilic Hebrew.[62] Materials from Qumran and Murabba'at reflect the increased use of the syndetic construction with preceding כל:[63]

3Q15 12.12–13	כל אחד ואח[ד]
11QT 15.1	כול יום ויום
11QT 22.12; 23.7	כול מטה ומטה
11QT 40.8	כול רוח ורוח
11QT 48.14	כול עיר ועיר
11QT 42.13	כול שנה ושנה
Mur 24, B16; C18	כול שנה ושנה

This development continues in rabbinic writings. Note, for example, the following illustrations:[64]

M. Soṭah 5.4 et passim[65]	כל דבר ודבר
M. Berakhot 6.6	כל אחד ואחד
M. Sheqalim 6.5	כל שנה ושנה
M. 'Avot 6.2	כל יום ויום
T. Berakhot 6.7	כל נפש ונפש
Sifre Ḥovah 9.2	כל אחת ואחת
Mekhilta Baḥodesh	כל אחד ואחד

In light of the above evidence, it is striking that 'J' source verses consistently employ the SBH formulation (of either the syndetic or asyndetic type) in preference to the LBH syndetic construction with כל:

Gen. 39.10	יום יום
Exod. 10.8	מי ומי
Exod. 16.5	יום יום

There are 3 examples in 'J' of the syndetic construction in which the repeated singular noun is joined by ־ב. Note the following:

---

62. Note Qimron's comment (*Hebrew of the Dead Sea Scrolls*, p. 81, §440.15): 'The construction 'X־ ו X כול (ב)', meaning "every X", is only attested in the Hebrew of the Second Temple period and thereafter; it is common in late biblical, Mishnaic, and Aramaic usage'.

63. References cited in Qimron, *Hebrew of the Dead Sea Scrolls*, p. 81, §440.15; Hurvitz, *Beyn Lashon le-Lashon*, pp. 72–73; and Bergey, 'The Book of Esther', p. 69. See also *HDHL*, plates 10398–424.

64. Most examples are cited in Hurvitz, *Beyn Lashon le-Lashon*, p. 72; and in Bergey, 'The Book of Esther', p. 70. See also *HDHL*, plates 10244–605.

65. See also M. Sukkot 5.4.

Exod. 5.13, 5.19   יום ביומו

Exod. 16.4   יום ביומו

These constructions are semantically equivalent to those in which the nouns are joined by ו־,[66] and further demonstrate the preference of 'J' for the SBH formulations. The difference between these SBH construction in 'J' and the LBH syntagm כל X ו־X reflects the chronological gap between pre- and post-exilic Hebrew; clearly the consistent use of the *quivis* syntagma without כל reflects a pre-exilic linguistic background for 'J.'

5. *לולי...שֶ־...אז/אזי*

The syntactic construction לולי...שֶ־...אזי 'unless...then' occurs only in late texts of the Bible.[67] Note the following:

Ps. 124.1–5   לולי יהוה שהיה לנו...לולי יהוה שהיה לנו
                  אזי חיים בלעונו...אזי המים שטפונו...אזי עבר על־נפשני

Ps. 119.92   לולי תורתך שעשעי אז אבדתי בעניי

The term לולי/לולא occurs elsewhere in the Bible to express negative conditions,[68] but without שֶ־. Note the following:

Gen. 31.42   לולי אלהי אבי...היה לי כי עתה ריקם שלחתני

1 Sam. 25.34   לולי מהרת ותבאתי לקראתי כי אם־נותר...מֹשְׁתִין בקיר

In neither of the above examples does לולא/לולי precede the relative marker שֶ־ or אשֶׁר. Only once in pre-exilic Hebrew is the apodosis introduced by אז (2 Sam. 2.24); but even then, it is preceded by resumptive כי, as in Gen. 31.42 and 1 Sam. 25.34, above.[69] Evidence from post-biblical Hebrew suggests that it is the use of the relative marker with לולי/ לולא (or the post-biblical equivalent אלולי) which is distinctively late.[70] Note the following:[71]

Mekhilta Beshallaḥ 180   אלולי שאמר משה...לא

---

66. See GKC, p. 394, §123c; and Joüon-Muraoka, *Grammar of Biblical Hebrew*, p. 499, §135d.

67. For a fuller discussion, see Hurvitz, *Beyn Lashon le-Lashon*, pp. 160–62.

68. BDB, p. 530a; KB, p. 477b; *HALAT*, p. 498b. See also Joüon-Muraoka, *Grammar of Biblical Hebrew*, p. 631, §167k.

69. Hebrew כי does not always precede the apodosis after לול/א/לולי; see Prov 27.13.

70. Note BDB, p. 530b: 'in the later language, Ps. 124.1,2 לוּלֵי׳ שֶׁ (apod. אֲזַי)'.

71. Examples are from *HDHL*, plate 11774; and Hurvitz, *Beyn Lashon le-Lashon*, pp. 160–61.

Mekhilta Mishpaṭim 310   ...אלולי ששתפו ישראל
כלים היו מן העלם

The use of the relative marker with לולא/לולי was probably due to
Aramaic influence, as evidenced by examples from post-biblical Syriac
and Aramaic:

Tg. Ps. 27.13	...אלולי די תימנית
(Compare MT:	(...לולי האמנתי
Peshitta Ps. 106.23	...אלולא מושא גביה דקם
(Compare MT:	(...לולי משה בחירו עמד

The construction with אזי occurs once in the Bar Kokhba letters:[72]

Mur 42.5   ואף אללי שהגיים קרבים אלנו אזי עלתי

The evidence indicates clearly that לולי...שׁ...אזי (or post-biblical
אלולי) is characteristic of LBH. Although לולא/לולי was employed in
classical Hebrew, it never preceded the relative marker (except in 2 Sam.
2.24), and it was often used with resumptive כי. Both the use of the
relative marker to subordinate the conditional clause and אז/אזי before
the apodosis represent developments in post-exilic Hebrew.

   The LBH syntactic construction לולי...שׁ...אזי never occurs in earlier
books of the Bible, including 'J.' The 'J' source has one example of לולא
used to introduce a negative condition, but without the relative marker or
אזי:

Gen. 43.10	כי לולא התמהמהנו כי־עתה שבנו זה פעמים
(Compare Tg. Onq.:	ארי אלוכון בדא אתעכבנא
and Tg. Yer. I:	(...ארום אלולפון שהינו

That 'J' does not reflect the post-exilic development in the syntax of לולי/
לולא phrases further attests to its pre-exilic background.

6. למען לא *'so that... not'*

The syntactic construction למען לא 'so that...not' occurs only in exilic
and post-exilic texts.[73] For example:

Ezek. 14.11	למען לא־יתעו עוד בית־ישראל אחרי
Ezek. 19.9	למען לא־ישמע קולו עוד
Ezek. 25.10	למען לא־תזכר בני־עמון
Ezek. 26.20	למען לא תשבי

---

72. See Pardee, *Handbook of Ancient Hebrew Letters*, pp. 123–124.

73. For a fuller discussion, see Hurvitz, *Beyn Lashon le-Lashon*, pp. 147–48. See also
Joüon-Muraoka, p. 634, §169d: 'למען לא as in LBH'; and BDB, p. 775a; KB, p. 549b;
HALAT, p. 581a.

Zech. 12.7	למען לא־תגדל תפארת בית-דויד
Ps. 119.11	למען לא אחטא־לך
Ps. 119.80	למען לא אבוש
Ps. 125.3	למען לא־ישלחו הצדיקים

This construction does not appear in early texts, where other constructions are employed to introduce a negative purpose or a negative wish:[74]
אשר לא, למען אשר לא, לבלתי, פן. Compare the verses above with
verses from earlier books in which other expressions are used in contrast
to למען לא:[75]

Zech. 12.7	למען לא־תגדל תפארת בית־דויד
(Compare Judg. 7.2	פן־יתפאר עלי ישראל
and Deut. 17.20	(לבלתי רום־לבבו מאחיו
Ezek. 14.10–11	ונשאו עונם כעון הדרש כעון הנביא יהה
	מאחרי עוד בית ישראל למען לא־יתעו
(Compare Josh. 23.6	לבלתי סור־ממנו ימין ושמאול
and Exod. 20.20	(לבלתי תחטאו
Ezek. 19.9	למען לא־ישמע קולו עוד
(Compare Deut. 17.12	לבלתי שמע אל הכהן
and Isa. 6.10	(פן...ובאזניו ישמע
Ps. 119.11	בלבי צפנתי אמרתך למען לא אחטא לך
(Compare Exod. 23.33	פן יחטיאו אתך
and Exod. 20.26	(אשר לא תגלה ערותך

The above examples demonstrate the similarity in meaning between the
classical expressions and late Hebrew למען לא. LBH למען לא itself
replaced the fuller expression למען אשר לא, as well as לבלתי plus the
infinitive, which declined in use during the post-exilic period.[76] Although
the classical expressions continue to appear sporadically in late texts, it is
the appearance of למען לא in exilic and post-exilic texts which marks a
development in the Hebrew language.

---

74. See Joüon-Muraoka, *Grammar of Biblical Hebrew*, pp. 634–36, §§168c-169f. For פן,
see BDB, p. 814b; KB, p. 764b; *HALAT*, p. 884a. For לבלתי, see BDB, p. 116b; KB, p.
131b; *HALAT*, p. 130a. For למען אשר לא, see BDB, p. 775b; KB, p. 549b; and Joüon-
Muraoka, *Grammar of Biblical Hebrew*, p. 636, §169f.

75. Several of the following examples were cited in Hurvitz, *Beyn Lashon le-Lashon*, pp.
147–148.

76. Hurvitz noted: 'The fact that the use of the infinitive underwent a gradual – but
consistent – retreat in the history of the Hebrew language cannot be denied. In classical
Hebrew it is prevalent and widespread, in LBH and in DSS its use is quite noticably reduced';
A Linguistic Study of the Relationship between the Priestly Source and the Book of Ezekiel, p.
121. This pattern of development naturally applied to לבלתי which is used with the
infinitive; post-classical Hebrew prefered לא plus the finite verbal form; Hurvitz, *A Linguistic
Study of the Relationship between the Priestly Source and the Book of Ezekiel*, p. 123.

The lateness of LBH למען לא is confirmed by its attestation in post-biblical Hebrew. This syntactic construction occurs occasionally in Ben Sira and in QH. Note the following:[77]

Ben Sira 38.8	למען לא ישבות מעשהו
Ben Sira 45.26	למען לא ישכח טובכם
11QT 13.35	למען לוא ישוגו הכוהנים

The SBH construction (with ־שׁ instead of אשׁר) occurs but once in post-biblical Hebrew.

Mekhilta Shim'on b. Yoḥai 6.2	ולמען שלא יתהלל שמי בהם

That למען לא occurs more commonly in post-biblical Hebrew than למען אשׁר לא indicates that the LBH phrase began to replace the classical construction.

The 'J' source consistently employs SBH פן or לבלתי to introduce a negative purpose or a negative wish. Subordinate clauses introduced by פן occur frequently in 'J'. Note the following examples:

Gen. 3.3	פן־תמתון
Gen. 19.15	פן־תספה בעון העיר
Gen. 19.17	פן־תספה
Gen. 19.19	פן תדבקני הרעה ומתי
Gen. 24.6	פן־תשׁיב את־בני שׁמה
Gen. 26.7	פן־יהרגני אנשׁי המקום
Gen. 26.9	פן־אמות
Exod. 5.3	פן־יפגענו בדבר או בחרב
Exod. 19.21	פן־יהרסו אל־יהוה
Exod. 19.22	פן־יפרץ בהם יהוה
Exod. 19.24	פן־יפרץ בם

There are also several examples of SBH לבלתי used to express a negative purpose. Note the following:

Gen. 3.11	לבלתי אכל־ממנו אכלת
Gen. 4.15	לבלתי הכות־אתו כל־מצאו
Gen. 19.21	לבלתי הפכי את־העיר
Exod. 8.25	לבלתי שׁלח את־העם לזבח ליהוה
Exod. 9.17	לבלתי שׁלחם

If the 'J' source were composed during the post-exilic period, one would expect it to display at least once LBH למען לא to introduce a negative purpose or wish, but such examples are lacking. That 'J' consistently displays SBH פן or לבלתי is further evidence that it must have been composed before the exile.

---

77. See *HDHL*, plates 14637–638.

Chapter 4

PHRASEOLOGY

This chapter discusses features of LBH that pertain to phraseology and can be compared to related features in 'J' source verses. The features discussed in this chapter are not simply syntactic constructions, as in the last chapter, but constitute distinctive expressions or formulae which represent Biblical Hebrew in the late period. For example, the phrase שלום על is an expression characteristic of LBH, even though the term שלום itself is not considered late. Items discussed in this chapter include:

Late Biblical Hebrew	*Standard Biblical Hebrew*
1)	Calendar Formulae
2) ברוך **אתה** יהוה	ברוך יהוה
3) ברך שם יהוה לעולם/עד עולם	(Not all four elements together)
4) דרש חוקים/פקודים/מצות	דרש (בדרך) יהוה
5) כול עולמימם	עד ,נצח ,עולם
6) נשא **אשה**	לקח אשה
7) עשה (ב)רצון	עשה הטוב/הישר בעינים
8) שלום על	שלום ל־

1. *(Calendar Formulae)*

Calendar formulae in BH display the order month-day or day-month, with or without the words יום or חדש. The following is a breakdown of the different patterns of calendar formulae as they appear in the Masoretic Text:

(a) month-day

(i) בחדש X ב־Y יום לחדש
Gen. 7.11, 8.4, 8.14; Numb. 9.11 (without לחדש), 28.16, 33.3; 1 Kgs 12.32; Esth. 3.12

(ii) בחדש X ב־Y לחדש
Gen. 8.5, 8.13; Exod. 40.17; Lev. 16.29, 23.5, 23.24; Numb. 10.11 (בחדש...), 29.1, 33.38; 2 Kgs 25.1; Jer. 39.2, 52.4, 52.6, 52.12; Esth. 3.9 (בחדש...)

(iii) ב־X (חדש) ב־Y (יום) לחדש

Deut. 1.3; 2 Kgs 25.27; Jer. 52.31; Hag. 2.1 (without חדש); 2 Chron. 3.2 (without לחדש or יום)

(iv) בחדש X ב־Y (יום) בו

Esth. 3.12, 8.9, 9.1, 9.17, 9.18 (3x), 9.21

(b) day-month

(i) יום לחדש Y(ב־)

Exod. 12.18 (עד יום), 16.1; Lev. 23.6, 23.34, 23.39; Numb. 9.3 (בחדש...), 9.5; Josh. 5.10; 1 Kgs 12.33 (בחדש...); Ezek. 45.21, 45.25

(ii) לחדש Y(ב־)

Exod. 12.3; Lev. 23.27, 25.9; Numb. 1.1, 1.18, 29.7, 29.12; Josh. 4.19; 2 Kgs 25.8; Ezek. 1.2, 8.1, 20.1, 24.1, 26.1, 29.1, 29.17, 30.20, 31.1, 32.1, 32.17, 33.21, 40.1, 45.18, 45.20; Hag. 2.20; Zech. 7.1; Ezra 6.19, 7.9; 2 Chron. 30.15, 35.1

(iii) X ביום Y לחדש (ו)[1]

Hag. 1.1, 1.15; Zech. 1.7; Esth. 9.15, 9.17, 9.21; Dan. 10.4; Ezra 3.6 (מיום), 10.16, 10.17 (עד־יום); Neh. 8.2, 9.1; 2 Chron. 7.10, 29.17 (2x)

The above lists demonstrate a clear pattern. SBH calendar formulae with יום never place יום at the beginning of the phrase (examples from [a]), whereas in LBH יום is often in initial position (examples from [b]):[2]

(a)	(i) Numb. 9.11	בחדש השני ארבעה עשר יום
	(ii) 2 Kgs 25.27	בשנים עשר חדש בעשרים ושבעה לחדש
	Deut. 1.3	ועשתי־עשר חדש באחד לחדש
	(iii) Jer. 52.31	בשנים עשר חדש בעשרים וחמשה לחדש
(b)	(iii) Hag. 1.1	ביום אחד לחדש
	Zech. 1.7	ביום עשרים וארבעה לעשתי־עשר חדש
	Esth. 9.17	ביום־השלשה עשר לחדש אדר
	Dan. 10.4	וביום עשרים וארבעה לחדש הראשין
	Ezra 10.16	ביום אחד לחדש העשירי
	Neh. 8.2	ביום אחד לחדש השביעי
	2 Chron. 29.17	וביום שמונה לחדש...
		וביום ששה עשר לחדש הראשון

---

1. In biblical Aramaic, see Ezra 6.15: יום תלתה לירח אדר. See also GKC, §134, pp. 435–36. Because Exod. 40.2 contains the unique usage לחדש ביום החדש הראשין באחד, it is excluded from the list. This is the only instance where phrase-initial יום is in construct with החדש, or is modified by ראשון, which is an ordinal and not a cardinal number.

2. Only few LBH calendar formulae with יום do not have יום in the initial position. See Esth. 3.12; and exilic Ezek. 45.21, 45.25.

Bergey noted that calendar formulae with יום in the DSS place יום at the beginning of the phrase:[3]

1Q22 3.10	עד יו[ם] עש[ור] לחודש
1Q22 3.11	וביום ע[שר ל]חודש
4Q503 12.13	ביום חמשה ו[עשרים לחדש...]

There is still one other calendar formula usage in the Bible, namely, the use of בו ('of it [the month]') in place of (ל/ב)חדש in the month-day ordering. This usage occurs only in Esther,[4] which at first glance might suggest that the use of בו in calendar formulae is a unique stylistic feature of this late book. However, the feature appears in the Mishnah, too.[5]

| M. Sheqalim 1.1 et passim[6] | באחד...בחמשה עשר בו |
| M. Rosh Hashanah 1.2(1) et passim[7] | בניסן...בחמשה בעשר בו |

According to Bergey, the SBH formula לחדש occurs once in the Mishnah:[8]

| M. Megillah 3.7(5) | בחדש השביעי באחד לחדש |

And once at Qumran:

| 1Q22 1.1–2[9] | בחודש ע[שתי | עשר] באחד ל[חו]דש |

This evidence suggests that the use of final בו in month-day calendar formulae is a late development characteristic of the Mishnah, occurring first only in the Book of Esther.

Neither the LBH calendar formula ending in בו nor the day-month formula beginning with ביום occurs in the 'J' source, which instead displays only SBH calendar formulae. Note the following examples:

(a)	(i) Gen. 7.11	בחדש השני בשבעה־עשר יום לחדש
	Gen. 8.4	בחדש השביעי בשבעה־עשר יום לחדש
	Gen. 8.14	ובחדש השני בשבעה ועשרים יום לחדש

---

3. Calendar formulae without יום are in 1Q22 1.1–2, 3.11; 1QT 17.6, 17.10, 25.10. יום never appears in day-month formulae in the Mishnah. see M. Ta'anit 4.6(5); M. Sheqalim 1.3. See Bergey, 'Late Linguistic Features in Esther', p. 73. This contrast helps to confirm Qimron's view that the Hebrew of the DSS is distinct from the dialect represented by TH. See Qimron, 'Observations on the History of Early Hebrew', pp. 349–61.

4. Striedl, 'Untersuchung zur Syntax und Stilistik des hebräischen Buches Esther', p. 78; and most recently, Bergey, 'Late Linguistic Features in Esther', p. 72.

5. Examples cited in Bergey, 'The Book of Esther', p. 73.

6. See also M. Sheqalim 1.3; M. Ta'anit 1.3, 4.6, 6(5, 5), 7, 7(5, 5).

7. Also in M. Sheqalim 1.3; M. Ta'anit 1.3, 4.6(5), 7(5).

8. Note, however, that M. Megillah 3.7(5) appears to be quoting Lev 23.24.

9. See D. Barthélemy, and J.T. Milik, *Qumran Cave I*, (DJD, 1; Oxford: Clarendon Press, 1955), p. 92. See also Charlesworth, *Graphic Concordance to the Dead Sea Scrolls*, p. 351.

(ii) Gen. 8.5   עד החדש העשירי בעשירי באחד לחדש

Gen. 8.13   בראשון באחד לחדש

(iii) Exod 12.18   בראשון בארבעה עשר יום לחדש

(b) (i) Exod 16.1   בחמשה עשר יום לחדש השני

If 'J' were composed during the Persian period, one would expect it to contain calendar formulae characteristic of LBH, but such examples are lacking.

2. ברוך אתה יהוה ('Blessed Are You, Yhwh')

The expression ברוך אתה יהוה occurs twice in the Hebrew Bible,[10] in post-exilic texts:

Ps. 119.12   ברוך אתה יהוה

1 Chron. 29.10–11   ויאמר דויד ברוך אתה יהוה...מעולם ועד־עולם

The expression also appears several times in post-biblical literature,[11] although יהוה is often replaced by the terms אדני or אלהים. Note the following examples from Qumran:[12]

1QH 5.20 et passim[13]   ברוך אתה אדוני

1QS 11.15   ברוך אתה אלי

4Q511 16 1.4[14]   בריך אנתה אל עליון

The expression is also common in the Mishnah. Note the following:

M. Berakhot 4.4 et passim[15]   ברוך אתה ייי

This same expression, but without אתה, is common in early texts:

Gen. 9.26 et passim[16]   ברוך יהוה

Note, however, that it occurs several times in late texts, also:

Ezra 7.27 et passim[17]   ברוך יהוה

---

10. For a fuller discussion, see Hurvitz, *Beyn Lashon le-Lashon*, pp. 144–145. See also *ThWAT*, I, pp. 815–816.

11. For the examples from Qumran and the Mishnah, see *HDHL*, plates 6009–10.

12. 1QH 5.20 and 1QapGen 20.12 are cited by Hurvitz, *Beyn Lashon le-Lashon*, p. 144.

13. See also 1QH 10.14, 16.8. S. Mowinckel has pointed out that 1QH 5.20 is actually the first line of the next hymn; Mowinckel, 'Some Remarks on Hodayot 39.5–20 1QH5', *JBL* 75 (1956), p. 266; also B. Kittel, *Hymns of Qumran*, p. 82.

14. See Baillet, *DJD*, VII, p. 229.

15. See also M. Pesaḥim 10.6, M. Ta'anit 2.4 (2x).

16. See also Gen. 24.27; Exod. 18.10; 1 Sam. 25.32, 25.39; 2 Sam. 18.28; 1 Kgs 1.48, 5.21, 8.15, 8.56; Ps. 28.6, 31.22, 72.18, 89.53, 106.48; Ruth 4.14. Psalms 28 and 106 each contain a single late feature; see above, p. 13, n. 68.

17. See also 1 Chron. 16.36; 2 Chron. 2.11, 6.4; Ps. 124.6, 135.21, 144.1; Zech. 11.5.

LBH ברוך אתה יהוה appears to be an expansion of SBH ברוך יהוה, which continued to be used in the post-exilic period alongside the LBH expression. Although LBH ברוך אתה יהוה appears only twice in later texts, its lateness is confirmed by the fact that it appears several times at Qumran and in the Mishnah. In the post-biblical period, however, equivalent phrases such as אדוני, אלוהים, and אל, were used instead of יהוה. We may safely conclude that ברוך אתה יהוה represents a development in late Hebrew, even though the earlier expression ברוך יהוה continues to appear in post-exilic and post-biblical texts.

In light of the above conclusion, note that 'J' employs SBH ברוך יהוה in preference to LBH ברוך אתה יהוה. Note the following examples:

Gen 9.26	ברוך יהוה
Gen 24.27	ברוך יהוה
(Note Tg. Yer. I:[18]	(בריך שמא דייי

That 'J' displays only the SBH expression ברוך יהוה further indicates the pre-exilic linguistic milieu in which 'J' was composed.

3. *ברך שם יהוה לעולם/עד עולם* (*'Blessed Be The Name of Yhwh Forever'*)

The expression ברך שם (יהוה) לעולם/עד עולם 'bless the name (of YHWH) forever' occurs three times in clearly late texts.[19] Note the following examples:

Ps. 72.19[20]	ובָרוך שם כבודו לעולם
Ps. 145.1	ואברכה שמך לעולם ועד
Ps. 145.21	ויברך כל־בשר שם קדשו לעולם ועד

And one example in Biblical Aramaic.

Dan. 2.20	להוא שמה די־אלהא מברך מן עלמא ועד עלמא

There is one examples of this expression in a text of uncertain date, but which is probably post-exilic:[21]

Ps. 113.2	יהי שם יהוה מברך מעתה ועד עולם

---

18.   The Targumic rendition is admittedly not the Aramaic equivalent of ברוך אתה יהוה. What is significant is that the early expression was modified because it no longer reflected normal post-exilic usage.

19.   This includes the Aramaic equivalent; see Dan 2.20 below. See also *ThWAT*, I, pp. 815–816.

20.   For the post-exilic date of the 'doxologies', including Psalm 72.19, see Hurvitz, *Beyn Lashon le-Lashon*, p. 171.

21.   Psalm 113 contains no other clearly late features, and thus Hurvitz refrained from calling this text post-exilic on linguistic grounds; Hurvitz, *Beyn Lashon le-Lashon*, p. 174.

In each of these verses, three elements occur together: ברך, שם (of יהוה),
and עד עולם/לעולם. Other combinations of these elements also occur in
the Bible. The combination ברך יהוה (without עולם or שם) occurs
frequently in pre-exilic texts:

Gen. 9.26   ברוך יהוה
Exod. 18.10   ויאמר יתרו ברוך יהוה
Deut. 8.10   וברכת את־יהוה
1 Sam. 25.32[22]   ברוך יהוה

Note, however, that this combination persists in late Hebrew. See the
following examples:

1 Chr 29.10[23]   ...ויברך דויד את־יהוה...ברוך אתה יהוה

Other verbs similar in meaning to ברך occur frequently with יהוה
(without עולם or שם) in both early and late texts:

Gen. 29.35[24]   אודה את־יהוה
Judg. 5.3[25]   אזמר ליהוה
Exod. 15.21[26]   שירו ליהוה
Ps. 22.27[27]   יהללו יהוה
Ps. 30.2[28]   ארוממך יהוה
Ps. 34.4[29]   גדלו ליהוה

Evidence indicates that at some point during the period of the monarchy,
some praise formulae began to substitute other terms for יהוה as the
direct object. Observe the following examples:

2 Sam. 22.50[30]   ולשמך אזמר

---

22. See also Gen. 24.27, 24.48; Judg. 5.2, 5.9; 1 Sam. 25.39; 2 Sam. 5.21, 8.15, 8.56, 18.28;
1 Kgs 10.9; Ps. 16.7, 26.12, 28.6, 31.22, 34.2, 68.27, 104.1, 134.1, 134.2, 135.20, 135.21.
23. See also Zech. 11.5; Ps. 72.18, 103.1, 103.20, 103.21, 103.22, 124.6, 144.1, 145.10; Ezra
7.27; Neh. 8.6; 1 Chron. 29.10; 2 Chron. 2.11, 6.4, 9.8, 20.26, 31.8.
24. For examples of ידה and יהוה, see also 2 Sam. 22.50; Isa. 12.1, 12.4; Jer. 33.11; Ps.
7.18, 9.2, 18.50, 28.7, 33.2, 92.2, 105.1, 105.2, 105.31, 106.1, 107.1, 107.8, 107.15, 108.4,
109.30, 111.1, 118.1, 118.29, 136.1, 136.2, 136.3, 138.4, 145.10; Ezra 3.11; 1 Chron. 16.41,
23.30, 25.3, 29.13; 2 Chron. 5.13, 7.3, 7.6, 20.20.
25. For זמר and יהוה, see also Isa. 12.5; Ps. 9.12, 27.6, 30.5, 33.2, 98.5, 101.1.
26. For שיר and יהוה, see also Exod. 15.1; Isa. 42.10; Jer. 20.13; Ps. 27.6, 96.1, 96.2, 98.1,
104.33; 1 Chron. 16.23.
27. For הלל and יהוה, see also Isa. 62.9; Jer. 20.13; Ps. 22.23, 22.24, 104.35, 106.1,
106.48, 109.30, 111.1, 112.1, 113.1, 115.18, 116.19, 117.1, 117.2, 135.1, 135.3, 135.21, 146.1,
146.2, 146.10; 148.1, 148.7, 149.1; Ezra 3.11; Neh. 5.13; 1 Chron. 16.4, 16.36, 23.5, 23.30,
25.3; 2 Chron. 5.13, 20.19, 29.30, 30.21.
28. For רום and יהוה, see also Isa. 25.1.
29. For גדל and יהוה, see also Ps. 69.31.
30. For ידה with שם (of יהוה), see also Ps. 7.18, 18.50, 92.2, 135.3.

1 Kgs 8.33[31]   והודו את־שמך
Ps. 74.21[32]   יהללו שמך
Ps. 22.23   אספרה שמך
Ps. 34.4   ונרוממה שמו
Ps. 105.1[33]   הודו ליהוה קראו בשמו

Verbs for praise occur in conjunction with עולם, with or without שם in place of the divine name, throughout the Bible:

Ps 30.13[34]   יהוה אלהי לעולם אודך
Ps 44.9[35]   ושמך לעולם נודה

Note, however, that verbs for praise with עולם do not occur in the first five books of the Bible.

It thus appears that the development of praise formulae in the Hebrew Bible went through three main stages. We find יהוה as the direct object of verbs for praise in the earlier texts. Second, in texts from the monarchic period and later, we find examples where שם appears in place of יהוה as the direct object. We also find during this stage that עולם was introduced into praise formulae. It is important to note that the formula represented by the first stage persisted in the period of the second stage. For example, ברוך יהוה, which represents the earliest stage of praise formulae for God, occurs still in clearly post-exilic texts (see above, p. 13, and p. 13, n. 68). It is not when each stage ends that is important, because it appears that neither does; it is when each stage begins that is significant.

The development of praise formulae for God which include ברך follows this pattern, except with the addition of a third stage. The first stage, where יהוה is the direct object of ברך, was discussed earlier. Instances where שם (of יהוה) is the direct object of ברך are mostly in post-exilic texts. Note the following examples:[36]

Ps. 103.1   ברכו נפשי את־יהוה וכל קרבי את־שם קדשו
Job 1.21   יהי שם יהוה מברך
Neh. 9.5   ויברכו שם כבודך

---

31. For ידה with שם (of יהוה), see also 1 Kgs 8.35; Isa. 25.1; Ps. 54.8, 99.3, 106.47, 122.4, 138.2, 140.14, 142.8.

32. For הלל and שם (of יהוה), see also Joel 2.26; Ps. 74.21, 113.1, 135.1, 145.2, 148.5, 148.13, 149.3.

33. See also Isa. 25.1.

34. For other examples of verbs for praise with עולם and יהוה, see also Ps. 45.18, 52.11.

35. For other examples of verbs for praise with עולם and שם (of יהוה), see also Ps. 86.12, 145.2.

36. For the post-exilic date of Job 1.21, see Hurvitz, 'The Date of the Prose-Tale of Job', pp. 17–34.

There are, however, examples of (יהוה) שם ברך in pre-exilic texts which anticipate the frequency of this construction in the late period. Note the following:

Ps. 96.2	ברכו שמו
Ps. 100.4	ברכו שמו

Finally, we may observe several examples wherein ברך appears with both יהוה and עולם:

Ps. 41.14	ברוך יהוה...מהעולם ועד העולם
Ps. 89.53	ברוך יהוה לעולם
Ps. 106.48	ברוך־יהוה...מן־העולם ופד העולם
Neh. 9.5	ברכו את־יהוה...מן־העולם ועד העולם

The combination ברך שם (יהוה) לעולם/עד עולם occurs, with one exception (Ps. 113.2), in clearly post-exilic texts. As seen above, it is not the use of עולם or שם for the deity which is distinctively late, but rather the use of ברך plus שם (of God) with עולם which is constitutes an expression characteristic of LBH. Furthermore, it stands in contrast to earlier expressions used for praising the deity.

Post-biblical evidence confirms that ברך שם (יהוה) לעולם/עד עולם is characteristic of the Hebrew of the post-biblical period.[37] This late expression is attested at Qumran. Note the following:

4Q511 2.4	ברוך שמכה	לעולם עד
11QBer 12.2	וברוך שם קודשו[ן]	לעולמת עד

See also the Aramaic equivalent of this expression in the following texts:[38]

Palmyra inscription C4002.1[39]	לבריך שמה לעלמא
Tg. Ps. 41.14	בריך שמיה דיוי...מן עלמא הדין ועד עלמא דאתי
(Note the MT:	ברוך יהוה...מהעולם ועד העולם)

The Septuagint also sometimes employs the equivalent expression in Greek. Note the following:[40]

Tobit 8.5 (B, A)	καὶ εὐλογητον τὸ ὄνομα σου... εἰς τοὺς αἰῶνας
LXX Ps. 72.17	ἔστω τὸ ὄνομα αὐτοῦ καὶ εὐλογημένον εἰς τοὺς αἰῶνας
(Note the MT:	יהי שמו לעולם)

Finally, note these examples from Tannaitic texts:

---

37. For examples from post-biblical Hebrew, see *HDHL*, plates 6009–12.

38. Cited in Hurvitz, *Beyn Lashon le-Lashon*, p. 96.

39. Cited in Hurvitz, *Beyn Lashon le-Lashon*, p. 96; D. Hillers and E. Cussini, *Palmyrene Aramaic Texts* (Baltimore MD: Johns Hopkins University Press, 1996), p. 79. The phrase *bryk šmh l'lm'* has its own dictionary entry; Hillers and Cussini, *Palmyrene Aramaic Texts*, p. 397a.

40. Cited in Hurvitz, *Beyn Lashon le-Lashon*, pp. 96–97, 97n.

M. Yoma 3.8, 4.1   ברוך שם כבוד מלכותו לעולם ועד
Sifre Deuteronomy 342   ברוך שם כבוד מלכותו לעולם ועד

The above evidence indicates clearly the vitality of the expression in the post-biblical period, and confirms that ברך שם (יהוה) לעולם/עד עולם is a chracteristic expression of LBH.

In light of the above evidence, it is significant that 'J' never uses all of the elements in the post-exilic expression. Several times 'J' employs יהוה as the direct object of ברך, without an interposed שם. See the following:

Gen. 9.26   ברוך יהוה
Gen. 24.27   ויאמר ברוך יהוה אלהי אדני אברהם
(Note Tg. Yer. I: בריך שמא ייי)
Gen. 24.48   ואברך את־יהוה אלהי אדני אברהם

Moreover, the praise formulae in 'J' do not include שם or עולם, which appear in praise formulae in the Bible in texts set in the monarchic period or later. Note the following example:

Gen 29.35   אודה את־יהוה

The absence of שם or עולם in praise formulae in 'J' is consistent not only with pre-exilic Hebrew, but also with the earliest texts of the Bible.

4. *דרש חוקים/פקודים/מצות* *('Seek/Consult (the) Laws/Statues/Commandments')*

The verb דרש 'seek, inquire' occurs frequently in early books of the Bible with God as the direct object.[41] Note the following examples:[42]

Gen. 25.22   ותלך לדרש את־יהוה
Exod. 18.15   לדרש אלהים
1 Sam. 9.9   בלכתו לדרוש אלהים
1 Kgs 22.8 (= 2 Chr 18.7) et passim[43]   לדרש את־יהוה
Isa. 31.1[44]   ואת יהוה לא דרשו

---

41. BDB distinguishes דרש with the meaning 'seek, consult, inquire' from 'seek deity in prayer and worship'; p. 205a. The following discussion will deal with the first use דרש. See also *HALAT*, p. 224b; and KB, p. 219a, which distinguishes דרש with the meaning of 'apply to Y. with demands a. prayers.'

42. The list below is not exhaustive. Note also Ps. 24.6, 78.34.

43. See also 2 Kgs 3.11, 8.8, 22.8, 22.13 (= 2 Chron. 34.21).

44. Isa 31.3 need not be excluded from the discussion even though here דרש occurs parallel to שוע 'cry for help'. J. Oswalt noted: '*dāraš*, "to seek", indicates the formal placing of an inquiry before the Lord with an answer expected through mechanical means (lots, Urim and Thumim, etc.) or prophetic oracle'; J. Oswalt, *The Book of Isaiah Chapters 1–39* (NICOT; Grand Rapids, MI: Eerdmans, 1986), p. 569, n. 1.

Jer. 21.2 et passim[45]   דרש־נא..את־יהוה

This linguistic usage continued in the exilic and post-exilic books, for example:

Ezek 20.1   לדרש את־יהוה
Ezek 20.3   כה אמר אנדי יהוה הלדרש אתי אתם באים
1 Chr 15.13 et passim[46]   כי־לא דרשנהו

By comparison, there are two examples where the word (דבר) of God is the object of דרש:

1 Kgs 22.5   דרש־נא כיום את־דבר יהוה
2 Kgs 1.16 (= 2 Chr 18.4)   אין־אהלים בישראל לדרש בדברו

The distinction to be drawn, however, is not only between דרש taking God as its direct object and דרש taking the word (דבר) of God as its direct object. The distinction is also between inquiring of God directly versus inquiring of God through an intermediary. In most of the above examples, human beings sought or inquired of God through one of his prophets. For example, in 1 Kgs 22.8, King Ahab informed King Jehoshaphat that he could inquire of Yahweh (לדרש את־יהוה) through Micaiah the prophet. In ancient Israel, the word of Yahweh was spoken by his prophets: to seek or inquire of Yahweh was to seek a word from him delivered through a prophet. Hence Jehoshaphat asked of King Ahab, 'Please inquire first of the word of Yahweh (דרש־נא כיום את־דבר יהוה)' (1 Kgs 22.5). And in 2 Kgs 1.16, Elijah asked rhetorically, 'Is there no God in Israel to inquire of his word (לדרש בדברו)?' when he heard that Ahab had sent to Ekron to inquire of Baal-zebub (לדרש בבעל זבוב) (2 Kgs 1.3, 1.6). Thus the examples wherein the word (דבר) of God is the direct object of דרש reflect the underlying theology of ancient Israel: human beings sought or inquired of God by seeking his word through a prophet of Yahweh.

Examples wherein God is the direct object of דרש are rare. In Gen. 25.22, Hagar sought God directly (ותלך לדרש את־יהוה), without seeking a prophetic word. 1 Sam. 9.9 suggests that early in Israel's history human beings inquired of God through the mediation of a seer:

לפנים בישראל כה־אמר האיש בלכתו לדרש אלהים לכו
ונלכה עד־הראה כי לנביא היום יקרא לפנים הראה

> Formerly in Israel, when a man went to inquire of God, he used to say, 'Come, and let us go to the seer'; for a "prophet" now was formerly called a "seer"'.

---

45. See also Jer. 37.7.
46. See also 1 Chron. 21.30.

Nevertheless, it appears that the idea of seeking or inquiring of God directly persisted. In 1 Chron. 15.13, after the death of Uzzah, David complains that they did not inquire of God according to the 'judgment' (כי־לֹא דרשנהו כמשפט); and in 1 Chron. 21.30, David could not inquire of God (no prophet is mentioned) because of the angel of death: ולֹא יכל דויד ללכת לפניו לדרש אלהים. Job, interestingly, expressed his desire to seek God: אולם אני אדרש אל־אל (Job 5.8). Nevertheless, one must note that examples of seeking God directly are comparatively rare in the Bible; more commonly, when God was sought, it was his word through a prophet that was sought.

In post-exilic books, however, we find examples of דרש being used with the תורה, חוקים, פקודים, or מצות of God.[47] Note the following:

Ps. 119.45	פקדיך דרשתי
Ps. 119.94	פקודיך דרשתי
Ps. 119.155	חקיך לא דרשו
Ezra 7.10	לדרוש את תורת יהוה
1 Chron. 28.8	שמרו ודרשו כל מצות יהוה

No longer did ancient Israelites seek God directly or through a prophetic word; as the above examples indicate, they sought or inquired of God through the written word, that is, through the study of texts. M. Gertner explained this post-exilic development thus:

> Instead of priest and prophet came rabbi and scholar, and instead of prophecy and the 'word of God' came interpretation and the 'word of Torah'. The old prophetic idea of 'inquiring of the Lord' (Hos. x, 12) was replaced by the new midrashic idea of 'inquiring of the Torah' (Ezra vii, 10).[48]

It is worth noting that the term מדרש 'interpretation,' in the sense of an inquiry into a text, occurs only in post-exilic Hebrew (2 Chr 13.22, 24.27).[49] Gertner expressed well the contrast between the classical idea of inquiring of (the word of) God and inquiring of the 'teaching', 'laws', 'ordnances', or 'commandments' of God:

> This [Ezra 7.10] is the first and only time that *darash* is used in this novel sense and referred to the *Torah*, in precisely the same phrasing as it is referred to *God* by King Hezekiah in his prayer for 'everyone who prepareth his heart to seek God' (*lidhrosh*, 2 Chron. xxx, 19).[50]

47. For a fuller discussion, see Hurvitz, *Beyn Lashon le-Lashon*, pp.130–134.

48. M. Gertner, 'Terms of Scriptural Interpretation: A Study in Hebrew Semantics', *BSO(A)S* 25 (1962), p. 1.

49. BDB, p. 205b: 'late; common in NH [late Hebrew].' The late character of מדרש is confirmed by its appearance in post-biblical literature; see Ben Sira (B) 51.23, and CD 13.22, and the many attestations in rabbinic literautre.

50. Gertner, 'Terms of Scriptural Interpretation', p. 5.

Although terms such as חוקות/חוקים and מצות occur in pre-exilic texts, they do not occur in conjunction with דרש. Note Deut. 6.17–18: ותשמרון **את** מצות יהוה...ועדתיו וחיו. In short, seeking or inquiring of the sacred text replaced seeking God directly or by means of a prophetic word.

The evidence suggests three stages in the use of דרש with reference to seeking or inquiring of God. Before the time of the prophets in ancient Israel, human beings could seek or inquire of God directly, as in Gen 25.22. After Moses (note Exod 18.15), prophets brought to the people the word of God, hence דרש is used with God only in the context of inquiring through a prophet. (The idea of inquiring of God directly may have persisted, however, as evidenced by 1 Chron. 21.30 and Job 5.8.) Finally, in the post-exilic period the word of the text replaced the word of God conveyed through the prophets.

The late character of דרש being used in conjunction with תורה, פקודים, מצות or חוקות/חוקים is confirmed by its attestation in post-biblical literature.[51] Such phraseology occurs at Qumran. Note the following examples:

1QS 5.11	ולוא דרשהו בחוקותו
1QS 6.6	איש דורש בתורה
4Q485 1.1	ידורשהו האיש הפקוד
4QCat[a] 10 + 1.5	דורש התורה

Rabbinic literature occasionally displays דרש in conjunction with תורה, for example:

Sifre Deuteronomy 237	דורש מן התורה

The above evidence demonstrates that דרש with direct objects תורה, פקודים, מצות represents both a theological and linguistic development in post-exilic Hebrew which continued into the post-biblical period.

The 'J' source has one example of דרש with יהוה as the direct object, the aforementioned example of Hagar:

Gen. 25.22	ותלך לדרש את־יהוה

Not only does this example of דרש in 'J' not display the LBH usage with חוקות/חוקים, פקודים, תורה, or מצות, but it reflects the earliest stage in which God is sought directly without the mediation of a prophet or seer. Gen. 25.22 reflects an especially early pre-exilic theological and linguistic background.

51. See *HDHL*, plates 6881–87.

5. כל עולמים (*'Everlastingness, Eternity'*)

The expression כל עולמים occurs once in Biblical Hebrew, in a clearly post-exilic text:[52]

Ps. 145.13   מלכותך מלצות כל־עלמים

Although the singular form עולם occurs commonly throughout the Hebrew Bible, the plural form occurs much less frequently. Note the following occurrences:[53]

---

52.   Cited in Hurvitz, *Beyn Lashon le-Lashon*, p. 100. For a fuller discussion of this item, see Hurvitz, ibid., pp. 100–04. See also *HALAT*, p. 754b; KB, p. 688a; BDB, p. 761b.

53.   The date of Isaiah 26 is debated by scholars. At one extreme, Duhm (*Jesaja*, xii, pp. 172–94) dated it to the early second century BCE., a position which is no longer tenable in light of the Isaiah scroll at Qumran (Oswalt, *Isaiah 1–39*, p. 441 and note). Other scholars see it as an integral part of First Isaiah (see E. Kissane, *The Book of Isaiah* (Dublin: Brown and Nolan, 1960; rev. edn), pp. 276, 303). Some scholars view it as belonging to the exilic period. W. Millar commented: 'The author [of Isaiah 24–27] emerges as one ... who shared in Second Isaiah's vision for the reconstruction of Israel. For that reason, we label the genre of Isaiah 24–27 proto-apocalyptic. A 6th-century date is not unreasonable'; Millar, 'Isaiah, Book of (Chaps. 24–27)', *ABD*, III, p. 489. See also W. Millar, *Isaiah 24–27 and the Origin of Apocalyptic*, (HSM, 11; Missoula, MT: Scholars Press, 1976). The issue of the date of Isaiah 26 is far from settled, but the possibility that it is an exilic text must be considered. Note, however, the recent work of S. Noegel, who demonstrated that Isaiah 26 displays several features of Israelian Hebrew; Noegel, 'Dialect and Politics in Isaiah 24–27', *Aula Orientalis* 12 (1994), pp. 177–92. This raises the possibility that עולמים in Isa. 26.4 may reflect not LBH but IH.

Psalm 77, one of the Asaph Psalms, contains features characteristic of IH, and is therefore classified as a northern Psalm. See Rendsburg, *Linguistic Evidence for the Northern Origin of Selected Psalms*, pp. 73–81. Note also the example of עולמים in 1 Kgs 8.13, in a narrative that contains other possible features of IH (such as such as K בנית 'you [csg] built' [Q בניתי] 'I [msg] built' in 1 Kgs 8.48 where context clearly requires us to read בנית as '*I* built'; see Rendsburg, *Linguistic Evidence for the Northern Origin of Selected Psalms*, p. 29). Rendsburg commented:

> Based on the use of the Phoenician month names Ziv, Bul, and Ethanim in 1 Kgs 6.1, 6.37–38, 8.2, it is most likely that the description of the construction and dedication of Solomon's Temple is the product of Phoenician scribes. In other words, not only did Phoenician architects and craftsmen build the Temple, their scribes also recorded the activity (ibid., pp. 29–30).

Ugaritic attests one example of the plural of *'lm* (*'lmt*); Gordon, *UT*, III, p. 456, §19.1858. Note also the Aramaic isogloss עלמין in Dan. 2.4 and passim. The plural of עלם (עולם) is attested in Northwest Semitic only in Imperial Aramaic and Nabatean; Jean-Hoftijzer, *DISO*, p. 213. Does the presence of עולמים in texts which contain other examples of non-Judahite Hebrew (Psalm 77 and 1 Kings 8), and in a text which some date to the beginning of the Exile, indicate that עולמים originated in IH, and became more common in Judahite Hebrew after the Exile?

Although some of the occurrences of עולמים are in pre-exilic texts or texts of uncertain date, Qimron (*Hebrew of the Dead Sea Scrolls*, p. 93) listed it as a word 'mainly attested in the DSS and in the Late Biblical Books' (p. 88).

1 Kgs 8.13 (= 2 Chr 6.2)	מכון לשבתך עולמים
Isa. 26.4	יהוה צור עולמים
Isa. 45.17	תשועת עולמים...עד־עולמי עד
Isa. 51.9	קדם דרות עולמים
Ps. 61.5	אגורה באהלך עולמים
Ps. 77.6	מקדם שנות עולמים
Ps. 77.8	הלעולמים יזרח אדני
Qoh. 1.10	היה לעלמים
Dan. 9.24	ולהביא צדק עלמים

BDB distinguished between the sense of עולמים 'years of ancient times, of olden times' in Isa. 51.9, Ps. 77.6, and Qoh. 1.10,[54] and that of עולמים 'everlastingness, eternity' in 1 Kgs 8.13 (= 2 Chron. 6.2), Isa. 26.4; 45.17, Ps. 61.5; 77.8, and Dan. 9.24.[55]

The Aramaic equivalent עלמין[56] occurs several times in the late book of Daniel. Note the following:

Dan. 2.4	מלכא לעלמין חיי
Dan. 2.44	די לעלמין...תקום לעלמיא
Dan. 3.9, 5.10, 6.22	מלכא לעלמין
Dan. 6.27	וקים לעלמין
Dan. 7.18	ועד עלם עלמיא

The term עולמים occurs frequently in post-biblical Hebrew, including the Hebrew of the DSS. Note the following examples:[57]

1QS 4.22	כיא בם בחר אל לברית עולמים
(Compare 2 Sam. 23.5:	ברית עולם)
1QS 4.7–8	ברכות עד ושמחת עולמים...באור עולמים
(Compare Isa.. 35.10:	שמחת עולם
and Isa. 60.19, 60.20:	אור עולם)
1QM 13.7	שמכה נברכה לעולמים
(Compare LBH Psalm 145.1	ואברכה שמך לעולם ועד)

Note also examples of עלמין in Aramaic texts from Qumran:[58]

In summary, I suggest that עולמים represents IH in 1 Kgs 8.13; Ps. 77.6, 77.8; the transition from SBH to LBH in the exilic texts Isa. 45.17, 51.19; and LBH in Qoh. 1.10; Dan. 9.24. This leaves Isa. 26.4, which may reflect IH as noted above; and Ps. 61.5. See recently Richard M. Wright, 'Further Evidence for North Israelite Contributions to Late Biblical Hebrew', pp. 132–35.

54. BDB, p. 762a.
55. See BDB, p. 762b: 'pl. intens.'
56. See BDB, p. 1106b; KB, p. 1109a.
57. See other examples in Charlesworth, *Graphic Concordance to the Dead Sea Scrolls*, pp. 367, 440–441, 451; and in *HDHL*, plates 14486–491.
58. See other examples in Charlesworth, *Graphic Concordance to the Dead Sea Scrolls*, p. 451.

1QapGen 21.2	וקרית תמן בשם מרה עלמיא
(Compare Gen. 21.33:	(ויקרא־שָׁם בשם יהוה אל עולם

The term עולמים occurs frequently in rabbinic literature, especially in the compound phrase בית עילמום, literally 'house of eternity' (= 'grave').[59] Note the following examples:[60]

M. Tamid 7.4	לחיי העולמים
T. Berakhot 3.24	בבית העולמים

There are several instances where the Targumim rendered Hebrew עולם with Aramaic עלמין:

Tg. Onq. Exod. 15.18	מלכותיה לעלמא ולעלמי
(Note MT:	יהוה ימלך לעלם ועד
Tg. Onq. Deut. 32.40	ואמרית קיים אנא לעלמין
(Note MT:	(ואמרתי חי אנכי לעולם
Tg. Isa. 25.8	יתמשון מותא לעלמין
(Note MT:	(בלע המות לנצח
Tg. Micah 7.18	לא החזיק לעלמין רוגזיה
(Note MT:	לא החזיק לעד אפו
Tg. Ps. 44.5	דלא תזוע לעלמי עלמין
(Note MT:	(בל־תימוט עולם ועד

The pleonastic expression כל עולמים, and its Aramaic equivalent, occurs several times at Qumran. Note the following:[61]

1QapGen 20.13–14	ברית אנתה אל עליין מדי לכול עלמים
1QapGen 21.10	ולזרעך לכול עולמים
1QapGen 21.12	וירחונה לכול עלמים

The Greek equivalent of כל עלמים occurs once in the New Testament:

Jude 1.25   πρὸ παντὸς τοὺς αἰῶνος... καὶ εἰς πάντας τοὺς αἰῶνας

And several times in apocryphal literature:

Daniel 3.52 (Greek)	εἰς πάντας τοὺς αἰῶνας
Tobit 8.15 (B, A) et passim[62]	εἰς πάντας τοὺς αἰῶνας

The above evidence indicates that עולמים was a rare synonym for עולם, נצח, or עד that became more widespread in LBH and post-biblical Hebrew and Aramaic. A pleonastic expression, כל עולמים, is character-

---

59. See A. Hurvitz, 'בית־קברות and בית־עולם: Two Funerary Terms in Biblical Literature and Their Linguistic Background', *Maarav* 8 (1992), pp. 59–68.
60. See *HDHL*, plates 14491–521.
61. See also Charlesworth, *Graphic Concordance to the Dead Sea Scrolls*, p. 451.
62. See also Tobit (B, A) 13.4, 18; (S) 8.5, 15; 11.14; 13.4, 17.

istic of LBH; its vitality in the post-biblical period is demonstrated by equivalent Greek and Aramaic expressions in post-biblical literature.

The expressions עולמים and כל עלמים never occur in the 'J' source, which consistently employs עולם in preference to the later expressions. Parallel phrases in post-biblical literature occasionally substitute עולמים or the Aramaic equivalent. Note the following:

Gen. 3.22	וחי לעלם
(Note Tg. Yer. I.	(הוי חי וקיים עד לעלמין
Gen. 6.3	לא־ידון רוחי באדם לעלם
Gen. 6.4	להם המה הגברים אשר מעולם אנשי השם
Gen. 13.15	לך אתננה ולזרעך עד־עולם
(Note 1QapGen 21.10:	(ולזרעך לכול עלמים
Exod. 14.13	לא תסיפו לראתם עוד עד־עולם

There is one sentence in the DSS which closely parallels a verse in 'J', but which adds עלמין where the biblical reference lacks the Hebrew equivalent:

1QapGen 21.13–14	קום הלך...ארי לך ולזרעך אנתננה
	אחריך עד כול עלמיא
Gen. 13.17	קום התהלך...כי לך אתננה

The evidence shows that, in contexts where late or post-biblical texts often employ עלמים or the equivalent, 'J' employs the SBH expression עולם or nothing at all. The preference of 'J' for עולם further demonstrates its pre-exilic linguistic character.

6. נשא אשה *('Take as Wife')*

The expression נשא אשה 'take as wife' occurs predominantly in late books,[63] 7 times in clearly post-exilic texts:[64]

Ezra 9.2	כי נשאו מבנתיהם להם
Ezra 9.12	ובנתיהם אל־תשאו
Ezra 10.44	כל־אלה נשאו נשים נכריות
Neh 13.25	ואם־תשאו מבנתיהם לבניכם
2 Chron. 11.21	כי נשים שמונה־עשרה נשא
2 Chron. 13.21	וישא־לו נשים ארבע עשרה

63. See BDB, pp. 669b-971a: '*take* as wife (usu. c. ל *for*), late'; KB, p. 636b; *HALAT*, p. 685: 'älter לָקַח.' In some instances נשא is used in the sense of 'take (as wife)' without אשה. Since it is this use of נשא – with or without אשה – that is important for the purposes of this discussion, examples where אשה is not present but is implied by context will be included. See further Kutscher, *A History of the Hebrew Language*, pp. 83–84, §123; Polzin, *Late Biblical Hebrew*, p. 146.

64. See Even-Shoshan, *A New Concordance of the Old Testament*, pp. 781–82.

2 Chron. 24.3   וישא־לו יהוידע נשים שתים

It occurs once in a text of uncertain date, but probably pre-exilic:[65]

Ruth 1.4   וישא להם נשים מאביות

And we find one example in a pre-exilic text:[66]

Judg. 21.23   וישאו נשים למספרם

Except for the examples in Ruth 1.4 and Judg. 21.23, this expression does not occur in earlier books, where instead the phrase לקח אשה 'take as wife' is employed to convey the same idea.[67] Note the following illustrations:[68]

Gen. 28.6 (2x) et passim[69]   וישלח אתו פדנה ארם לקחת־לו משם
אשה...לא תקח אשה מבנות כנען

Exod. 6.25[70]   לקח־לו מבנות פוטיאל לו לאשה

Lev. 20.14 et passim[71]   ואיש אשר יקח את־אשה ואת־אמה זמה הוא

Numb. 12.1 (2x)   על־אדות האשה הכשית אשר לקח כי־אשה כשית לקח

Deut. 24.4 et passim[72]   לא־יוכל בעלה הראשון...לקחתה להיות לו לאשה

---

65. Driver lists נשא נשים in Ruth 1.4 along with other linguistic traits of the book that occur primarily, but not exclusively, in exilic and post-exilic writings. He further commented, 'In reference to [most of these linguistic traits], it may be remembered that words, with Aramaic or late Hebrew affinities, occur, at least sporadically, in passages admittedly of early date... It is possible that the Book, in spite of its interest in Bethelehem and David, was yet written in the N. kingdom, and preserved words current there dialectally'; see Driver, *Introduction to the Literature of the Old Testament*, p. 455. If Driver is correct, נשא נשים in Ruth 1.4 might represent a feature of non-Jerusalemite Hebrew that became more common in the post-exilic period. I am unconvinced that Ruth is a northern text, and would prefer to see this as an example of an expression that was rare and unproductive in SBH during the pre-exilic period.

66. Driver argued that the use of נשא with אשה in Judg. 21.23 should be understood differently as 'carry away, secure', rather than acquire by normal means; see Driver, *Introduction to the Literature of the Old Testament*, p. 455. I prefer to see this, like נשא אשה in Ruth 1.4, as further evidence that although the expression occurred occasionally in the pre-exilic period, it was rare and unproductive. It was not until the post-exilic period that this alternative expression for 'acquire a wife' began to replace SBH לקח אשה.

67. See BDB, pp. 542b-543a; KB, p. 485b; *HALAT*, p. 507: 'später > נָשָׂא אִשָּׁה.' As in the case of נשא אשה, what is important is the use of לקח in the sense of 'take (as wife)'; in many instances אשה is implied but not present, and these examples are included in the discussion.

68. 'J' source verses have been excluded from the following list.

69. See also Gen. 20.3, 21.21, 21.27, 25.20, 28.1, 31.50, 34.9, 34.16, 34.21, 36.2.

70. See also Exod. 21.10.

71. See also Lev. 18.17, 20.17, 20.21, 21.7 (2x), 21.13, 21.14 (2x).

72. See also Deut. 7.3, 20.7, 21.11, 22.13, 22.14, 23.1, 24.1, 24.3, 24.5, 25.5, 25.7, 25.8.

Judg. 14.3 et passim[73]   כִּי־אַתָּה הוֹלֵךְ לָקַחַת אִשָּׁה מִפְּלִשְׁתִּים

1 Sam. 25.40 et passim[74]   דָּוִד שְׁלָחָנוּ אֵלַיִךְ לְקַחְתֵּךְ לוֹ לְאִשָּׁה

2 Sam. 3.15 et passim[75]   וַיִּשְׁלַח אִישׁ בֹּשֶׁת לְקָחָהּ מֵעִם אִישׁ

1 Kgs 7.8   וּבֵית יַעֲשֶׂה לְבַת־פַּרְעֹה אֲשֶׁר לָקַח שְׁלֹמֹה

Ezek. 44.22   וְאַלְמָנָה וּגְרוּשָׁה לֹא־יִקְחוּ לָהֶם לְנָשִׁים

This expression continues to occur occasionally in post-exilic writings.
Note the following:

Ezra 2.61   בְּנֵי בַרְזִלַּי אֲשֶׁר לָקַח מִבְּנוֹת בַּרְזִלַּי הַגִּלְעָדִי אִשָּׁה

Neh. 6.18 et passim[76]   לָקַח אֶת־בַּת־מְשֻׁלָּם בֶּרֶכְיָה

1 Chron. 4.18 et passim[77]   וְאֵלֶּה בְּנֵי בִתְיָה בַת־פַּרְעֹה אֲשֶׁ֯ר לָקַח

2 Chron. 11.20   וְאַחֲרֶיהָ לָקַח אֶת־מַעֲכָה בַת־אַבְשָׁלוֹם

The distribution of לקח אשה 'take as wife' and נשא אשה 'take as wife'
suggests that the latter may have been a rare dialectal form that became
more common in the post-exilic period; it did not displace completely the
earlier expression לקח אשה, but the fact that it occur almost exclusively
in post-exilic texts suggests that it is a feature of Late Biblical Hebrew.
The use of the later expression in post-exilic books may reflect
developments in the meaning and use of verbs meaning 'take'. Kutscher
noted that the verb לקח in SBH normally meant 'take', but already by the
post-exilic period we see examples where it means 'buy'. To avoid
misunderstanding, post-exilic writers began to use נשא, which earlier
meant 'carry', in the same contexts in which earlier writers had used
לקח.[78] The shift from לקח אשה to נשא אשה thus reflected a parallel
development in the use of נשא 'take' for לקח, since לקח had come to be
used for 'buy' as well as 'take'.[79]

Post-biblical evidence confirms the late character of נשא אשה 'take as
wife'. We find the expression in Ben Sira and in the literature of Qumran.
Note the following examples:[80]

Ben Sira 7.23   וּשָׂא לָהֶם נָשִׁים בִּנְעוּרֵיהֶם

TS 57.15[81]   וְאִשָּׁה לוֹא יִשָּׂא מִכּוֹל | בְּנוֹת הַגּוֹיִים

---

73. See also Judg. 14.8, 15.6.

74. See also 1 Sam. 12.9, 25.39.

75. See also 2 Sam. 11.4, 12.9.

76. See also Neh. 7.63.

77. See also 1 Chron. 7.15.

78. Kutscher, *A History of the Hebrew Language*, pp. 82–83, §123.

79. Similarly, LBH began to employ קבל 'receive' in place of לקח, since לקח מן in the
post-exilic period could be understood as 'buy from'; Kutscher, *A History of the Hebrew
Language*, pp. 83–84, §123; also see below, p. 127.

80. See *HDHL*, plates 5030–73.

81. On נשא אשה in the DSS, see Qimron, *Hebrew of the Dead Sea Scrolls*, p. 93.

Although the earlier expression survived in Qumran Hebrew, it appears primarily in biblical quotes and allusions.[82] The late idiom נשא אשה is particularly common in Tannaitic literature.[83] See the following examples:[84]

M. Berakhot 8.1	מי שלא לו בנים ונשא אשה שכבר ילדה
M. Ketuvot 13.11	נשא אשה בארץ־ישרא׳ וגירשה בארץ־ישרא׳
M. Yebamot 10.8	נשא אשה ומת
Mekhilta R. Shim'on ben Yoḥai 13.15 (44)	מנין אתה אומ׳ שאם נשא חמש נשים

The above evidence suggests that, except for two rare and possibly dialectal forms in earlier books, the expression נשא אשה 'take as wife' was coined in the post-exilic period as an alternative to SBH לקח אשה. The SBH idiom continued to be employed alongside its LBH equivalent in the Hebrew Bible and in the Qumran literature. In Mishnaic Hebrew it appears to have disappeared completely. The eventual disappearance of SBH לקח אשה in TH may reflect not so much a chronological trend as much as the fact that biblical style had a greater influence on QH than it did on TH.

The LBH construction נשא אשה does not occur at all in 'J', which instead employs consistently only the SBH equivalent לקח אשה. Note the following:

Gen. 4.19	ויקח־לו למך שתי נשים
Gen. 6.2	ויקחו להם נשים
Gen. 11.29	ויקח אברם ונחור להם נשים
Gen. 24.48	...לקחת את־בת־אחי אדני לבנו
Gen. 24.67	ויקח את־רבקה ותהי־לו לאשה
Gen. 25.1	ויסף אברהם ויקח אשה
Gen. 26.34	ויקח אשה יהודית

If the 'J' source were composed during the post-exilic period, we should expect to see LBH נשא אשה in at least some of the verses listed here. That 'J' uses only the SBH idiom is further evidence it was composed prior to the post-exilic era.

---

82. For example, see TS 57.16, 57.17, 65.7, 66.12. Three examples of לקח אשה which do not appear to be allusions to the Hebrew Bible are CD 4.21, 7.7, 19.3.

83. See Polzin, *Late Biblical Hebrew*, p. 146.

84. See *HDHL*, plates 13367–81.

7. עשׂה (כ)רצון ('Act According to The Will [of Someone]')

The expression עשׂה (כ)רצון 'to act according to the will (of someone)' occurs several times in post-exilic contexts:[85]

Ps. 145.19[86]	רצון־יראיו יעשׂה
Esth. 1.8	לעשׂות כרצון איש־ואיש
Esth. 9.5	ויעשׂו בשׂנאיהם כרצונם
Dan. 8.4	ועשׂה כרצונו
Dan. 11.3	ומשׁל...ועשׂה כרצונו
Dan. 11.16	ויעשׂ הבא אליו כרוצנו
Dan. 11.36	ועשׂה כרצונו המלך
Ezra 10.11	ועשׂו רצונו
Neh. 9.24	לעשׂות בהם כרצונם

The noun רצון is based on the root רצה, which in biblical Hebrew originally meant 'to satisfy, please'; apparently under the influence of the Aramaic cognate רעה, the noun came to signify 'will, desire, pleasure.'[87] This may be seen in a similar expression in the Aramaic portion of Ezra: כרעות אלהכם העבדון (7.18). There are a few expressions semantically equivalent to עשׂה (כ)רצון in earlier contexts:[88]

Deut. 12.8	לא תעשׂון ככל אשׁר אנחנו עשׂים פה היום
	אישׁ כל־הישׁר בעיניו
Judg. 17.6	אין מלך בישׂראל אישׁ הישׁר בעיניו יעשׂה
2 Sam. 10.12	ויהוה יעשׂה הטוב בעיניו

---

85. The following examples are cited in Hurvitz, *Beyn Lashon le-Lashon*, p. 73; and Bergey, 'The Book of Esther', p. 153. For further discussion see Hurvitz, ibid., pp. 74–78. For discussion of related expressions, see also A. Hurvitz, 'History of a Legal Formula', *VT* 32 (1982), p. 264; and Kutscher, *History of the Hebrew Language*, p. 83, §123. The noun רצון, with similar meaning, also appears in 2 Chron. 15.15 and Gen. 49.6 but without the verb עשׂה.

86. The expression עשׂה (כ)רצון also occurs in three psalms of uncertain date: (103.21); ברכו יהוה...מׁשרתיו עשׂי רצונו (Ps. 40.9); לעשׂות רצונך אלהי חפצתי למדני לעשׂות רצונך (143.10); see Hurvitz, *Beyn Lashon le-Lashon*, p. 78.

87. See *BDB*, p. 958b; *HALAT*, p. 1193a; and Hurvitz, who commented: 'This semantic change occurred apparently under the influence of the Aramaic influence of רעה. In any event, this development is evident in the Bible in the later books, especially in light of the use of the expression עשׂה (כ)רצון, which is found nowhere else but in the books of Daniel, Esther, and Nehemiah'; Hurvitz, *Beyn Lashon le-Lashon*, p. 74 (translated in Bergey, 'The Book of Esther', p. 153). See however Ian Young, 'Late Biblical Hebrew and Hebrew Inscriptions', in Ian Young (ed.), *Biblical Hebrews: Studies in Typology and Chronology* (London: T. and T. Clark, 2003), pp. 292–93. Note that although Young raised the possibility that רצה was used in a pre-exilic Judahite inscription, the form רצון is still unattested in pre-exilic Hebrew.

88. Examples cited are in Hurvitz, *Beyn Lashon le-Lashon*, p. 74; and Bergey, 'The Book of Esther', p. 154.

2 Sam. 19.19	לעביר את ־בית המלך לעשׂות הטוב בעינו
Josh. 9.25	הננו בידך כטוב וכישׁר בעיניך לעשׂות לנו עשה
Exod. 15.26	והישׁר נעיניו תעשׂה

These expressions do occur occasionally in exilic and post-exilic contexts as well. Note, for example:

Jer. 34.15	ותשׁבו אתם היום ותעשׂו את־הישׁר בעיני
Esth. 3.11	לעשׂות בו כטוב בעיניך
1 Chron. 19.13	הטוב בעיניו יעשׂה

We may observe the similarity between the early expressions and עשׂה (ב)רצון) by comparing these two verses:

Dan 11.36	ועשׂה כצרונו המלך
2 Sam 9.11	ויאמר ציבא...ככל אשׁר יצוה אדני המלך...
	יעשׂה עברך

The above evidence shows that עשׂה (ב)רצון) penetrated biblical Hebrew after the Exile, and it was used in contexts where SBH employed other, semantically equivalent expressions: עשׂה הישׁר/הטוב בעינים and עשׂה חפץ.

Extra-biblical literature reveals that עשׂה (ב)רצון) is a genuinely late expression that became widely used after the period of the Exile. Note the following post-biblical examples:

Ben Sira 50.22 (B)[89]	המגדל אדם מרחם ויעשׂהו כרצונו
T. Pesaim 3(2).19	שׁשׁה דברים עשׂו אנשׁי יריחי שׁלשׁה
	כרצון חכמים ושׁלשׁה שׁלא כרצון חכמים

Both biblical Aramaic and the Targumim employ the Aramaic equivalent of עשׂה (ב)רצון):

Dan. 4.32	וכמצביה עבד בחיל שׁמיא
Ezra 7.18	כרעות אל הכם תעבדון
Tg. 1 Sam. 2.35	כדמימרי וכרעותי יעביד
(Compare MT:	(כאשׁר בלבבי ובנפשׁי יעשׂה

Note also the use of the LBH phrase in the DSS and the Mishnah:

1QS 9.13	לעשׂות את צרון אל
1QS 9.23	לעשׂות רצון בכול משׁלח כפים
CD 3.12	עשׂות אישׁ את רצונו
M. 'Avot 2.4	עשׂה רצונו כרצנך שׁיעשׂה רצונך כרצונו
M. 'Avot 5.22(20)	לעשׂות רצון אביך שׁבשׁמים

---

89. Examples cited in Hurvitz, *Beyn Lashon le-Lashon*, p. 75. Ben Sira (B) 5.22 [*sic*] cited by Bergey ('The Book of Esther', p. 154) should be 50.22 (נ,כב).

As Bergey aptly summarized:

> The evidence presented above clearly portrays a linguistic development which is characteristic of the later literature. The semantic development of רצה from 'satisfied, pleased' in EBH [= SBH] to 'desire, want' - as is evidence in the expression עשׂה כרצון in LBH - permitted this idiom's usage in contexts which, in EBH [= SBH], featured other expressions.[90]

The 'J' source, however, uses only an equivalent early expression in preference to the LBH idiom:

Exod. 15.26[91]   והישׁר בעיניו תעשׂה

True, we have seen a few instances where late biblical sources also employ עשׂה הישׁר בעינים (or the like), and one may argue that the absence of עשׂה (כ)רצון from 'J' is therefore a coincidence. However, two points must be kept in mind. First, coincidence or not, 'J' includes one example of an expression which is clearly characteristic of SBH. Second, the reader must remember that this is a single example among many where J uses an early feature of biblical Hebrew in preference to an equivalent late expression. It is the cumulative effect of such single examples (as Exodus 15.26) which demonstrates that 'J' consistently reflects the linguistic background of Standard Biblical Hebrew.

8. שׁלום על (*'Peace Be Unto/Be Well With (Someone or Something)'*

The expression שׁלום על, with שׁלום governing the preposition על, occurs 3 times in the Bible,[92] twice in clearly late texts:

Ps. 125.5   שׁלום על ישׂראל
1 Chron. 22.9   ושׁלום...על ירשׂאל

And once in a text which is probably post-exilic:[93]

---

90. Bergey, 'The Book of Esther', p. 155.

91. The reader might also consider the following other examples: Gen. 7.5, ויעשׂ נח ככל אשׁר־צוהו יהוה; and Gen. 18.19, ושׁמרו דרך יהוה לעשׂות צדקה ומשׁפט. Neither Hurvitz nor Bergey treated these expression as equivalent to עשׂה רצון, but I have included them in a footnote for consideration.

92. For a fuller discussion, see Hurvitz, *Beyn Lashon le-Lashon*, p. 154. See also BDB, p. 1022b; KB, p. 973b; *HALAT*, pp. 1395a-99a.

93. Psalm 128 contains no other features of late Hebrew, but the 'Songs of Ascent' collection is usually viewed as post-exilic; see R. Preuss, 'Der zeitgeschichtliche Hintergrund der Wallfahrtspsalmen', *Theologische Zeitschrift* 14 (1958), pp. 401–15; C. Keet, *A Study of the Psalms of Ascents: A Critical and Exegetical Commentary Upon Psalms CXX to CXXIV* (Greenwood: Attic, 1969); and K. Seybold, *Die Wallfahrtspsalms: Studien zur Entstehungsgeschichte von Psalm 120–134* (Neukirchen-Vluyn: Neukirchener Verlag, 1978).

Ps. 128.6 שלום על ישראל

Elsewhere in the Bible, שלום governs the bound preposition ־ל rather than על. The expression שלום ל־ occurs frequently in early books:

Judg. 6.23 et passim[94] ויאמר לו יהוה שלום לך

And twice in texts of uncertain date:

Ps. 72.3 שלום לעם
Isa. 26.12[95] יהוה תשפת שלום לנו

The noun שלום with ־ל occurs also in exilic and post-exilic texts:

Isa. 57.19 et passim[96] שלום שלום לרחוק ולקרוב

Although שלום with ל־ occurs in both early and late books, the appearance of שלום על in two late texts suggests that it represents a development in post-exilic Hebrew.

There are occasional appearances of שלום על in post-biblical Hebrew.[97] It occurs at Qumran. Note the following:[98]

4Q503 29 11 שלום על [ע]ל יכה ישראל
4Q503 51 10 שלום עליכה
11QPs[a] 23.11 (= Ps. 133.3, not in MT) שלום על ישראל

Finally, it occurs sporadically in rabbinic literature, for example:

M. Middot 1.2 שלום עליך

In sum, שלום על ישראל does not occur in early books of the Bible. The expression שלום על is characteristically late, as can be seen in from the aforementioned late biblical and post-biblical texts.

The 'J' source, by contrast, displays only שלום with the preposition־ל, instead of LBH שלום על. Note the following:

Gen. 29.6 השלום לו
Gen. 43.23 ויאמר שלום לכם
(Compare later Jewish usage: שלום עליכם)
Gen. 43.28 ויאמרו שלום לעבדך לאבינו

That שלום always governs the preposition ־ל in 'J' is consistent with SBH usage, and attests to the early linguistic character of 'J'.

---

94. See also Gen. 29.6, 43.23, 43.28; Judg. 19.20; 1 Sam. 20.7; 2 Sam. 18.29, 18.32; 2 Kgs 4.26; Isa. 26.12.
95. For the uncertain dating of Isaiah 26, see above, p. 68, n. 54.
96. See also Jer. 12.12; 1 Chron. 12.19; 2 Chron. 15.5.
97. See *HDHL*, plates 17750–753.
98. Also in a partially fragmentary line, 4Q503 35.5.

Chapter 5

LEXEMES

During the exilic and post-exilic periods, new words entered the Hebrew language, rare terms began to be used more frequently, certain roots were used in different conjugations with new meanings. This chapter discusses such characteristic features of LBH that pertain to lexicography and that can be compared to similar features in the 'J' source. The items discussed in this chapter are as follows:

Late Biblical Hebrew	*Standard Biblical Hebrew*
1) אֲנִי	אָנֹכִי
2) בהל	חפז, מהר
3) בכן	אז
4) נבעת	ירא, פחד
5) נזר על	צוה
6) זקף	רום, נצב, נשׂא, קום
7) יקר	כבוד
8) כנס	אסף, בקץ
9) מהלך	ארך, רחב, דרך
10) מערב	מבוא, ים
11) סוף	אחדית, קצה, קץ
12) קבל	לקח
13) שבח	הגיד, הודה, הלל, ברך
14) שלט	משל, מלך
15) תאב	כסף, אוה, תשׁוקה

1. אֲנִי *(First Person Singular Pronoun)*

There are two forms of the 1st person singular independent pronoun in Biblical Hebrew: אֲנִי and אָנֹכִי.[1] Both forms are common in earlier books of the Bible, as the following statistics indicate:[2]

---

1. For אֲנִי, see BDB, p. 59a; KB, p. 68b; *HALAT*, p. 69a. For אָנֹכִי, see BDB, p. 59a; KB, p. 69b; *HALAT*, p. 69b. See also GKC, p. 105, §32.2c; p. 105, n. 1; Joüon-Muraoka, *Grammar of Biblical Hebrew*, pp. 119–120, §32.A.a; p. 121, n. 2.

2. See Even-Shoshan, *A New Concordance of the Old Testament*, pp. 94–95, s.v. אֲנִי; p. 96, s.v. אָנֹכִי. Books of problematic date have been excluded from the following discussion.

	אני	אנכי
Genesis-Deuteronomy (excluding 'J')	138	68
Former Prophets (Joshua-Kings)	111	74
Jeremiah	54	37

Thus אני and אנכי occur alongside each other throughout pre-exilic and late pre-exilic writings, although אני occurs more frequently than אנכי. This situation changes dramatically in late books of the Bible, where אני predominates and אנכי almost disappears. Note the following distributions of אני and אנכי in late texts:

	אני	אנכי
Isaiah 40–66	67	17
Ezekiel	138	1
Jonah	5	2
Haggai	4	0
Zechariah	10	4
Malachi	7	1
late Psalms	8	4
Job (prose portions)	4	1
Qohelet[3]	28	0
Lamentations	4	0
Esther	6	0
Ezra	2	0
Nehemiah	15	1
1–2 Chronicles	30	1

The above statistics indicate that in early books of the Bible, אני and אנכי occur with nearly equal frequency, but in exilic and post-exilic texts, אני predominates to the near exclusion of אנכי.[4]

The form אני occurs once in a late pre-exilic Hebrew inscription (Arad 88.1), whereas אנכי is absent from Hebrew epigraphic remains; Aharoni, *Arad Inscriptions*, pp. 103–04.

3. D. Fredericks, while acknowledging that אני predominates in post-exilic Hebrew, argued that the exclusive use of אני instead of אנכי in Qohelet is due to the genre and style of the book, rather than LBH; Fredericks, *Qoheleth's Language*, pp. 39–40, 63–64, 66, 69–81, 89, 97, 128, 141–46, 157, 257, 265; see also Young, *Diversity in Pre-Exilic Hebrew*, pp. 140–57. A. Schoors, however, pointed out that even if the use of אני in Qohelet is a characteristic of the author's vernacular, that does not exclude the possibility of a late date; Schoors, *The Preacher Sought to Find Pleasing Words: A Study of the Language of Qoheleth*, (Orientalia Lovaniensa Analecta, 41; Leuven: Peeters, 1992), pp. 47–48, §1.1.1.1.

4. See BDB, p. 59a, s.v. אנכי: 'In later books the preponderance of אני is evident'; KB, 70a: 'Thus later on אנכי lessens, אני increases'. But see cautionary remarks by Rezetko, 'Dating Biblical Hebrew', pp. 224–25.

The reasons for and the difference between the two forms – אני and אנכי – have been the subject of scholarly discussion. Cognates of אנכי are present in Egyptian (*ink*), Moabite (אנך), Phoenician (אנך), Sam'alian (אנך), and Akkadian (*anāku*). Cognates of אני can be found in Aramaic (אנה), Eblaite, Amorite, and Arabic (*'anā*).[5] Rendsburg noted there is insufficient evidence to suggest that אני or אנכי is a dialectal form,[6] or that one form represents colloquial Hebrew as opposed to the written form.[7] E.J. Revell recently attempted to elucidate the principles which govern the use of אני versus אנכי (in pre-exilic texts):[8] 'אני is typically used by status-marked human [or divine] speakers, אנכי by others.... אני is the 'marked' form for a non-status speaker, used to show that the pronoun carries some meaning additional to its basic content "speaker".'[9] Thus status-marked speakers ordinarily use אני except to deemphasize their status (that is, to express politeness) or the importance of their speech, or where the speech 'concerns the addressee on a personal level'. Non-status speakers ordinarily use אנכי, except when adding special emphasis to their speech, such as expressing emotion, emphasizing the speaker, or making a special appeal to a status-marked addressee.[10] Revell intended this explanation to apply only to pre-exilic texts, and offered the following suggestions why in late Hebrew אני is used exclusively:

> The fact that אני, the marked form, eventually replaced the unmarked may result from excessive use in the effort to speak expressively... or some social development such as that which appears to have led to the use of 'you' in place of contrasting 'thou' and 'you' in address to an individual in English. The development was no doubt hastened by the

5. See W.R. Garr, *Dialect Geography of Syria-Palestine, 1000–586 BCE* (Philadelphia, PA: University of Pennsylvania Press, 1985), pp. 79–80; Jean-Hoftijzer, *DISO*, pp. 18–19; and references in Rendsburg, *Diglossia in Ancient Hebrew*, pp. 141–44, nn. 11–17.

6. Rendsburg points out that cognates to both forms appear in Ugaritic (*ank* and *an*). See Rendsburg, *Diglossia in Ancient Hebrew*, p. 148; *contra* C.F. Burney, who in his analysis of the language of Kings argued that אני represents the language of Northern Israel; idem, *Notes on the Hebrew Text of the Book of Kings* (Oxford: Clarendon Press, 1903), p. 207.

7. Rendsburg, *Diglossia in Ancient Hebrew*, p. 148.

8. See Revell, 'The Two Forms of First Person Singular Pronoun in Biblical Hebrew' *JSS* 40 (1955), pp. 199–217.

9. Revell, 'The Two Forms of the First Person Singular Pronoun', pp. 202, 204. Elsewhere Revell explained what is meant by 'status-marked': the speaker is of greater or equal 'rank' than the addressee, 'rank' descending from (1) God, to (2) kings or 'men of God' (איש אלהים), (3) those addressed as 'lord', or parents, to (4) all others. Contrast Revell's conclusions to Waltke-O'Connor, *An Introduction to Biblical Hebrew Syntax*, p. 292, §16.3a: 'There is no functional difference between [אני and אנכי]'.

10. Revell, 'The Two Forms of the First Person Singular Pronoun', pp. 203–14.

similarity of אֲנִי to the first person pronoun of Aramaic, increasingly common as a second language for Hebrew speakers as the biblical period progressed.[11]

Thus in pre-exilic books a distinction was maintained between אֲנִי and אָנֹכִי, but after the Babylonian exile this distinction was lost, and אָנֹכִי all but disappeared from normal use.

That the predominance of אֲנִי over אָנֹכִי is a characteristic of LBH is confirmed in post-biblical literature.[12] Only אֲנִי occurs in Ben Sira. The SBH form אָנֹכִי is rare in QH, appearing only in the Temple Scroll and in 1Q22.[13] Rabbinic literature never employs אָנֹכִי – only אֲנִי – except in direct allusions to biblical passages.[14] Except when imitating classical Hebrew (as in the DSS) or alluding to biblical passages (as in TH), אֲנִי is the only form of the 1st person singular independent pronoun used in post-biblical Hebrew.

The use of אֲנִי and אָנֹכִי in 'J' differs greatly from that of later Hebrew. Not only is אָנֹכִי common in 'J' source verses, it occurs more frequently than the predominant LBH form אֲנִי. The SBH form אָנֹכִי occurs 28 times in 'J': Gen. 3.10, 4.9, 7.4, 16.5, 18.27, 19.19, 24.3, 24.24, 24.27, 24.31, 24.34, 24.37, 24.42, 24.43, 25.22, 26.24, 27.19, 28.15, 28.16, 38.17, 38.25, 43.9, 47.30; Exod. 4.23, 7.17, 7.27, 8.24, 8.25. And אֲנִי occurs 16 times. Gen. 18.13, 18.17(2x), 24.45, 27.24, 27.32, 27.34, 28.13, 34.30(2x); Exod. 7.17, 8.18, 9.14, 10.1, 10.2, 11.4. The frequent appearance of אָנֹכִי alongside אֲנִי in 'J' conforms strongly to the pre-exilic usage of the 1st person singular independent pronouns.

2. בהל ('Hasten')

The verb בהל occurs in the Bible with two distinct meanings: 'disturb, terrify', and 'hasten'.[15] The verb with the former meaning occurs

---

11. Revell, 'The Two Forms of the First Person Singular Pronoun', p. 216. Revell later explained that the 'social upheaval' was the capture of Jerusalem by the Babylonians in 597 BCE; ibid.

12. See *HDHL*, plates 4669–716, s.v. אֲנִי; plates 4716–18, s.v. אָנֹכִי.

13. Qimron, *Hebrew of the Dead Sea Scrolls*, p. 56, §321.11: 'In the 1st person singular the form אֲנִי (57 times) is normal. אָנֹכִי occurs only in TS (22 times) and in 1Q22 2.4 (and perhaps also *ib.* 1.7, 9). Both TS and 1Q22 are written in the style of the Pentateuch (and especially of Deuteronomy), and in them אָנֹכִי always refers to God'.

14. Segal, *Grammar of Mishnaic Hebrew*, p. 39, §67.

15. For a fuller discussion, see Bergey, 'Esther', pp. 111–12; Polzin, *Late Biblical Hebrew*, p. 129. See also BDB, p. 96a, 'late, cf. Aram'.; KB, p. 110a; *HALAT*, p. 107a.

16. Note Driver, *Introduction to the Literature of the Old Testament*, 445; and L. Paton, *A Critical and Exegetical Commentary on the Book of Esther* (ICC: Edinburgh: T. & T. Clark, 1908), p. 62: 'In these late passages the word [בהל] means "hasten," ordinarily "terrify" '.

throughout the Bible, but בהל with the sense of 'hasten' occurs 7 times, 5 times in clearly late texts:[16]

Esth. 2.9	ויבהל את־תמרוקיה ואת־מנותה לתת לה
Esth. 6.14	ויבהלו להביא את־המן
Esth. 8.14	יצאו מבהלים ודחופים בדבר המלך
2 Chron. 26.20	ויבהלוהו משם
2 Chron. 35.21	ואלהים אמר לבהלני

And 2 times in texts of uncertain date, but which are probably pre-exilic:

| Ps. 48.6[17] | המה ראו כן תמהו נבהלו נחפזו |
| Prov. 20.21[18] | נחלה מבהלת(Q) בראשנה |

The verb occurs in BA, meaning 'hasten' in the Hitpaal.[19] Hebrew בהל 'hasten' does not occur in early books of the Bible, which instead employ מהר or חפז to convey the same meaning.[20] Note the following examples:

| Gen 27.20 | מה־זה מהרת למצא בני |
| 1 Sam 23.26 | ויהי דוד נחפז ללכת מפני שאול |

The diachronic contrast between בהל 'hasten' on the one hand, and מהר and חפז on the other, can be seen in the follow pairs of passages:[21]

Josh 8.14	וימהרו...ויצאו אנשי־העיר
(Compare Esth 8.14	(הרצים...יצאו מבהלים
Exod 2.18	מדוע מהרתן בא היום
(Compare Esth 6.14	(ויבהלו להביא את־המן

The above evidence suggests that although the root בהל occurred during the pre-exilic period in northern texts, it was during the post-exilic period that it became more widespread and began to compete with SBH מהר in similar contexts.

The post-exilic character of בהל 'hasten' is confirmed by its appearance in rabbinic literature, though admittedly the evidence is scanty. Although the term occurs several times in post-biblical literature (with the meaning 'disturb, terrify'),[22] it occurs once with the meaning 'hasten, hurry':

| M. 'Avot 5.7 | ואינו נבהל להשים |

---

17. Psalm 48 is one of the Korah psalms, and is considered to be northern in origin; Rendsburg, *Linguistic Evidence for the Northern Origin of Selected Psalms*, pp. 51–60.

18. Evidence exists that the book of Proverbs is also northern; see Rendsburg, *Linguistic Evidence for the Northern Origin of Selected Psalms*, p. 10.

19. Dan. 2.25, 3.24, 6.20; BDB, p. 1084a; KB, p. 1056b.

20. For מהר, see BDB, p. 554b; KB, p. 500a; *HALAT*, p. 524b. For חפז, note BDB, p. 342a; KB, p. 320b; *HALAT*, p. 325b.

21. Examples are from Bergey, 'The Book of Esther', p. 112.

22. *HDHL*, plate 5310.

Bergey concluded:

> The evidence gathered from the Hebrew literary sources points to the semantic development of בהל 'hasten' in post-exilic times, resulting in its extension to the semantic sphere of two other lexemes occurring in EBH [SBH] – מהר and חפז. This development, no doubt, contributed to the decline of חפז, which nowhere occurs in LBH prose.[23]

The LBH term בהל 'hasten' appears nowhere in the so-called 'J' source, which uses only the SBH equivalent מהר. Note the following illustrations:

Gen. 18.6	וימהר אברהם האהלה אל־שׂרה
Gen. 18.7	וימהר לעשׂות אתו
Gen. 24.18	ותמהר ותרד כדה על־ידה
Gen. 27.20	מה־זה מהרת למצא בני
Gen. 43.30	וימהר יוסף כי־נכמרו רחמיו אל־אחיו
Gen. 44.11	וימהרו ויורדו אישׁ את־אמתחתו ארצה
Exod. 2.18	מדוע מהרתן בא היום
Exod. 10.16	וימהר פרעה לקרא למשׁה ולאהרן

Since בהל 'hasten' occurs alongside מהר in post-exilic Hebrew, one might expect at least one example of בהל 'hasten' in 'J' if it were composed after the exile. But such examples are lacking. 'J''s use of מהר in contrast to SBH בהל 'hasten' is further evidence of its pre-exilic linguistic background.

3. בכן *('Thereupon, Then')*

The term בכן (כ + ב) 'thereupon, then'[24] occurs twice in Biblical Hebrew, both times in clearly late texts.[25] Note the following examples:

| Esth. 4.16 | ובכן אביא אל המלך |
| Qoh. 8.10 | ובכן ראיתי שׁעים קברים |

This term does not appear in early texts, which instead use אז.[26] Note the following illustrations:[27]

---

23. Bergey, 'The Book of Esther', p. 112.
24. See KB, p. 443a; BDB, p. 486b: 'late. T[argumim] בְּכֵין oft. for אָז; e.g. Ex 15.1'; *HALAT*, p. 460a. Fredericks has argued against the late character of בכן in Qohelet; *Qoheleth's Language*, pp. 193, 216, 219–20. But see rebuttal by Hurvitz, review of D. Fredericks, *Qoheleth's Language*, pp. 150–152.
25. For a fuller discussion, see Bergey, 'The Book of Esther', p. 132.
26. See KB, p. 24a; BDB, p. 23a; *HALAT*, p. 26a. BDB, p. 23a, also mentions אֲזַי as a 'dialectal form' in Ps. 124.3, 124.4, 124.5 and compares it to Aramaic אֱדַיִן. The Targumim render Hebrew אז in the examples below with Aramaic בכן.
27. For a fuller list, see Even-Shoshan, *A New Concordance of the Old Testament*, pp. 29–30.

Exod. 15.1	אז ישיר־משה ובני ישראל
Josh. 8.30	אז יבנה יהושע מזבח
1 Kgs 8.12	אז אמר שלמה

Hebrew אז continues to appear in late books. Note the following:

| Jer. 11.15 | אז תעלזי |
| 1 Chron. 15.2 | אז אמר דויד |

The late character of בכן is confirmed by its attestation in postbiblical Hebrew. It occurs once in the Qumran literature:[28]

| 1QSa 1.11 | ובכן תקבל להעיד עליו |

The above evidence indicates that בכן began to appear in postexilic texts alongside earlier אז, which continued to be employed in postexilic and Qumran Hebrew.[29]

LBH בכן does not appear anywhere in passages attributed to 'J', which instead employs only SBH אז. Note the following examples:

Gen. 4.26	אז הוחל לקרא בשם יהוה
(Compare Tg. Onq.:	(בכין ביומוהו חלו...
Exod. 4.26	אז אמרה חתן דמים למולת
(Compare Tg. Onq.:	(בכין אמרת אלולי דמא ומהולתא

The absence of LBH בכן in 'J', which uses only the SBH equivalent אז, is further evidence of the the pre-exilic date of 'J'.

4. נבעת *'Be Terrified [of Someone or Something]')*

The Niphal of בעת 'be terrified (of someone or something)'[30] occurs only in late books of the Hebrew Bible.[31] Note the following examples:

Esth. 7.6	והמן נבעת מלפני המלך והמלכה
Dan. 8.17	ובבאו נבעתי ואפלה על־פני
1 Chron. 21.30	כי נבעת מפני חרב מלאך יהוה

---

28. Otherwise the DSS use אז extensively. See for example 1QS 3.11; 1QM 1.10; 1QH 6.29; CD 20.17.

29. Hebrew בכן does not appear in TH. In the Mishnah, אז is replaced by בשעה זו. See Segal, *Grammar of Mishnaic Hebrew*, p. 134, §294.

30. See KB, p. 141a; *HALAT*, p. 141a; BDB, p. 130a: 'late prose'. The Piel of בעת occurs 4 times in early books (1 Sam. 16.14, 2 Sam. 22.5, Ps. 18.5, Isa. 21.4), and elsewhere in Job. See also Driver, *Introduction to the Literature of the Old Testament*, p. 507: נבעת *not the ordinary word*; Paton, *A Critical and Exegetical Commentary on the Book of Esther*, p. 62: 'only in late books'.

31. For a fuller discussion, see Bergey, 'The Book of Esther', pp. 137–38.

The term נבעת does not occur in early books, which instead use (a) פחד[32] or (b) ירא[33] in similar contexts. See the following illustrations:[34]

(a) Isa. 19.16   ופחד מפני תנופת יד־יהוה צבעות
       (Compare 1 Chron. 21.30   נבעת מפני חרב מלאך יהוה)
(b) 1 Kgs 1.50   ואדניהו ירא מפני שלמה
       (Compare Esth. 7.6   והמן נבעת מלפני המלך)

Although the terms פחד and ירא do continue in postexilic texts,[35] the above evidence suggests that the Niphal of בעת began to be used instead of פחד and ירא in the post-exilic period.

The Niphal of בעת continued to be employed in postbiblical Hebrew,[36] thus confirming its late character. It occurs 3 times in the literature of the DSS. Note the following illustrations:

     1QH 1.23   נבעתי במשפטי צדק
     1QH 3.14   ביורדי ימים נבעתים מהמון מים
     1QS 7.1   ואם קלל או להבעת מצרה

It also appears sporadically in Tannaitic literature. Note the following:

     T. Rosh Hashanah 1.15   נבעתתי ונפלתי לאחורי
     Sifra Qedoshim 1.3 (4.87)   נבעת
     Sifre Devarim 192 (233)   שמע קול הגפת תריסין ונבעת

The early terms פחד and ירא continue to appear in post-biblical texts,[37] but the distribution of the Niphal of בעת in postexilic and postbiblical literature and its contrast with earlier פחד and ירא clearly show that the Niphal of בעת 'be terrified' is a feature of LBH.

The 'J' source, however, never employs the LBH form נבעת. Instead it uses only the SBH term ירא to describe being afraid of a person or thing.[38] Note the following examples:

     Gen. 3.10   ויאמר את־קלך שמעתי בגן ואירא כי־עירם אנכי
     Gen. 43.23   ויאמר שלום לכם אל־תיראו
     Exod. 34.30   וירא אהרן וכל־בני ישראל את־משה

---

32. See BDB, p. 808a; KB, p. 757a; *HALAT*, p. 871a.

33. See BDB, p. 931a; KB, p. 399b; *HALAT*, p. 414a.

34. See also the examples given in Bergey, 'The Book of Esther', p.137; and Even-Shoshan, *A New Concordance of the Old Testament*, pp. 489–91, 941–42.

35. See Even-Shoshan, *A New Concordance of the Old Testament*, pp. 489–91, 941–42.

36. See *HDHL*, plate 5960.

37. See Bergey, 'The Book of Esther', p. 138, n. 1.

38. Other instances of ירא in the 'J' source which do not resemble the use of later נבעת are Gen. 18.15, 19.30, 26.7, 26.24, 32.8, 32.12, 43.18, Exod. 14.13, 34.10.

If the 'J' source were indeed written during the post-exilic period, one would expect to see examples of the later form נבעת to express being afraid of a thing or a person, but such examples are lacking.

5. *גזר על* *('Decree [that]')*

The lexeme גזר occurs throughout the Bible with the meaning 'divide, cut off',[39] but twice in the niphal with the meaning 'decree',[40] once in a clearly post-exilic text:

Esth. 2.1   זכר את־ושתי ואת אשר־עשתה ואת אשר־נגזר עילה

And once in a text of uncertain date, but which is probably post-exilic:

Job 22.28   ותגזר־אומר ויקם לך

The Aramaic noun גזר 'decree' occurs twice in BA.[41] Note the following:

Dan. 4.14   בגזרת עירין פתגמא
Dan. 4.21   וגזרת עליא היא

In Esth. 2.1, גזר occurs with על to express a prohibitive command or decree, whereas the example of גזר in Job 22.28 appears to have no prohibitive force.[42]

The expression גזר (על) 'decree' is not used in early texts of the Bible, which instead employ צוה 'command',[43] sometimes in a prohibitive sense. Note the following examples:

Gen. 28.6   ויצו עליו...לא־תקח אשר מבנות כנען
1 Kgs 2.43   ומדוע לא שמרת...אשר צויתי עליך
1 Kgs 11.10–11   וצוה אליו...לבלתי־לכת אחרי אלהים אחרים...
                             ולא שמרת...אשר צויתי עליך

Note however that צוה 'command (against)' occurs also in exilic and post-exilic books:

Jer. 35.6   צוה עלינו לאמר לא תשתו יין
Esth. 2.10   כי מרדכי צוה עליה אשר לא־תגיד

---

39. BDB, p. 160a; KB, p. 178b; *HALAT*, p. 179b.
40. For a fuller discussion, see Bergey, 'The Book of Esther', pp. 109–110. See also BDB, p. 160a: Aramaism, cf. BAram'.; and Paton, *A Critical and Exegetical Commentary on the Book of Esther*, p. 166: 'an Aramaism'.
41. BDB, p. 1086a; KB, p. 1061b.
42. New International Version: 'What you decide on [ותגזר] will be done'.
43. BDB, p. 845b; KB, p. 797a; *HALAT*, p. 947b.

Although צוה 'command, decree' continued to be employed in post-exilic Hebrew, the above evidence demonstrates that גזר 'decree' began to replace it during the post-exilic period.

Post-biblical literature attests to the late character of גזר 'decree'. It occurs several times in rabbinic writings. Note the following examples:[44]

M. Ma'aser Sheni 5.13	עשינו שגזרתה עלינו
M. Soṭah 9.14	גזרו על עטרות חתנים ועל האֵרוס
T. Shevi'it 3.10	גזרו עליה שלא תזרע

Thus גזר with the meaning 'decree' represents a development in post-exilic Hebrew which continued in the post-biblical period.

LBH גזר 'decree' does not appear in the so-called 'J' source, which uses instead SBH צוה for the same purpose. Note the following illustration:

Gen 2.16–17	ויצו יהוה אלהים על־האדם...לא תאכל ממנו

The absence of LBH צוה 'decree' in 'J' source verses is further evidence that 'J' conforms to pre-exilic and not post-exilic usage.

6. *זקף* ('Raise Up')

The root זקף[45] 'raise up' occurs twice, in the book of Psalms: Ps 145.14, 146.8. As noted before, Psalm 145 contains several other features of LBH and can be considered post-exilic[46]; Psalm 146 is of uncertain date, but most likely it is post-exilic.[47]

Ps. 145.14	סומך יהוה לכל־הנפלים ויזקף לכל־הכפופים
Ps. 146.8	יהוה פקח עורים יהוה זקף כפופים

The use of זקף contrasts with several other expressions in Biblical Hebrew which express the same meaning, such as the roots קום, נשׂא, נצב, and רום. Aramaic translations of several biblical passages show how these expressions are all similar in meaning to זקף:[48]

Ps. 20.9	המה כרעו...ואנחנו קמנו
(Note Targum:	(אנון גחנו...ואנחנא אזדקפנא
Ps. 110.7	על כן ירים ראש
(Note Targum:	(מטול היכנא יזקוף רישי

---

44.   See *HDHL*, plates 6248–50.

45.   See BDB, p. 279a: '(late) raise up... only fig. of יהוה's dealing with prostrate men'; KB, 264b; *HALAT*, p. 267b: '? aram. lw.'. See also E. Kautzsch, *Aramaismen im alten Testament* (Halle, 1902), pp. 28–29.

46.   See above, p. 13.

47.   Besides זקף, Psalm 146 contains one other feature of LBH. See Hurvitz, *Beyn Lashon le-Lashon*, pp. 93, 165, 175.

48.   These examples are cited in Hurvitz, *Beyn Lashon le-Lashon*, pp. 94–95.

Isa. 5.26   וְנָשָׂא ־נֵס לַגּוֹיִם

(Note Targum: יִזְקוֹף אֵת לְעַמְמַיָא)

Rabbinic literature provides us with examples which show the vitality of זקף in the post-biblical period:[49]

M. Sukkot 4.5   וְזוֹקְפִים אוֹתָם לְצִדְדֵי הַמִּזְבֵּחַ

Sifre Deuteronomy 80   וְזָקְפוּ אֶת עֵינֵיהֶן

T. Baba Batra 1.6   זוֹקֵף אֶת הַסּוּלָם

Two examples show particularly how much the term זקף was used in the post-biblical period instead of earlier SBH constructions which conveyed the same meaning:

Y. Berakhot 1.4   הַמֶּלֶךְ מְשֶׁהוּא כּוֹרֵעַ אֵינוּ נִזְקַף עַד שֶׁהוּא מַשְׁלִים

כָּל תְּפִילָּת מַאי טַעֲמָא?

וַיְהִי כְּכַלּוֹת שְׁלֹמֹה לְהִתְפַּלֵּל...קָם מִלִּפְנֵי

(1 Kgs 8.54) מִזְבַּח יהוה מִצּוֹרֵעַ עַל בִּרְכָּיו

Talmud Shabbat 62b   יַעַן כִּי גָבְהוּ בְּנוֹת צִיּוֹן (Isa 3.16)

...שֶׁהוּא הוֹלְכוֹת בְּקוֹמָה זְקוּפָה

In light of the evidence that the root זקף became more frequently used in the Hebrew language from the post-exilic period on, it is significant that the root זקף is never employed in similar contexts in 'J'. Note that the Aramaic translations of several of the following examples use זקף to convey the sense of the SBH constructions:

Gen. 13.10   וַיִּשָּׂא־לוֹט אֶת־עֵינָיו וַיַּרְא

(Note Tg. Yer. I: וּזְקַף לוֹט יַת עֵינוֹי לְזָנָן וַחֲמָא)

Gen. 13.14   שָׂא נָא עֵינֶיךָ וּרְאֵה

(Note Tg. Yer. I: זְקוֹף כְּדוֹן עֵינָךְ וְתֶחֱמֵי)

Gen. 18.2   וַיִּשָּׂא עֵינָיו וַיַּרְא

(Note Tg. Yer. I: וּזְקַף עֵינוֹי וַחֲמָא)

Gen. 24.63   וַיֵּצֵא יִצְחָק...וַיִּשָּׂא עֵינָיו וַיַּרְא

(Note Tg. Yer. I: וּנְקַף יִצְחָק...וּזְקַף עֵינוֹי וַחֲמָא)

Gen. 37.7   וְהִנֵּה קָמָה אֲלֻמָּתִי וְגַם נִצָּבָה

(Note Tg. Onq.:   ...וְאַף אִזְדְּקִיפַת)

Gen. 37.25   וַיִּשְׂאוּ עֵינֵיהֶם וַיִּרְאוּ

(Note Tg. Yer. I: וּזְקַפוּ עֵינֵיהִין וַחֲמוֹן)

Gen. 39.7   וַתִּשָּׂא אֵשֶׁת־אֲדֹנָיו אֶת־עֵינֶיהָ אֶל־יוֹסֵף

(Note Tg. Yer. I: וּזְקַפַת אִיתַת רִיבּוֹנֵיהּ יַת עֵינָהּ בְּיוֹסֵף)

Gen. 43.29   וַיִּשָּׂא עֵינָיו וַיַּרְא

(Note Tg. Onq.:   וּזְקַף עֵינוֹהִי שְׁחֶזָא

---

49. There are two occurrences of the root זקף in the DSS: וְ]חִ]יכַף עֵץ וִיזְקֵף [...] (4Q385 2 1.10); זֹקְפִין[:] וְעַל וֹן[:] מִין (1Q65 1 1.2). For examples in post-biblical literature, see *HDHL*, plates 8051–53.

And compare Sifre Deuteronomy 80:[50]   (וזקפו את עיניהן

Exod. 14.10a   וישאו בני־ישראל את־עיניהם

(Note Tg. Yer. I.   (וזקפו בני ישראל ית עיניהין

The above evidence indicates that זקף is a characteristically late lexeme, meaning 'raise up'. It intrudes upon the semantic domain of SBH expressions such as הקים, נשא, רומם, and הציב; this is especially clear where the Targumim employ זקף to translate the standard expressions in Hebrew. The vitality of the root in post-biblical Hebrew is evident in examples from rabbinic literature. The fact that 'J' consistently employs semantically equivalent SBH expressions instead of LBH זקף is further evidence that 'J' reflects a pre-exilic linguistic background.

7. יקר *('Honor')*

The term יקר occurs throughout the Bible,[51] but with the sense of 'honor' 9 times in the post-exilic book of Esther.[52] Note the following:

Esth. 1.4   ואת־יקר תפארת גדולתו

Esth. 1.20   וכל־הנשים יתנו יקר לבעליהן

Esth. 6.3   מה־נעשה יקר וגדולה למרדכי

Esth. 6.6   למי יחפץ המלך לעשות יקר

Esth. 6.6, 6.7, 6.9, 6.11   אשר המלך חפץ ביקרו

Esth. 8.16   אורה ושמחה וששן ויקר

The meaning of 'honor' for יקר in these passages is clear; the Septuagint employs δόξα 'glory, honor' to translate יקר in Esth 1.4, 6.3, and δοξάζω 'honor, glorify' in rendering Esth. 6.6, 6.6, 6.7, 6.9, 6.11. Hebrew יקר 'honor' does not occur in pre-exilic texts, however, which employ כבוד to convey the same meaning.[53] Note the following examples which illustrate the diachronic contrast:[54]

Esth. 1.3–4   ...בהראתו...יקר תפארת

---

50. See also Mekhilta Deuteronomy 12.1.

51. Besides the meaning of 'honor' discussed below, יקר signifies 'precious, (costly things)' in two texts c. 586 BCE: Jer. 20.5; Ezek. 22.25; and in one text of uncertain date (although see above, p. 13, n. 64), Prov. 20.15; and 'price' in post-exilic Zech. 11.13; Job 28.10; see BDB, p. 430a, 'late'; KB, p. 399a; *HALAT*, p. 412b.

52. For a fuller discussion, see Bergey, 'The Book of Esther', pp. 92–93; and Paton, *A Critical and Exegetical Commentary on the Book of Esther*, p. 63: 'late word and Aram'. This discussion will not take into account the examples of יקר in Ps. 49.13, 49.21, where it is unclear that יקר signifies 'honor'. (The Septuagint employs ἐν τιμῇ to render יקר in Ps. 49.13, 49.21.) KB, p. 399a, proposes כבקר for ביקר in Psalm 49. See also Rendsburg, *Linguistic Evidence for the Northern Origin of Selected Psalms*, pp. 57–58.

53. BDB, p. 458b; KB, p. 420a; *HALAT*, pp. 436–437.

54. Examples are from Bergey, 'The Book of Esther', p. 92.

(Compare Exod. 28.2   וְעָשִׂיתָ בִגְדֵי־קֹדֶשׁ לְאַהֲרֹן אָחִיךָ

(לְכָבוֹד לְתִפְאָרֶת

Esth. 1.20   וְכָל־הַנָּשִׁים יִתְּנוּ יְקָר לְבַעְלֵיהֶן

(Compare 1 Sam. 6.5   (וּנְתַתֶּם לֵאלֹהֵי יִשְׂרָאֵל כָּבוֹד

Although Hebrew כבוד 'honor' continued to be used in post-exilic Hebrew, the above evidence suggests that יקר 'honor' began to replace it during the post-exilic period, most likely due to Aramaic influence.[55]

The post-exilic character of Hebrew יקר is demonstrated by its occasional appearance in the Hebrew of the Dead Sea Scrolls. Note the following:

1QM 11 1.14   לוא כבשר תא >ותי...<כול יקרי לי בכבוד

1QS 8.7   הואה חומת הבחן פנת יקר

11QSS 2–1-9 2[56]   ש[לו]חֲמיו במשפטי]...[רחמיו ביקר

The *qᵉtāl* noun pattern is an Aramaic form which occurs primarily, although not exclusively, in post-exilic Hebrew.[57] In addition to יקר, other examples are כְּתָב, שְׁאָר, קְרָב, סְפָר, and מְצָד. Hebrew קְרָב occurs in Zech. 14.3; Ps. 78.9; Job 38.23, and Qoh. 9.18; סְפָר occurs only in 2 Chron. 2.16; and מְצָד appears in 1 Chron. 11.7 (|| 2 Sam. 5.9 מְצֻדָה), 12.16, and in 1 Sam. 23.15 (plural). כְּתָב occurs exclusively, and שְׁאָר occurs primarily (see below), in post-exilic texts, and are discussed elsewhere by Bergey.[58] Because יקר is an example of the Aramaic form *qᵉtāl*, which occurs chiefly in late Hebrew, the lexeme יקר is both phonologically and lexically late. Regarding the appearance of קְטָל forms in Hebrew, Kutscher commented:

> It is remarkable that one noun of this pattern, namely שְׁאָר 'remnant', figures prominantly in Isaiah. Perhaps despite the fact that the common Judean did not yet understand Aramaic, we may posit that [this] noun pattern reached Hebrew via the Judean intelligentsia.[59]

---

55. Aramaic יקר 'honor' is well attested in BA: Dan. 2.6, 2.37, 4.27, 4.33, 5.18, 5.20, 7.14. See BDB, p. 1096b; KB, p. 1083a.

56. For the reading and translation of this passage, see Newsom, *Songs of the Sabbath Sacrifice*, p. 374.

57. Joüon-Muraoka, *Grammar of Biblical Hebrew*, p. 250, §88Ef; GKC, pp. 231–32, §84an; see also Hurvitz, *Beyn Lashon le-Lashon*, pp. 58–59; 59, n. 158. GKC, pp. 213–32, §84an, suggested that only יקר, כתב, קרב are loan words from Aramaic.

58. 'The Book of Esther', pp. 103–05, 142–44, respectively.

59. Kutscher, *History of the Hebrew Language*, p. 75, §103. The appearance of the Aramaic form שְׁאָר in pre-exilic texts actually emphasizes the late nature of the *qᵉtāl* pattern in Biblical Hebrew. Such a form could only appear when employed by a member of the 'Judean intelligentsia', and would not become more widespread until the post-exilic period, when Aramaic began to exert a much stronger influence on Biblical Hebrew.

Yet LBH יקר never occurs in the 'J' source; instead, the Yahwist employs only the SBH lexeme כבוד 'honor, glory'. Note the following:

Gen. 31.1	עשׂה את כל ־הכבד הזה
(Compare Tg. Yer. I:	(עבד ליה ית כל יקר
Gen. 49.6	בקהלם אל ־תחד כבדי
(Compare Tg. Onq.:	...לא נחתית מן יקרי
and Tg. Yer. I.	(לא אתיחד יקרי אדום ברגזהון
Exod. 33.22	והיה בעבר כבדי ושׂמתיך בנקרת הצור
(Compare Tg. Onq.	...ויהי במיעבר יקרי
and Tg. Yer. I:	(ויהי במעיבר יקרי שׁכינתי
Numb. 14.21	וימלא כבוד ־יהוה את ־כל ־הארץ
(Compare Tg. Onq.:	...ומליא יקרא דייי
and Tg. Yer. I:	(ומליא יקרא דייי ית ארעא
Numb. 14.22	כי כל ־האנשׁים הראים את ־כבדי...
(Compare Tg. Onq.:	ארי כל גבריא דחזו ית יקרי
and Tg. Yer. I:	...די חמון ית יקרי)

Were the 'J' source composed during the post-exilic period, we would expect to see at least one example of LBH יקר 'honor' in place of SBH כבוד, but such examples are lacking.

8. כנס *'(Gather, Collect)'*

The Piel and Qal forms of the verb כנס 'gather, collect' occur 8 times in exilic and post-exilic texts:[60]

Ezek. 22.21[61]	וכנסתי אתכם ונפחתי עליכם באשׁ עברתי
Ezek. 39.28	וכנסתים על ־אדמתם
Qoh. 2.8	כנסתי לי גם ־כסף וזהב
Qoh. 2.26	ולחוטא נתן ענין לאסוף לכנוס
Qoh. 3.5	עת להשׁליך אבנים ועת כנוס אבנים
Esth. 4.16	לך כנוס את ־כל ־היהודים הנמצאים בשׁושׁן
Neh. 12.44	לכנוס בהם לשׂדי הערים
1 Chron. 22.2	לכנוס את ־הגרים אשׁר בארץ ישׂראל

And twice in texts of uncertain date:

Ps. 33.7	כנס כנד מי הים
Ps. 147.2	נדחי ישׂראל יכנס

---

60. For a fuller discussion, see Bergey, 'The Book of Esther', pp. 129–30; Hurvitz, *A Linguistic Study of the Relationship between the Priestly Source and the Book of Ezekiel*, pp. 123–35. See also q.v. כנס, BDB, p. 488b: 'late'; KB, p. 443b; *HALAT*, p. 461b.

61. Compare the Septuagint and Peshitta renditions of this verse, where the word for 'gather' is missing; see *BHS*, q.v.; Hurvitz, *A Linguistic Study of the Relationship between the Priestly Source and the Book of Ezekiel*, p. 125, n. 203; and commentaries on this verse.

It also occurs in Aramaic portions of the Bible (= כנש 'assemble').[62] The verb כנס in the above examples is employed to describe gathering crops (Nehemiah), people (Ezekiel, Chronicles), and raw materials (Qohelet). Besides the distribution of the Qal and Piel forms of כנס above, the Hithpael of 'gather oneself' occurs once in an early text:[63]

Isa. 28.20   והמסכה צרה כהתכנס

The Qal and Piel of כנס do not appear in undisputably early books of the Bible, which employ instead אסף or קבץ with the same meaning of 'gather (crops or people)'.[64] Note the following illustrations:

(a) 1 Sam. 5.8   ויאספו את־כל־סרני פלשתים אליהם
         Deut. 11.14   ואספת דגנך ותירשך ויצהרך
         (Compare Gezer Tablet 1:[65]   (ירחו אסף
(b) Gen. 41.35   ויקבצו את־כל־אכל השנים הטבת
         1 Sam. 7.5   קבצו את־כל־ישראל המצפתה

Both (a) אסף and (b) קבץ continue to appear in exilic and post-exilic texts, for example:

(a) Jer. 16.5[66]   כי־אספי את־שלומי מאת העם־הזה
(b) Jer. 29.14[67]   וקבצתי אתכם מכל־הגוים ומכל־המקומות

Nevertheless, the evidence suggests that the qal and piel of כנס entered the Hebrew language during the exilic period (perhaps due to Aramaic influence), and began to replace אסף and קבץ in similar contexts. Note

---

62. See BDB, p. 1097a; KB, p. 1086a.

63. Note Hurvitz, who commented: 'הִתְכַּנֵּס, which is found in *Is.* XXVIII, 20, should be excluded from discussion since (semantically) its exact meaning is unclear and (morphologically) it belongs to a different conjugation (*Hithpa'el*)'; *A Linguistic Study of the Relationship between the Priestly Source and the Book of Ezekiel*, p. 124. However, the root כנס also appears in Aramaic (כנש; see below), and its appearance in Isaiah 28 might be an example of addressee-switching in a prophecy addressed to the tribe of Ephraim. On the phenomenon of addressee-switching in the Bible, see Rendsburg, 'The Strata of Biblical Hebrew', 96–97. Biblical passages set in Ephraimite contexts often display non-standard forms and vocabulary. Regarding such evidence for a distinctive Ephraimite dialect of ancient Hebrew, see Rendsburg, *Linguistic Evidence for the Northern Origin of Selected Psalms*, pp. 7, 14, 20, 22, 24–25, 70, and references. Since the tribes of Ephraim and Manasseh are associated with Joseph, note the presence of IH features in the blessing of Joseph in Genesis 49; G.A. Rendsburg, 'Israelian Hebrew Features in Genesis 49', *Maarav* 8 (1992), pp. 161–70, especially pp. 167–69. See recently Wright, 'Further Evidence for North Israelite Contributions to Late Biblical Hebrew', pp. 138–40.

64. For אסף, see BDB, p. 62a; KB, p. 71; *HALAT*, p. 71b. For קבץ, see BDB, p. 867b: 'syn. אסף'; KB, p. 820a; *HALAT*, p. 994a.

65. Gibson, *Textbook of Syrian Semitic Inscriptions*, I, pp. 2–3.

66. See also Ezek. 11.17; Dan. 11.10; Ezra 3.1; Neh. 8.13; 1 Chron. 15.14.

67. See also Ezek. 22.20; Esth. 2.3, 2.8, 2.19; Ezra 7.28; Neh. 4.14; 2 Chron. 15.19.

how the book of Ezekiel uses SBH אסף and קבץ, as well as LBH כנס, to describe the gathering of the Exiles:

Ezek. 11.17	וקבצתי אתכם...ואספתי אתכם מן־הארצות
But Ezek. 39.28	וכנסתים על־אדמתם

The above distribution of the Qal and Piel forms strongly suggest that they are characteristic of the post-classical stage of BH.[68]

The post-classical character of the Qal and Piel of כנס is confirmed by its attestation in post-biblical literature.[69] It occurs occasionally in the texts from Qumran,[70] for example:

4QOrd 2.4	ואוכל נה וכנס לו
11QT 34.7	ויהיו כונסים את הדם במזרקות

Hebrew כנס is more widespread in rabbinic literature. Note the following examples:

M. Baba Batra 3.1	כנס את תבואות כנס את ק(ו) [י]צו
M. Toharot 9.13	כינסן לאוכל מטמאין
M. Shavu'ot 4.8	הבאיש כונס לתוך ביתו

Thus LBH כנס appeared alongside and began to replace SBH אסף and קבץ in the exilic and post-exilic, although all three roots continued to be used in post-biblical Hebrew.

Recently, however, Joseph Naveh has published what may be attestation of the verb כנס in a pre-exilic text from Jerusalem.[71] The text in question is a jar inscription that is dated paleographically to the First Temple period.[72] The third and second lines of the three line inscription read:

2 [י]הו.בן.חסדיהו.הכנס.כס[ף.]
3 [י]הון.בן.י[דעיהו.הכנס.]

Naveh has suggested the translation: "PN son of PN₂ who gathers silver [and gold]... PN₃ son of PN₄ who gathers [silver and gold]".[73] If the date, provenance, and reading of the text are correct, then the verb כנס was

68. Note also Paton, *A Critical and Exegetical Commentary on the Book of Esther*, p. 63: 'as NH. and Aram.'; and Driver, *Introduction to the Literature of the Old Testament*, p. 446.
69. See *HDHL*, plates 10694–723.
70. DSSH more frequently employs אסף (rarely קבץ) for 'gather'; Bergey, 'The Book of Esther', p. 130, n. 1.
71. J. Naveh 'Hebrew and Aramaic Inscriptions', in D.T. Ariel (ed.), *Excavations at the City of David 1978–1985 Directed by Yigal Shiloh*, VI, *Inscriptions* (Qedem, 41; Jerusalem: Hebrew University, 2000); pp. 1–14. I would like to thank Drs. Ian Young and Gary Rendsburg for bringing this item to my attention.
72. Naveh, 'Hebrew and Aramaic Inscriptions', pp. 1, 2–3.
73. Naveh, 'Hebrew and Aramaic Inscriptions', p. 2.

present in pre-exilic Jerusalemite Hebrew and therefore is not a feature of either LBH or IH. I would suggest this evidence is too recent to draw any firm conclusions. More important is the unusual form הסרט in line 1 – if this stands for שרט (> סרט in later Hebrew) then the text may come from outside of Jerusalem and therefore might not represent evidence for the use of כנס in pre-exilic Judahite Hebrew.

The possibly late character of כנס (Qal and Piel) contrasts strongly with the linguistic situation in the 'J' source, where only אסף appears. Note the following:

Gen. 29.3	ונאספו־שמה כל ־העדרים
(Compare Tg. Onq. and Yer. I:	(ומתכנשין תמן כל עדריא
Gen. 29.7	לא־עת האסף המקנה
(Compare Tg. Onq.:	לא עידן למכנש
and Tg. Yer. I:	(לא עידן למיכנוש...
Exod. 3.16	לך ואספת את־זקני ישראל
(Compare Tg. Onq. and Yer. I:	(ותיכנוש ית סבי ישראל
Exod. 9.19	ולא ואסף הביתה
(Compare Tg. Onq. and Yer. I:	(ולא יתכניש לביתא

Note that 'J' only uses אסף in contexts where כנס could have been an option. However, the possible attestation of כנס in a pre-exilic text from Jerusalem could mean that we cannot use this datum as evidence for early language in 'J'.

9. מהלך *('Walk, Journey, Distance')*

Although the verb הלך is exceedingly common throughout the entire Bible, the noun מהלך 'walk, journey, going' occurs only 5 times, all in exilic and post-exilic texts.[74] Note the following examples:

Ezek. 42.4	מהלך עשר אמות
Jonah 3.3	עיר גדולה לאלהים מהלך שלשת ימים
Jonah 3.4	בעיר מהלך יום אחד
Zech. 3.7	ונתתי לך מהלכים בין העמדים
Neh. 2.6[75]	עד־מתי יהיה מהלכך

---

74. For a fuller discussion, see Hurvitz, *A Linguistic Study of the Relationship between the Priestly Source and the Book of Ezekiel*, pp. 91–94.

75. Note New American Standard Bible: 'How long shall your journey be?'

In all of the above examples, except Zech. 3.7,[76] the noun מהלך is employed to measure distance (Jonah 3.3, 3.4; Neh. 2.6) or dimension (Ezek. 42.4). The term does not appear in any pre-exilic books, where other terms – such as דרך,[77] רחב,[78] and ארך[79] – are used to measure distance. For example, in early texts רחב and ארך are used with אמה to measure dimensions. Note the following:[80]

Gen. 6.15	שלש מאות אמה ארך התבה חמשים אמה רחבה
Exod. 25.23	אמתים ארכו ואמה רחבה

The expressions רחב and ארך continue in exilic and post-exilic Hebrew. For example:

Ezek. 42.2	והרחב חמשים אמות
Ezek. 41.12	וארכו תשעים אמה

For examples of דרך in early books used with יום to measure the distance of a journey, note the following examples:

Deut. 1.2	אחד עשר יום מחרב דרך הר־שעיר
1 Kgs 19.4	והוא־הלך...דרך יום
2 Kgs 3.9	ויסבו דרך שבעת ימים

Note that in these examples, the length of a journey or distance is measured in days (יום), just as in Jonah 3.3 and 3.4. The distribution of מהלך in late books, and the similarity to how דרך, רחב, and אמה are used in early books, suggest that מהלך represents post-classical usage.

The lateness of the term מהלך is confirmed by its frequent use in post-biblical Hebrew and Aramaic. It occurs in rabbinic literature with the same meaning as דרך in the examples above.[81] For example:

M. Ma'aser Sheni 5.2	לירושלם מהלך יום אחד
M. Rosh Hashanah 1.9	שעל מהלך לילה ויום מחללים את השבת
Mekhilta Pesha 14 (47)	והלך מהלך ארבעים יום

Note especially the following example where the rabbinic commentators used מהלך to explain a biblical passage which contained דרך:[82]

---

76. The sense of the plural of מהלך in Zech. 3.7 is that of 'goings, free access'; BDB, p. 237b. Although it is not used here to measure distance, it is the distribution of מהלך in mostly post-exilic texts that is significant. On this point, see Hurvitz, *A Linguistic Study of the Relationship between the Priestly Source and the Book of Ezekiel*, p. 93.

77. BDB, p. 203, §2; KB, p. 218, §2; *HALAT*, p. 222a.

78. BDB, p. 931b; KB, p. 884a; *HALAT*, p. 1311a.

79. BDB, p. 73b; KB, p. 87b.; *HALAT*, p. 86a.

80. For examples of אמה with רחב or ארך, see also BDB, p. 52a; and KB, p. 59a.

81. See *HDHL*, plate 7461.

82. See also Sifre Deuteronomy 2, cited in Hurvitz, *A Linguistic Study of the Relationship between the Priestly Source and the Book of Ezekiel*, p. 93.

T. Pesaḥim 8.3   "דרך רחוקה" שומע אני
מהלך יום אחד או שני ימים או שלשה ימים

'"a distant journey (דרך)" I understand (as) a journey (מהלך) of
one day or two days or three days'

Occasionally the Targumim introduce Aramaic מהלך when translating a
passage that does not contain דרך, for example:

Tg. Onq. Deut. 1.2   מהלך חד עסר יומין מחורב
(Compare MT: אחד עשר יום מחרב)

Although SBH expressions such as דרך, רחב, and ארך continue to be
used alongside LBH מהלך in post-exilic texts, it is the appearance of LBH
מהלך in exilic and post-exilic Hebrew, and its attestation in post-biblical
Hebrew and Aramaic which confirm that it is a characteristic feature of
post-classical Hebrew.

The 'J' source never displays LBH מהלך, but instead employs SBH
דרך in a similar manner. Note the following examples:

Gen. 30.36   וישם דרך שלשת ימים בינו ובין יעקב
(Note Tg. Onq.:   ושוי מהלך תלתה יומין
and Tg. Yer. I: (ושוי מהלך תלתה יומין)
Exod. 3.18   נלכו־נא דרך שלשת ימים
(Note Tg. Onq.:   ניזיל כען מהלך תלתה יומין
and Tg. Yer. I: (נזיל כדון מהלך תלתא יומין)
Exod. 5.3   נלכו נא דרך שלשת ימים
(Note Tg. Onq.:   ניזיל כען מהלך תלתה יומין
and Tg. Yer. I: (נטייל כדון מהלך תלתה יומין)
Exod. 8.23   דרך שלשת ימים נלך
(Note Tg. Onq.:   מהלך תלתה יומין ניזיל
and Tg. Yer. I: (מהלך תלתא יומין נטייל)

Note that the Targumim consistently render SBH דרך with Aramaic
מהלך, in accordance with late usage. That 'J' only employs SBH דרך –
and not LBH מהלך – further reflects its early background.

10. מערב ('West')

The term מערב meaning 'west' occurs 13 times in the Hebrew Bible,[83] 11
times in texts which are clearly late:

Isa. 43.5   וממערב אקבצך
Isa. 45.6   למען ידעו ממזרח־שמש וממערבה

---

83. For a fuller discussion, see Hurvitz, *Beyn Lashon le-Lashon*, pp. 113–116.

Isa. 59.19	וייראו ממערב את־שם יהוה
Ps. 103.12	כרחק מזרח ממערב
1 Chron. 7.28	ולמערב
1 Chron. 12.16	ולמערב
1 Chron. 26.16	לשפים ולחסה למערב
1 Chron. 26.18	לפרבר למערב
1 Chron. 26.30	מעבר לירדן מערבה
2 Chron. 32.30	ויישרם למטה־מערבה
2 Chron. 33.14	בנה חומה...לעיר־דויד מערבה

And twice in texts of uncertain date:[84]

Ps. 75.7	כי לא ממוצא וממערב
Ps. 107.3	ומארצות קבצם ממזרח וממערב מצפון ומים

Note the several instances where מערב 'sunset, the West'[85] appears alongside מזרח 'rising (of the sun), the East'.[86] The late character of the term מערב is confirmed by its contrast with the use of (a) ים and (b) מבוא to express the same meaning in early texts.[87] Note the following examples:[88]

(a)   Josh. 11.3   הכנעני ממזרח ומים

---

84.   See Hurvitz, *Beyn Lashon le-Lashon*, p. 175. Psalm 75 is one of the Asaph Psalms, identified by Rendsburg and others as being northern in origin; see Rendsburg, *Linguistic Evidence for the Northern Origin of Selected Psalms*, pp. 73–81, especially pp. 76–78. This raises the question of whether מערב was a feature of IH which penetrated the Judahite dialect of LBH in the post-exilic period. Note the isogloss between it and Sam'alian, below, 166. Ugaritic displays *m'rb* 'sunset', but it is unclear whether this lexeme also can mean 'west'; see Gordon, *UT*, III, §1915, p. 461. I have noted elsewhere instances where a feature of LBH also appears in non-Judahite texts; see above, pp. 68, n. 54. Psalm 107 contains two other late expressions; see Hurvitz, *Beyn Lashon le-Lashon*, pp. 173 and 173, n. 308.

85.   See BDB, p. 788a, מערב: 'west (late), place of sun*set*'; KB, 550a, II (which mentions Ugaritic *m'rb*); *HALAT*, p. 582a: 'Sonnenuntergang, Westen'. For the root from which מערב is derived, see BDB, p. 787b, ערב V, which associates Hebrew ערב with Akkadian *erêbu* 'enter, go in', Arabic *ġarbu* 'place of sunset, west' (notwithstanding *ġ* for ', probably due to the influence of nearby *r*), and Sabean מערבם, מערבי 'west, western'. With respect to the Akkadian cognate, note the expression *erêb šamši* 'sunset'; see *CAD* E, pp. 258, 269. The Semitic root *'rb* and its meaning of 'west' is reflected in Greek Εὐρόπα and the myths which surround her; see M. Bernal, *Black Athena*, II (New Brunswick, NJ: Rutgers University Press, 1991), pp. 93, 497–498, and references.

86.   See KB, p. 510b; BDB, p. 280b; *HALAT*, p. 536b.

87.   For the use of ים to mean 'west', see BDB, p. 411a: 'west, westward (orig. sea-ward, fr. position of Mediterr. with ref. to Palestine'; KB, p. 383b; *HALAT*, p. 396b. For the use of מבוא (normally 'entrance') to express 'west', see BDB, p. 100b: 'sunset = west'; and KB, p. 491a.

88.   For other references where ים means 'west' and not 'sea', see Even-Shoshan, *A New Concordance of the Old Testament*, pp. 470–72. For מבוא, see Even-Shoshan, *A New Concordance of the Old Testament*, p. 617.

Josh. 12.7   בעבר הירדן ימה
    (Compare 1 Chron. 26.30:   (מעבר לירדן מערבה
Josh. 16.6   ויצא הגבול הימה
Isa. 11.14   ועפו בכתף פלשתים ימה
Zech. 14.4   מזרחה וימה
(b) Deut. 11.30 et passim[89]   בעבר הירדן אחדי דרך מבוא השמש

As seen above, the use of ים and מבוא for 'west' is common in early texts, but although these terms continue to be employed in post-exilic texts, the distribution of מערב clearly indicates that it began to displace the earlier terms ים and מבוא. This is especially clear in phrases where the early texts employ יום or מבוא (see Josh. 12.7 and Deut. 11.30, above), but the late text inserts מערב in an identical context (1 Chron. 26.30). The increased use of מערב in LBH most likely is due to Aramaic influence. Note that מערב appears in a Samalian inscription from Zengirli:[90]

Panammu 13   מן מוקא שמש ועד מערב

and in Middle Aramaic as well (see below, for example, the evidence from the Targumim).

The lateness of the term מערב is confirmed by its frequent appearance in post-biblical literature such as the DSS, the Bar Kokhba letters, and rabbinic writings.[91] Note examples of מערב at Qumran:[92]

11QT 10.35   ועשיתה מקום למערב ההיכל
11QT 13.31   מהמזרח ומהצפון מהמערב

And one example from the Bar Kokhba letters:

Bar Kokhba 15   שעלו מהמערב

The term מערב is also commonly employed in Tannaitic texts. Note the following examples:

M. Ma'aser Sheni 3.5   באו מן המערב
T. 'Erubin 4.6   זה הוא מזרח ומערב
Sifre Numbers 73   תוקע לצפון ולמערב
Mekhilta Pesḥa 1.7   ליושבי מזרח במערב

The distribution of מערב in almost exclusively post-exilic texts in the Bible, and the frequent appaearance of the term in post-biblical literature,

---

89. Elsewhere see Josh. 1.4, 23.4; Zech. 8.7; Mal. 1.11; Ps. 50.1, 104.19, 113.3.

90. Gibson, *Textbook of Syrian Semitic Inscriptions*, II, pp. 76–86; Donner-Röllig, *KAI*, II, pp. 31–34.

91. For examples of מערב from post-biblical literature, see *HDHL*, plates 14765–68; and examples cited in Hurvitz, *Beyn Lashon le-Lashon*, pp. 114–16.

92. In Aramaic, see 1QapGen 17.8: למערבא לאשור.

demonstrates that מערב 'west' is a characteristic of LBH, as opposed to SBH ים and מבוא 'west'.[93]

It is significant, in light of the above, that 'J' never employs מערב, but always uses the SBH term ים for 'west'. Note the following:

Gen 12.8	ויט אהלה בית־אל מים
(Note Tg. Yer. I:	ופרסיה משכיה ביתאל מן מערבא
and Tg. Onq.:	ופרסיה משכניה ביתאל ממערבא)
Gen 13.14	וראה...צפנה ונגבה וקדמה וימה
(Note Tg. Yer. I:	זקוף צדון עינך...ומערבא
and Tg. Onq.:	וחזי...ולמערבא)
Gen 28.14	ופרצת ימה וקדמה וצפנה ונגבה
(Note Tg. Yer. I:	ותיתקף למערבא
and Tg. Onq.:	ותתקף למערבא)
Exod 10.19	ויהפך יהוה רוח־ים
(Note Tg. Yer. I:	נשא היקון רוח מערבא
and Tg. Onq.:	והפך יוי רוח מערבא)

Compare the list of directions in Gen 13.14 and 28.14 with the short list of directions in 11QT 13.31: מהמזרח ומהצפון ומהמערב (see above). Note also how the Targumim consistently render Hebrew ים with Aramaic מערבא, bringing the verses into agreement with Aramaic and post-exilic usage. The fact that 'J' always uses SBH ים in preference to LBH מערב is further evidence of the pre-exilic linguistic character of the 'J' source.

---

93. I respectfully disagree with the argument of Martin Ehrensvärd, who wrote recently: 'So with eight out of its 14 BH occurrences found in clear LBH texts and with its continuity in post-BH, it is possible that the word [מערב] indicates LBH. However, with five occurrences in otherwise EBH texts, it is doubtful that the word was not an option also in EBH'; idem., 'Linguistic Dating of Biblical Texts', in Ian Young (ed), *Biblical Hebrew: Studies in Typology and Chronology* (JSOTSup, 369; London: T. & T. Clark, 2003), p. 181. Part of the problem is that Ehrensvärd relies too much on the conclusion of Mark Rooker that Isaiah 40–66 'consistently shows EBH usage'; see Rooker, 'Dating Isaiah 40–66: What Does the Linguistic Evidence Say?', *WTJ* 58 (1996), pp. 303–312. Rooker did demonstrate successfully that in several instances Isaiah 40–66 'shows EBH usage... where LBH usage is found in Ezekiel' (Ehrensvärd, 'Linguistic Dating of Biblical Texts', p. 181). But one could just as easily argue that such features as מערב and עולמים in Isaiah 40–66, which Rooker did not discuss in his article, reflect LBH beginning to appear in exilic period writings – and therefore Isaiah 40–66 does not consistently reflect SBH. This is not to deny that some LBH terms (such as מערב) did occur sporadically in early texts. Where I disagree with Ehrensvärd and others is how to interpret the evidence. In at least some cases LBH features in early texts may indicate dialectal variation in pre-exilic ancient Hebrew; see R. Wright, 'Further Evidence for North Israelite Contributions to Late Biblical Hebrew', pp. 142–44, 146–48, especially pp. 146–48. I hope to address the issue of late language in Isaiah 40–66 in a future study.

11. סוֹף ('End')

The lexeme סוֹף 'end' occurs five times in Biblical Hebrew,[94] four times in late texts:

Qoh. 3.11	אֶת־הַמַּעֲשֶׂה אֲשֶׁר־עָשָׂה הָאֱלֹהִים מֵרֹאשׁ וְעַד־סוֹף
Qoh. 7.2	בַּאֲשֶׁר הוּא סוֹף כָּל־הָאָדָם
Qoh. 12.13	סוֹף דָּבָר הַכֹּל נִשְׁמָע אֶת־הָאֱלֹהִים יְרָא
2 Chron. 20.16	וּמְצָאתֶם אֹתָם בְּסוֹף הַנַּחַל

And once in a text of uncertain date:[95]

Joel 2.20	אֶת־פָּנָיו אֶל־הַיָּם הַקַּדְמֹנִי וְסֹפוֹ אֶל־הַיָּם הָאַחֲרוֹן

The above examples demonstrate how סוֹף was used to express the 'end' of a geographical area (2 Chron. 20.16; Joel 2.20), or of an abstraction (the 'end' of what God has done in Qoh. 3.11; the 'end' of humankind in Qoh. 7.2; the 'end' of the matter in Qoh. 12.13). The term also occurs in Aramaic portions of the Hebrew Bible with the same meanings.[96]

This expression does not however occur anywhere in earlier books of the Bible, which instead employ (a) קֵץ,[97] (b) קָצֶה,[98] or (c) אַחֲרִית[99] to convey the same meaning. Note the following examples of such usages:[100]

(a)	Gen. 6.13	קֵץ כָּל־בָּשָׂר בָּא לְפָנַי
	(Compare Qoh. 7.2	בַּאֲשֶׁר הוּא סוֹף כָּל־הָאָדָם)
	2 Sam. 15.7	מִקֵּץ אַרְבָּעִים שָׁנָה
(b)	Josh. 15.2	וַיְהִי לָהֶם גְּבוּל נֶגֶב מִקְצֵה יָם הַמֶּלַח
	(Compare 2 Chron. 20.16	וּמְצָאתֶם אֹתָם בְּסוֹף הַנַּחַל)
	Jer. 51.31	לְהַגִּיד לְמֶלֶךְ בָּבֶל כִּי־נִלְכְּדָה עִירוֹ מִקָּצֶה
	(Compare Qoh. 3.11[101]	אֶת־הַמַּעֲשֶׂה אֲשֶׁר־עָשָׂה הָאֱלֹהִים
		מֵרֹאשׁ וְעַד־הַסּוֹף)

---

94.   BDB, p. 693a: 'end, late synon. of קֵץ'; KB, p. 652b: 'aram. = hebr. קֵץ'; *HALAT*, p. 705b: ':: he. קֵץ . . . Ende'. For a fuller discussion, see Polzin, *Late Biblical Hebrew*, pp. 146–147.

95.   On the uncertain but probably post-exilic date of Joel, see the introductory chapter above, p. 13, n. 62.

96.   Dan. 4.8, 4.19, 6.27, 7.26, 7.28. The phrase עַד־סוֹפָא 'until the end' (that is, 'forever') in Dan. 6.26 suggests that BA סוֹף could also signify the end of a period of time. See BDB, p. 1104a; KB, p. 1103b.

97.   BDB, p. 893b; KB, p. 846a; *HALAT*, p. 1045a: 'Ende'.

98.   BDB, p. 892a: 'end, extremity'; KB, p. 846b: 'end, border, limit'; *HALAT*, p. 1046b: 'Band, Ende, Äusserstes'.

99.   BDB, p. 31a: 'after-part, end'; KB, p. 33b: 'end (of time, of a matter, the future)'; *HALAT*, p. 35b: 'Ende, Ausgang'.

100.   See Even-Shoshan, *A New Concordance of the Old Testament*, p. 42 s.v. אַחֲרִית; p. 1023 s.v. קֵץ, קָצֶה.

101.   In both Jer. 51.31 and Qoh. 3.11 the word for 'end' is used to convey the notion of totality. See BDB, p. 892a.

(c) Prov. 14.12   יֵשׁ דֶּרֶךְ יָשָׁר לִפְנֵי־אִישׁ וְאַחֲרִיתָהּ דַּרְכֵי־מָוֶת
(Compare Qoh. 12.13 סוֹף דָּבָר הַכֹּל נִשְׁמָע אֶת־הָאֱלֹהִים יְרָא)

These terms continued to appear in exilic texts, but are especially rare in post-exilic texts. Note the following illustrations:

(a) Ezek. 7.2   לְאַדְמַת יִשְׂרָאֵל קֵץ
     Ezek. 29.13   מִקֵּץ אַרְבָּעִים שָׁנָה אֲקַבֵּץ
     Qoh. 4.8   וְאֵין קֵץ לְכָל־עֲמָלוֹ
     2 Chron. 8.1   מִקֵּץ עֶשְׂרִים שָׁנָה
(b) Isa. 62.11   אֶל־קְצֵה הָאָרֶץ
(c) Qoh. 7.8   טוֹב אַחֲרִית דָּבָר מֵרֵאשִׁיתוֹ
                     (Compare Qoh. 12.13 סוֹף דָּבָר הַכֹּל נִשְׁמָע אֶת הָאֱלֹהִים יְרָא)

The above evidence indicates that LBH סוֹף entered Hebrew during the post-exilic period (probably due to Aramaic influence), and began to replace SBH קֵץ, קְצֵה, and אַחֲרִית in similar contexts.

The post-exilic character of סוֹף is confirmed by its widespread attestation in post-biblical literature. It occurs sporadically in Ben Sira and the DSS:[102]

Ben Sira 8.18   כי לא תדע מה ילד ספו
1QH 18.30[103]   סוף וקצי שלום לאין ח<קר...>
4Q171 1 2.6   פשרו על כול הרש?ע?ה לסוף ארבעים השנה
                        אשר ותמו ולאו ימצא בארץ
papMur 45.9[104]   <...> עד סוף הזמן
Apocryphal Psalm 2.10   את גבורות ימינך ולהבין את סוף דרבי
                        קודשך
Mur 24 2 14   חכרתי המך ?מ?ן ?ה־<יום | ע<ד? סוף ע?ר?ב השמטה

But סוֹף 'end, limit' is common throughout Tannaitic literature. Note the following examples:

M. Kil'ayim 3.3   מפני שהוא ניראה כסוף שדהו
M. Yebamot 1.1   צרותיהן מן החלוצה ומן היבום עד סוף העולם

·

102. See *HDHL*, plates 13632–44. For סוֹף = 'end' in the DSS, see E. Qimron, *HDSS*, 93.

103. '[For un]ending [seasons of joy] and un[numbered] ages of peace'; S. Holm-Nielsen, *Hodayot Psalms from Qumran*, (Acta Theologica Danica, 2; Aarhus, Denmark: Universitetsforlaget, 1960), pp. 253, 257, n. 50.

104. So *HDHL*, but see D. Pardee, who reads this line differently: "'d hswp d[gn "until the g]rain] is finished"'; Pardee, *Handbook of Ancient Hebrew Letters*, pp. 134–35.

Although קץ continued to occur in post-biblical texts,[105] the above evidence is sufficient to demonstrate that סוף 'end' is a lexeme characteristic of post-exilic Hebrew.

The LBH lexeme סוף does not occur anywhere in 'J'. Instead, the Yahwist source consistently employs only the SBH expressions (1) קץ, (2) קָצֶה.[106] Note the following:

(a) Gen. 4.3   ויהי מקץ ימים
        (Compare Tg. Onq.:   והוה מסוף ימין
        and Tg. Yer. I: (והוה מסוף יומיא
      Gen. 8.6   ויהי מקץ ארבעים יום
        (Compare Tg. Onq. and Tg. Yer. I: (והוה מסוף ארבעין יומין
(b) Gen. 19.4   ואנשי העיר...נסבו על-הבית מנער
                           ועד-זקן כל-העם מקצה
        (Compare Tg. Onq.:   ...כל עמא מסופיה
        and Tg. Yer. I: (...כל עמא מסיפא
      Gen. 47.21   מקצה גבול-מצרים ועד-קצהו
        (Compare Tg. Onq.:   מסוף תחום מרצים ועד סופיה
        and Tg. Yer. I: (מסיפי תחום מרצים ועד סופיה

Whereas the lexeme סוף became widespread in late biblical and post-biblical Hebrew and Aramaic, it is significant that 'J' consistently avoids LBH סוף in favor of its earlier equivalents קץ and קָצֶה. Thus 'J' reflects the pre-exilic linguistic situation.

12. קבל ('Receive, Take')

The Piel of קבל 'receive, take'[107] occurs 8 times in the Hebrew Bible,[108] 7 times in clearly post-exilic texts:

---

105. SBH קץ occurs commonly – sometimes with the meaning 'time, epoch' – in Ben Sira and the DSS, for example: Ben Sira 43.27; 46.20; CD 1.5; 1QM 1.4; 1QS 4.25. See Qimron, *Hebrew of the Dead Sea Scrolls*, p. 95; L. Ginzberg, *An Unknown Jewish Sect* (New York: Jewish Theological Seminary, 1970; German original, 1922), p. 29. It is, however, rare in TH; but see M. 'Eduyyot 2.9; Mekhilta Pesaḥim 14 (51). See *HDHL*, plates 16304–305, s.v. קץ.

106. SBH קָצֶה occurs in Gen. 47.2 ('J'), but not with the meaning 'end, limit', and is not listed here.

107. See KB, p. 819b; BDB, p. 867a: '(late) Aram. loan word'; *HALAT*, 993a: 'althe. vb. doch durch לקח verdrängt u. unter aram. Einfluss wieder gebraucht'. This discussion does not include the Hiphil of קבל 'to correspond', which occurs in early texts (Exod. 26.5, 36.12).

Hurvitz rightly argued that the presence of the root *qbl* in the Amarna texts does not obviate the late character of Piel קבל in Hebrew; Hurvitz, *A Linguistic Study of the Relationship between the Priestly Source and the Book of Ezekiel*, p. 22, n. 21; W.F. Albright and William Moran, 'A Re-interpretation of an Amarna Letter', *JCS* 2 (1948), p. 240; R. Gordis, *The Book of God and Man* (Chicago: University of Chicago, 1965), pp. 163–64; 345, n. 32; but also Hurvitz, 'The Chronological Significance of Aramaisms in the Bible', p. 236.

Job 2.10 (2x) גַם אֶת־הַטּוֹב נְקַבֵּל מֵאֵת הָאֱלֹהִים וְאֶת־הָרַע לֹא נְקַבֵּל

Esth. 9.23 וְקִבֵּל הַיְּהוּדִים אֵת אֲשֶׁר־הֵחֵלּוּ לַעֲשׂוֹת

Esth. 9.27 וְקִבֵּל יְהוּדִים עֲלֵיהֶם

1 Chron. 12.19 וַיְקַבְּלֵם דָּוִיד

1 Chron. 21.11 כֹּה־אָמַר יְהוָה קַבֶּל־לָךְ

2 Chron. 29.16 וַיְקַבְּלוּ הַלְוִיִּם לְהוֹצִיא

And once in a text of problematic date:

Prov. 19.20[109] שְׁמַע עֵצָה וְקַבֵּל מוּסָר

The Aramaic cognate קבל with the same meaning occurs 3 times in the Aramaic portions of Daniel:

Dan. 2.6 et passim[110] תְּקַבְּלוּן מִן־קֳדָמַי

The Piel of קבל occurs nowhere in early books of the Hebrew Bible, which instead employ the common lexeme לקח 'to take'. Note the similarities in usage between לקח in early texts and קבל in later texts:

Gen 33.10, 11 אִם נָא מָצָאתִי חֵן...וְלָקַחְתִּי מִנְחָתִי...וַיִּקַּח

(Compare Esth 4.4 וַתִּשְׁלַח בְּגָדִים לְהַלְבִּישׁ אֶת מָרְדֳּכַי...וְלֹא קִבֵּל)

Exod 24.6 וַיִּקַּח מֹשֶׁה חֲצִי הַדָּם...וַחֲצִי הַדָּם זָרַק עַל הַמִּזְבֵּחַ

(Compare 2 Chr 29.22 וַיְקַבְּלוּ הַכֹּהֲנִים אֶת־הַדָּם וַיִּזְרְקוּ הַמִּזְבֵּחָה)

The equivalence between לקח and קבל is reinforced by comparing BH idioms with similar phrases in TH and the Targumim. Note the following illustrations:[111]

Gen. 23.13 נָתַתִּי כֶּסֶף הַשָּׂדֶה קַח מִמֶּנִּי

(Compare M. Sheqalim 5.4 וְנוֹתֵן לוֹ מָעוֹף וּמְקַבֵּל מִמֶּנּוּ חוֹתָם)

Lev. 14.15 וְלָקַח...מִלֹּג הַשֶּׁמֶן וְיָצַק עַל כַּף הַכֹּהֵן הַשְּׂמָאלִית

(Compare T. Zebaḥim 1.11 לוֹג שֶׁמֶן שֶׁל מְצוֹרָע מְקַבֵּל בִּימִינוֹ)

---

108. For a fuller discussion, see Bergey, 'The Book of Esther', pp. 145–147; Hurvitz, 'The Date of the Prose Tale of Job Linguistically Reconsidered', pp. 20–23; Polzin, *Late Biblical Hebrew*, p. 150; Kutscher, *History of the Hebrew Language*, pp. 83–84, §123.

109. This may represent another example of an IH isogloss with Aramaic which becomes part of the literary dialect during the post-exilic period. On IH features in Proverbs, see W.F. Albright, 'Some Canaanite-Phoenician Sources of Hebrew Wisdom', in *Wisdom in Israel and in the Ancient Near East*, ed. M. Noth and D.W. Thomas, (VTSup, 3; Leiden: E.J. Brill, 1960), pp. 1–15; H.L. Ginsberg, *The Israelian Heritage of Judaism* (New York: Jewish Theological Seminary, 1982), p. 36; and Rendsburg, *Linguistic Evidence for the Northern Origin of Selected Psalms*, p. 10 and nn. 39–40.

110. See also Dan. 6.1, 7.18.

111. Examples are drawn from Hurvitz, 'The Date of Job Linguistically Reconsidered', p. 21.

(ונותן בשמעלו)

Deut. 16.19   ולא תקח שחד

    (Compare Tg. Onq.:   (ולא תקביל שוחדא

Ps. 6.10   יהוה תפלתי יקח

    (Compare Targum: (ייי צלותי יקבל

Compare the phrase לקחת ברכה in classical BH to לקבל בכרה (and its Aramaic equivalent) in post-biblical Hebrew:[112]

Gen. 27.35   בא אחיך במרמה ויקח ברכתך

    (Compare Tg. Onq.:   (על אחוך בחוכמא וקביל ברכתך

Numb. 23.20   הנה ברך לקחתי

    (Compare Tg. Onq.:   הא בירכן קבילית

    (and 11QPs[a] Zion 13:   (וברכות נכבדים תקבלי

Although לקח appears frequently in postexilic texts,[113] the above evidence suggests clearly that the Piel of קבל began to be employed alongside earlier לקח in similar contexts.

Extra-biblical literature further demonstrates that the Piel of קבל is a characteristic of LBH. The term occurs several times in postbiblical texts.[114] Note the following examples:

Ben Sira 15.2   וכאשת העורים תקבלנו

1QSa 1.11   תקבל להעיד עליו

4QpPs[a] 171 2.9   יקבלו את מועד התענית

The Piel of קבל is also widespread in TH:

M. Berakhot 2.2   אלא יקבל עליו מלכות שמים תחילה ואחד

     כך יקבל

T. Ma'aserot 1.6   אבל לא וקבל בכלי להיות משתמש ממנו

Sifre Deuteronomy 54 (122)   קיבלתם מלכותי קבלו גזירותי

Regarding the above evidence, Bergey commented:

> לקח remains the preferred form throughout LBH, including Esther where it appears twice as often as קבל. Also קחל is the more frequently used term of the two [קחל and קבל] in the DSS. So from the literary evidence, it seems that קבל never thoroughly permeated the language until Tannaitic times. Nevertheless, its appearance in Esther, Ezra, and Chronicles is the earliest indication of this lexeme's penetration into the Hebrew literary sources, an entrance which was the harbinger of its gradually increased use as is evident especially in the Mishnah.[115]

112. See Hurvitz, 'The Date of Job Linguistically Reconsidered', p. 22.
113. See Even-Shoshan, *A New Concordance of the Old Testament*, p. 607.
114. See *HDHL*, plates 15868–83. See also Bergey, 'The Book of Esther', p. 146.
115. Bergey, 'The Book of Esther', pp. 146–147.

The LBH term קִבֵּל appears nowhere in verses attributed to the 'J' source. Instead of LBH קִבֵּל, 'J' uses only SBH לקח in the following verses:

> Gen. 2.21, 2.22, 3.6, 3.22, 4.11, 4.19, 6.2, 7.2, 8.9, 8.20, 9.23, 11.29, 18.5, 18.7, 18.8, 19.14, 19.15, 24.22, 24.37, 24.38, 24.40, 24.48, 24.51, 24.61, 24.65, 24.67, 25.1, 26.34, 27.9, 27.13, 27.14, 27.15, 27.35, 27.36, 27.45, 30.37, 31.46, 32.24, 34.2, 38.2, 38.6, 38.20, 38.23, 38.28, 39.20, 43.11, 43.12, 43.13, 43.15 (2x), 43.18, 44.29, 47.2
> Exod. 4.9 (2x), 4.20, 4.25, 5.11, 7.15, 7.19, 14.6

If the 'J' source were composed during the post-exilic period, we should expect to see at least one example of 'J' using LBH קִבֵּל instead of SBH לקח in the above verses.

13. שבח ('Laud, Praise')

The lexeme שבח, meaning 'laud, praise',[116] occurs four times in clearly late contexts:[117]

Ps. 117.1	שבחוהו כל־האמים
Ps. 145.4	דור לדור ישבח מעשיך
Qoh. 4.2	ושבח אני את־המתים... מן־החיים
Qoh. 8.15	ושבחתי אני את־השמחה

And twice in texts of uncertain date:[118]

Ps. 63.4	שפתי ישבחונך
Ps. 147.12	שבחי ירושלם את־יהוה

Except for the two references in Qohelet, the Piel form of the verb שבח is used to express praise for either the deity or his acts. The meaning of שבח is somewhat different from the sense of 'laud, praise' in the Psalms, since the object of the praise is the dead.[119] In the above examples, it occurs in poetic parellism with ברך[120] (Ps. 63.4), הלל[121] (Ps. 117.1, 147.12), and הגיד[122] (Ps 145.4). Both the verb and its meaning appear to be due to Aramaic influence. The Aramaic cognate שבח occurs in the Pael in Dan

---

116. See שבח II in BDB, p. 986b: 'late Aramaism, cf. Aram. (incl. O.Aram.) שבח'; and שבח I, in KB, p. 940b. Koehler-Baumgartner compares the root to Arabic *sabba*, but does not comment on its lateness. See also *HALAT*, p. 1290b.

117. Examples cited in Hurvitz, *Beyn Lashon le-Lashon*, p. 90.

118. Psalm 63 contains a single late feature, and Psalm 147 contains two features of LBH. See Hurvitz, *Beyn Lashon le-Lashon*, p. 175.

119. See BDB, p. 986b: 'commend, congratulate'. KB distinguishes the sense of שבח in Qoh. 4.2 ('congratulate') from that of Qoh. 8.15 ('praise, laud'); p. 941a.

120. See *HALAT*, p. 153a; KB, p. 153a; BDB, p. 138b.

121. See *HALAT*, p. 238b; KB, p. 235a; BDB, p. 237b.

122. See *HALAT*, p. 629a; KB, p. 591a; BDB, p. 616b.

2.23, 4.31, 4.34, 5.4, 5.23.[123] In contrast to this late use of שבח (or the nominal form תשבחה; see below), other passages employ a variety of other expressions – such as זמר ,שיר, and פסר – to praise the deity or his works:

2 Sam. 22.50	אודך...לשמך אזמר
(Note Targum:	(אודך...ולשמך אימר תשבחא
Isa. 12.5	זמרו יהוה
(Note Targum:	(שבחו קדם יוי
Isa. 14.7	פצחו רנה
(Note Targum	(יבעו תושבחו
Isa. 42.10–12	שירו ליהוה שיר חדשתהלת מקצה הארץ...
	ירנו ישבי סלע...ישימו ליהוה כבוד ותהלתו באיים יגידו
(Note Peshitta:	תשבוחתא דאשעיא שבחו למירא תשוחתא
	חדתא תשבוחתה מן סופיה דארעא... נשבחון יתבי שקיפא...
	(ונתלון תשבוחתא למירא ותשבחתה נחוון בגזרתא
Ps. 22.23	אספרה שמך לאחי בתוך קהל אהללך
Ps. 79.13	נודה לך לעולם לדר ודר נספר תהלתך

The Aramaic and the Syriac rendition of various Hebrew expressions with the verb שבח or the nominal form תשבוחא shows how they are equivalent in meaning to Hebrew שבח. The evidence that indicates Aramaic שבח was borrowed into Biblical Hebrew in the post-exilic period, and that it began to supplant other expressions for praising God or proclaiming his actions in history. Evidence from post-biblical literature shows that the emergence of שבח in LBH reflects the larger linguistic picture. The widespread popularity and use of שבח and the nominal form תשבחה in late and post-biblical Hebrew (and Aramaic) can be seen in several examples from Ben Sira, the DSS, and the Mishnah.[124] Thus in Ben Sira:[125]

Ben Sira (B) 51.14	הודו לאל התשבחות כי לעולם חסדו
Ben Sira (B) 51.30	ברוך יהוה לעולם ומשובח שמו לדר ודר
Ben Sira (B) 44.(title)	שבח אבות עולם

The root שבח occurs frequently in the DSS. Note the following:

1QM 8.4	תשבוחת אל
4Q403 1 1.2–3	שבח לאלוהי גבורות
4Q403 1 1.32	כול אלוהים שבחו לאלוהין

---

123. See BDB, p. 1114a, which relates it to Hebrew שבח ('Aramaism'); and KB, p. 1128a.

124. For post-biblical examples of שבח, see *HDHL*, plates 17366–72. For examples of תשבחה, see *HDHL*, plate 17372.

125. Also cited in Hurvitz, *Beyn Lashon le-Lashon*, p. 89.

11QShirShabb 2–1-9 3–4   ובהדר תשבוחותו בכול רקי]עי...[ם
אור וחושך

And in the Mishnah, see the following:[126]

     M. Pesaḥim 10.5   לפיכך אנו חייבים להודות להלל
                                         לשבח לפאר לרומם
     M. Sanhedrin 5.2   כל המרבה בדיקות הרי זה משתביח
     M. Pesaḥim 10.4   מתחיל בגנות ומסיים בשבח
     M. Sukkot 5.4   ואומרין לפניהם דברי תושבחות

The earlier expressions for praising the deity (based on הלל, ספר, זמר, שיר, רום, רנן) continue to be used in LBH and in post-biblical Hebrew. By contrast, the root שבח never appears in the Bible in early contexts, but it emerges in the post-exilic period to replace semantically equivalent expressions. It is, therefore, a characteristic of LBH.

The 'J' source, notably, never once uses the root שבח. In contexts where it could use שבח, it consistently employs one of the earlier expressions listed above. Note the following instances where a person is praised:

     Gen. 12.15[127]   ויהללו אתה אל פרעה
     Exod. 9.16   ולמען ספר שמי בכל הארץ

Note further how the Targumim employ שבח to translate הלל in Gen 12.15:

     Tg. Yer. I: ושבחו יתה לפרעה
     Tg. Onq.:   ישבחו אתה לפרעה

Whereas the use of the root שבח becomes widespread in the language of late and post-exilic Hebrew and Aramaic, it is significant that 'J' consistently prefers the earlier equivalents. Thus it fails to reflect the post-exilic linguistic situation.

14. שלט *('Rule, Have Dominion')*

The verb שלט occurs 8 times in the Bible, always in late texts.[128] It occurs 5 times in the Qal stem:

     Qoh. 2.19   וישלט בכל־עמלי
     Qoh. 8.9   ונתון את־לבי לכל מעשה...אשר שלט האדם באדם
     Esth. 9.1   אשר שברו...לשלוט בהם...אשר ישלטו היהודים

---

126. Examples also cited in Hurvitz, *Beyn Lashon le-Lashon*, p. 89.

127. Compare to the above sense of שבח 'commend' in Qoh. 4.2, 8.15.

128. BDB, p. 1020b: 'late'; KB, p. 977a: 'aram. LW'; *HALAT*, p. 1408b. For a fuller discussion, see Hurvitz, *Beyn Lashon le-Lashon*, pp. 134–36. For the meaning and use of שלט especially in Qohelet, see C.-L. Seow, *Ecclesiastes*, pp. 13–14.

Neh. 5.15   שׁלטוּ עַל־הָעָם

And 3 times in the Hiphil:

Qoh. 5.18   וְהִשְׁלִיטוֹ לֶאֱכֹל מִמֶּנּוּ
Qoh. 6.2   וְלֹא יַשְׁלִיטֶנּוּ הָאֱלֹהִים לֶאֱכֹל מִמֶּנּוּ
Ps. 119.133   וְאַל־תַּשְׁלֶט־בִּי כָל־אָוֶן

The verb שׁלט also occurs several times in Biblical Aramaic.[129] The Hebrew root occurs in nominal forms which occur, with one exception, in exilic or post-exilic texts:[130] שַׁלִּיט 'ruler'. in Gen. 42.6;[131] Ezek. 16.30; Qoh. 7.19, 8.8, 10.5; and שִׁלְטוֹן 'mastery' in Qoh. 8.4.

The verb שׁלט does not appear in early books. Instead, other terms, especially מָשַׁל, are employed to convey the idea of rulership or dominion. Note the following examples:[132]

Deut. 15.5   וּמָשַׁלְתָּ בְּגוֹיִם רַבִּים וּבְךָ לֹא יִמְשֹׁלוּ
      (Compare Tg. Onq.:   וְתִשְׁלוֹט בְּעַמְמִין סַגִּיאִין וּבָךְ לֹא יִשְׁלְטוּן)
Judg. 15.11   הֲלֹא יָדַעְתָּ כִּי מֹשְׁלִים בָּנוּ פְּלִשְׁתִּים
      (Compare Esth. 9.1:   ...אֲשֶׁר שִׂבְּרוּ...לִשְׁלוֹט בָּהֶם...
                            (אֲשֶׁר יִשְׁלְטוּ הַיְּהוּדִים
2 Sam. 23.3   מוֹשֵׁל בָּאָדָם צַדִּיק
      (Compare Qoh. 2.19, 8.9; Neh. 5.15, above)
1 Kgs 5.1   וּשְׁלֹמֹה הָיָה מוֹשֵׁל בְּכָל הַמַּמְלָכוֹת
      (Compare Dan. 5.7:   וְתַלְתִּי בְמַלְכוּתָא יִשְׁלַט)

The distribution of the verb שׁלט in late texts, and its contrast with earlier terms such as מָשַׁל, suggest that שׁלט is characteristic of LBH.

The lateness of שׁלט is confirmed by its frequent appearance in post-biblical Hebrew and Aramaic.[133] Note the following examples:

129. In the Peal, in Dan. 2.39, 3.27, 5.7, 6.25; and in the Haphel, in Dan. 2.38, 2.48. See BDB, p. 1115b, 'late'; and KB, p. 1131a.

130. For שַׁלִּיט, see BDB, p. 1020b; KB, p. 977b; *HALAT*, p. 1411a. For שִׁלְטוֹן, see BDB, p. 1020b; KB, p. 977b; *HALAT*, p. 1410a. For their Aramaic equivalents, שַׁלִּיט and שָׁלְטָן, respectively, see BDB, p. 1115b; and KB, p. 1131a.

131. See BDB, p. 1020b: 'prob. late substitution for original word of E'. However, in view of the attestation of the term *šlyṭ* in Ugaritic, this position of BDB no longer is tenable (regardless of how one interprets the *y* of *šlyṭ*); see Gordon, *UT*, §2423, p. 490. The appearance of שַׁלִּיט in Gen. 42.6 may be due to dialectal variation, intentionally utilized by the author to portray the foreignness of the scene; see Hurvitz, 'The Chronological Significance of "Aramaisms"', p. 239, n. 27. On 'style switching' in general, see G.A. Rendsburg, 'Linguistic Variation and the "Foreign" Factor in the Hebrew Bible', *Language and Culture in the Near East*, ed. S. Izre'el and R. Drory (Israel Oriental Studies, 15; Leiden: E.J. Brill, 1996), pp. 177–190; Rendsburg, 'The Strata of Biblical Hebrew', pp. 92–96.

132. Cited in Hurvitz, *Beyn Lashon le-Lashon*, pp. 135–136. See BDB, מָשַׁל III, p. 605b; KB, מָשַׁל II, p. 576a; *HALAT*, p. 611a. See also BDB, שַׂר, p. 978a; KB, p. 929a; *HALAT*, p. 1259a.

133. See *HDHL*, plates 17718–19.

Sifre Deuteronomy 323   ישראל...לא שלטה בהן

Mekhilta R. Shim'on ben Yoḥai 15.18   ייי מלך עולם ועד'

לא שלטה בהם אומה ומלכות

Sifre Deuteronomy 105   אבל אם רצה אתה תשלט בו

שנ' ואתה תמשל בו'

M. Menaḥot 10.4   היה מנוקב כדי שיהא האור שולט בכולן

The examples from Mekhilta R. Shim'on ben Yoḥai 15.18 and Sifre Deuteronomy 105 are especially illuminating. Biblical passages with משל or מלך are cited, and are explicated by the late term שלט. The evidence suggests that although lexemes based on שלט did occur in pre-exilic and exilic Hebrew, it was not until the post-exilic period, probably due to the influence of Aramaic, that the verb שלט was employed in place of earlier expressions like משל, and מלך. The verb שלט continued to be employed in post-biblical Hebrew, and rabbinic commentators used it to explain verses containing, for example, SBH משל or מלך. Thus we may conclude that the use of the verb שלט for 'rule, have dominion' is characteristic of LBH.

The term does not appear in verses commonly attributed to 'J', which displays only SBH usages such as שלט. Note the following examples:

Gen. 3.16   והוא ימשל־בך

(Compare Tg. Onq.:   והוא שלוט ביך

and Tg. Yer. I: (והוא יהי שליט ביך

Gen. 4.7   ואתה תמשל־בו

(Compare Tg. Yer. I: (ואנת תהי שליט ביה

Gen. 24.2   עבדו...המשל בכל־אשר־לו

(Compare Tg. Onq.:   לעבדיה...דקליט בכל דליה

and Tg. Yer. I: (...דשליט בכל אפותיקי דליה

Note also that the Targumim in these examples render משל with the root שלט, in accordance with post-exilic and post-biblical usage. That 'J' consistently displays משל in preference to LBH שלט further indicates its early linguistic character.

15. תאב ('Long For')

The verb תאב 'long for' is rare in Biblical Hebrew. Most likely it derives secondarily from אבה by means of the late noun תאבה.[134] This new verb תאב occurs twice in a clearly late text:[135]

134. KB, p. 1051b; BDB, p. 1060a; *HALAT*, p. 1542b: 'das vb. תאב ist eine sekundäre Stammbildung von אבה wollen, wahrscheinlich vermittelt durch das vs. 20 gennante sbst. יתאבה'.

135. For a fuller discussion, see Hurvitz, *Beyn Lashon le-Lashon*, pp. 148–49. The single occurrence of מתאב in Amos 6.8 is not to be related to תאב 'long for', but is a rare example of aleph-ayin interchange in Hebrew; S. Paul, *Amos*, (Hermeneia; Minneapolis: Fortress Press, 1991), p. 213, n. 4.

Ps. 119.40   תָּאַבְתִּי לְפִקֻּדֶיךָ

Ps. 119.174   תָּאַבְתִּי לִישׁוּעָתְךָ יהוה

The related noun תַּאֲבָה 'longing' occurs once in the same late text:[136]

Ps. 119.20   לְתַאֲבָה אֶל מִשְׁפָּטֶיךָ בְכָל עֵת

The root תאב also occurs several times in post-biblical Hebrew. Note the following examples from rabbinic literature:[137]

Mekhilta Pesḥa 16   תאב לאכל

Mekhilta Shirah 8   יתאב לחכמה נותן לו

T. Horayot 1.5   אף תעושה דבר שאין היצר תאב לו

The root does not occur, however, in early books of the Bible. Early Hebrew uses other terms to express the idea of longing, such as (a) תְּשׁוּקָה,[138] (b) אוה,[139] and (c) כסף.[140] Compare the use of these terms in SBH to the use of תאב in post-biblical Hebrew and Aramaic:[141]

(a)   Gen. 3.16   וְאֶל־אִישֵׁךְ תְּשׁוּקָתֵךְ

      (Compare Tg. Onq.:   ולות בעליך תהי תיובתיך)

(b)   Deut. 12.20   כי תאוה נפשך לאכל...בכל אות נפשך תאכל

      (Compare Mekhilta Beshallaḥ 160:   תאבים היו ישראל לאכל

      and Mekhilta Beshallaḥ 143: ...תאב לחכמה...אדם תאב לבנים.

      תאב לנסכים)

(c)   Ps. 84.3   נכספה וגם כלתה נפשי

      (Compare Targum: רגגת ולחהד תאיבת נפשי)

Eating is the object of the root אוה in Deut. 12.20 and of תאב in Mekhilta Beshalla 160. Note also that the Targumim employ the root תאב to translate תְּשׁוּקָה in Gen. 3.16 and כסף in Ps. 84.3. Evidence from the Targumim and post-biblical Hebrew show that the root תאב began to replace earlier terms such as תאב, אוה, and כסף in similar expressions.

The 'J' source, however, never displays תאב, but uses earlier expressions with the same meaning. Note the following:

Gen. 3.6   וכי תאוה־הוא לעינים...ותאכל

      (Compare Mekhilta Beshallaḥ 160:   תאבים היו ישראל לאכל)

---

136. See above, p. 13.

137. See *HDHL*, plates 18358–59.

138. See BDB, p. 1003b: 'longing'; KB, p. 1043b: 'impulse, urge'; *HALAT*, p. 1658: 'Begehren, Verlangen'.

139. BDB, p. 16a; KB, pp. 18b-19a; *HALAT*, p. 20: '[piel] wünschen, begehren'.

140. BDB, p. 493b; KB, p. 448a; *HALAT*, p. 467a: 'verlangen'.

141. See *HDHL*, plates 18358–59; and examples in Hurvitz, *Beyn Lashon le-Lashon*, pp. 148–49.

Gen. 3.16 וְאֶל־אִישֵׁךְ תְּשׁוּקָתֵךְ

(Compare Tg. Onq.: (ולות בעליך תהי תיובתיך)

Gen. 4.7 וְאֵלֶיךָ תְּשׁוּקָתוֹ

That fact that 'J' uses SBH expression for 'desire, longing' instead of the LBH equivalent חאב reflects the early linguistic background of 'J'.

Chapter 6

PERSIAN LOAN-WORDS

There are 22 words in Biblical Hebrew which are widely accepted to be of Persian origin. Note the following words, their meanings, and where they occur in the Hebrew Bible:[1]

1)	אֱגוֹז nut(s)[2]	Song 6.11
2)	אַנְרְטֵל bag[3]	Ezra 1.9 (2x)
3)	אֲדַרְכֹנִים daric[4]	Ezra 8.27; 1 Chron. 29.7
4)	אֲחַשְׁדַּרְפְּנִים satrap(s)[5]	Esth. 3.17, 8.9, 9.3; Ezra 8.36
5)	אֲחַשְׁתְּרָן royal[6]	Esth. 8.10, 8.14
6)	אַפֶּדֶן palace[7]	Dan. 11.45
7)	גִּזְבָּר treasurer[8]	Ezra 1.8
8)	גְּנָזִים treasures[9]	Esth. 3.9, 4.7
9)	גֶּנֶז treasury[10]	1 Chron. 28.11
10)	דָּת decree[11]	Esth 1.8, 1.13, 1.15, 1.19, 2.8, 2.12, 3.8 (2x), 3.14, 3.15, 4.3, 4.8, 4.11, 4.16, 8.13, 8.14, 8.17, 9.1, 9.13; Ezra 8.36
11)	זְמָן time[12]	Qoh. 3.1; Esth. 9.27, 9.31; Neh. 2.6
12)	זַן kind[13]	2 Chron. 16.14; Ps. 144.13 (2x)
13)	כַּרְמִיל crimson[14]	2 Chron. 2.6, 2.13, 3.14

1. See Seow, 'The Dating of Qohelet', pp. 646–50.
2. BDB, p. p. 8a; KB, p. p. 9a; *HALAT*, p. 10: 'Lw. < pe. *ganz*'.
3. BDB, p. 173b; KB, p. 9b: 'Gk. κάρταλος'; *HALAT*, p. 11: 'Lw. < pe. *hirāl*'. Note BDB, p. 174a: 'But κάρταλλος itself is possible a Pers. or Shemit. loan-word'.
4. BDB, p. 204a; KB, p. 15a: '<δαρ(ε)ικῶν'; *HALAT*, p. 16: 'pers. Goldmünze *Darike*'.
5. BDB, p. 31b: 'Pers. *Khshat_apân, protectors of the realm*'; KB, p. 34a; *HALAT*, p. 36.
6. BDB, p. 31b: 'Pers. *Khshat_a, lordship, realm*'; KB, p. 34a; *HALAT*, p. 36.
7. BDB, p. 66a: 'Pers. *apadâna*'; KB, p. 76b; *HALAT*, p. 75.
8. BDB, p. 159a; KB, p. 177b: 'pers. LW *ganzabara*'; *HALAT*, p. 178.
9. BDB, p. 170b; KB, p. 190a; *HALAT*, p. 191: 'pe. Lw. *ganz*'.
10. BDB, p. p.170b; KB, p. 190a; *HALAT*, p. 191.
11. BDB, p. 206b: 'Old-Pers. *dâta, law*'; KB, p. 220b; *HALAT*, p. 225.
12. BDB, p. 273b; KB, p. 259b: 'aram. LW'; *HALAT*, p. 262: 'ad. < ape. *jamān*, mpe. *zamān*'. Although the word was borrowed probably from Aramaic, it is ultimately of Persian origin; see below, pp. 117–119.
13. BDB, p. 275a; KB, p. 260b: 'pers. LW'; *HALAT*, p. 263.
14. BDB, p. 502a; KB, p. 455b: 'pers. *kirmis v. kārm... worm*'; *HALAT*, p. 474.

14) כרפס cotton[15]   Esth. 1.6
15) נשתון document[16]   Ezra 4.7, 7.11
16) פרבר court[17]   1 Chron. 26.18
17) פרדס park[18]   Song 4.13; Qoh. 2.5; Neh. 2.8
18) פרתמים nobles[19]   Esth. 1.3, 6.9; Dan. 1.3
19) פתבג portion[20]   Dan. 1.5, 1.8, 1.13, 1.15, 1.16, 11.26
20) פתגם word, sentence[21] Qoh. 8.11; Esth. 1.20
21) פתשגן copy[22]   Esth. 3.14, 4.8, 8.13
22) תרשתא excellency[23]   Ezra 2.63; Neh. 7.65, 7.69

Two observations can be made concerning the presence of Persian loan-words in the Hebrew Bible.[24] First, they occur only in the following books: Song of Songs, Qohelet (450–350 BCE),[25] Esther (which on internal grounds must be at least as late as 486–465 BCE, possibly as late as the 2nd century BCE), Daniel (also of disputed date, but probably 165–164 BCE), Ezra-Nehemiah (450–400 BCE), and Chronicles (on the basis of 1 Chron. 3.19–24, between 400–350 BCE). Ezra and Nehemiah describe the second wave of Jews who returned to Eretz-Israel. Books associated with the first wave of returnees (Haggai, Zechariah, Malachi, perhaps Jonah and Joel) do not contain any Persian loan-words. Second, Persian proper names occur only in the books of Esther, Daniel, Ezra, Nehemiah, and Chronicles. It is clear than Persian loan-words and proper names appear

---

15. BDB, p. 502b: 'Sk. *karpâsa, cotton*'; KB, p. 456b: 'pers. *kirpās, fine linen*'; *HALAT*, p. 475.

16. BDB, p. 677a; KB, p. 641a; *HALAT*, p. 691: 'ni-štâ-van'.

17. BDB, p. 826b, s.v. פרור; KB, p. 776a: 'pers. *frabada*'; *HALAT*, p. 905: '< pers. *fra-bar*'. On the reasons why פרבר in 1 Chron. 26.18 should not be equated with פרור in 2 Kgs 23.11, see Seow, 'The Dating of Qohelet', p. 648.

18. BDB, p. 825b: 'loan word from Zend *pairi-daêza, enclosure*'; 776b; *HALAT*, p. 907.

19. BDB, p. 832b: 'OPers. *fratama, first*'; KB, p. 784a; *HALAT*, p. 920.

20. BDB, p. 834b: 'Pers. loan-word, cf. Skr. *prati-bhâga*, Zend [*pati-baga*]'; KB, p. 786a; *HALAT*, p. 925: 'pe. Lw., ape. *patibaga*'.

21. BDB, p. 834a: 'OPers. *patigâma (patigam, come to arrive)*, NPers. *paigâm*, message'; KB, p. 786a; *HALAT*, p. 925.

22. BDB, p. 832a, s.v. פרשגן: 'loan-word from Persian through Aram'.; KB, p. 789b: altpers. *patij* again'; *HALAT*, p. 930: 'patšagn'.

23. BDB, p. 1077a; KB, p. 1042b: 'pers…. awest. *taršta the reverend*'; *HALAT*, p. 1655.

24. Concerning the subject of loan-words in the Bible, see most recently Mats Eskhult, 'The Importance of Loanwords for Dating Biblical Hebrew Texts', in Ian Young (ed.), *Biblical Hebrew: Studies in Typology and Chronology* (JSOTSup, 369; London: T. and T. Clark, 2003), pp. 8–23.

25. See Seow, 'The Dating of Qohelet', p. 666.

only in texts which are later than the second half of the fifth century BCE[26]
The absence of any such Persianisms in 'J' is itself noteworthy, even when
a contrast cannot be demonstrated between a Persianism in LBH and an
equivalent expression in SBH that appears in 'J'.[27] There are, however,
three Persian loan-words for which a contrast can be shown, and these are
discussed in greater detail below.

1. דת ('Law, Decree')

The lexeme דת 'law, decree'[28] occurs only in the post-exilic books of Ezra
and Esther. Note the following examples:[29]

Esth. 1.8[30]   והשתיה כדת אין אנס
Ezra 8.36   ויתנו את־דתי המלך לאחשדרפני המלך

The term is well attested also in Aramaic passages of the Hebrew Bible:[31]

Dan. 2.13[32]   ודתא נפקת
Ezra 7.14[33]   כדת אלהך די בירך

In the above examples, דת is used to describe a decree issued by a king
(Ezra 8.36) or by God (Ezra 7.12).

The word דת does not occur in early books. Instead, the terms חק/
חקה, תורה, משפט are used in semantically similar contexts. Note the
following examples:

Josh. 24.25   וישם לו חק ומשפט בשכם

---

26. This sets aside for the moment when Song of Songs and Qohelet were composed,
since these books do not mention explicitly any dateable events. Of course, given the
observation that Persian words and names appear in books that refer to events at least as late
as the second half of the fifth century BCE, it is likely that Song of Songs and Qohelet were
composed no earlier than that time period.

27. For a different interpretation see Young, 'Late Biblical Hebrew and Hebrew
Inscriptions', pp. 284–85.

28. See BDB, p. 206a: 'decree, law, usage, only in Persian period... Pers. loan-w., Old
Pers. *dâta*, law'; and KB, p. 220a: 'pers. LW'; *HALAT*, p. 225a: 'Lw. dāta'.

29. For a fuller discussion, see Bergey, 'The Book of Esther', pp. 116–18.
The list of examples does not include the problematic אשדת in Deut 33.2. Compare the
Samaritan (אש דת) version – which is the same as the Qere of Deut 33.2 – and the Latin
(*ignea lex*) version. See *BHS*, 349, critical apparatus. Rendsburg has discussed אשדת in light
of Ugaritic *išdym*, which occurs in a mythological text describing the radiant qualities of the
sun goddess *špš*; G.A. Rendsburg, 'Hebrew *'šdt* and Ugaritic *išdym*', *JNSL* 8 (1980), pp. 81–
84; also Rendsburg, 'Late Biblical Hebrew and the Data of "P"', p. 80.

30. See also Esth. 1.13, 1.15, 1.19, 2.8, 2.12, 3.8, 3.14, 4.3, 4.8, 4.16, 8.13, 8.14, 8.17, 8.36,
9.1.

31. See BDB, p. 1089a; KB, p. 1067b: 'LW dātam'.
32. See also Dan. 2.15, 6.6, 6.9, 6.13, 6.16, 7.25.
33. See also Ezra 7.12, 7.21, 7.25, 7.26.

Gen. 47.26	וישם אתה יוסף לחק...על־אדמת מצרים
(Compare Esth. 3.14	(להנתן דת בכל־מדינה ומדינה
Numb. 15.16	תורה אחת ומשפט אחד
(Compare Esth. 4.11	(אחת דתו
1 Sam. 8.9	והגדת להם משפט המלך
(Compare Ezra 8.36	(ויתנו את־דתי המלך
Josh. 24.26	ויכתב...בספר תורת אלהים
(Compare Esth. 1.19	(ויכתב בדתי פרס־ומדי
2 Kgs 17.26	אינם ידעים את־משפט אלהי הארץ...
2 Kgs 17.34	ואינם עשים כחקתם וכמשפטים
2 Kgs 22.11	ויהי כשמע המלך את־דברי ספר התורה
(Compare Esth. 3.8	(ואת־דתי המלך אינם עשים

Although the terms חקה/חק, תורה, משפט occur in late books,[34] the distribution of דת indicates that it entered Biblical Hebrew from Persian (perhaps via Aramaic influence) during the post-exilic period, and began to replace חקה/חק, תורה, משפט in similar contexts.

The late character of דת is confirmed by its attestation in postbiblical texts. Note the following illustrations:[35]

M. Ketuvot 7.6	העוברת על דת משה יהודים אי־זו היא
	דת משה...ואי־זו היא דת יהודים
T. Ketuvot 7.6	ויתן כתובה מנפי שלא נהג עמה כדת משה

Whereas דת in Esther and Ezra is used to refer to Persian customs and law (but note the references to דתא די־אלה in Ezra 7.12, and כדת אלהך in Ezra 7.14), the above examples show that in rabbinic literature the term had taken on a broader application.[36] Compare דת משה in M. Ketuvot 7.6 and T. Ketuvot 7.6 to תורת משה in Josh. 8.31 et passim.[37]

The LBH lexeme דת is never employed in 'J', which instead uses SBH חק. Note the following example:

Gen. 47.26	וישם אתה יוסף לחק...על־אדמת מצרים

---

34. See Jer. 44.10; Ezek. 5.7; Ezra 7.10; Neh. 8.11; 2 Chron. 19.10, 33.8.
35. See *HDHL*, plate 6892.
36. Note the following comment by Bergey, 'The Book of Esther', 118, n. 1:

   An analogy to the penetration of the Persian loanword דת into the Hebrew legal, and then later the religious, vocabulary can be drawn from the French influence upon Middle English. French loan-words in the paradigm of government terms are: government, assembly, authority, council, court, crown, empire, majesty, mayor, parliament, reign, royal, state, statute, tax, and treaty. In the field of law: assault, judge, justice, plaintiff, prison, sentence, and trespass; L.M. Myers, *The Roots of Modern English* (Boston: Little, Brown, and Company, 1966), 129. A number of these terms made their way into religious contexts, e.g., assembly, council, and trespass.

37. See also Josh. 8.32, 23.6, 1 Kgs 2.3, 2 Kgs 14.6, 23.25.

(Compare Esth. 3.14   לְהִנָּתֵן דָּת בְּכָל־מְדִינָה וּמְדִינָה)

That 'J' uses only SBH חֹק instead of LBH דָּת further attests to its prexilic linguistic character.

2. זְמָן ('*Appointed Time, [Period of] Time*')

The noun זְמָן 'appointed time, (period of) time'[38] occurs 4 times in late texts. Note the following instances:[39]

Qoh. 3.1	לַכֹּל זְמָן וְעֵת לְכָל־חֵפֶץ תַּחַת הַשָּׁמָיִם
Esth. 9.27	כְּכְתָבָם וּכִזְמַנָּם בְּכָל־שָׁנָה וְשָׁנָה
Esth. 9.31	לְקַיֵּם אֶת־יְמֵי הַפֻּרִים הָאֵלֶּה בִּזְמַנֵּיהֶם
Neh. 2.6	וָאֶתְּנָה לוֹ זְמָן

In each case זְמָן refers to a specific time: in Qohelet, there is an appointed time or season for everything to occur (described at greater length in Qoh. 3.2–9); in Esther, זְמָן in 9.27 and 9.31 refers to the appointed time for Purim; in Nehemiah, it answers the king's question of how long Nehemiah would be away from Susa (Neh. 2.5). The word also occurs in Aramaic portions of the Bible with the same meaning (= זְמָן, זְמַן).[40]

The Hebrew term does not occur in pre-exilic or exilic books of the Hebrew Bible, which instead employ מוֹעֵד as the standard expression for (i) 'appointed time', including (ii) a time for festival.[41] Note the following illustrations:[42]

(i) Gen. 17.21	וְאֶת־בְּרִיתִי אָקִים אֶת־יִצְחָק אֲשֶׁר תֵּלֵד לְךָ שָׂרָה לַמּוֹעֵד הַזֶּה
1 Sam. 13.11	וְאַתָּה לֹא־בָאתָ לְמוֹעֵד הַיָּמִים
Jer. 46.17	קָרְאוּ שָׁם פַּרְעֹה מֶלֶךְ־מִצְרַיִם שָׁאוֹן הֶעֱבִיר הַמּוֹעֵד
(ii) Lev. 23.2	מוֹעֲדֵי יְהוָה אֲשֶׁר־תִּקְרְאוּ אֹתָם מִקְרָאֵי קֹדֶשׁ אֵלֶּה הֵם מוֹעֲדָי
Hos. 9.5	מַה־תַּעֲשׂוּ לְיוֹם מוֹעֵד וּלְיוֹם חַג־יְהוָה
Lam. 2.7	קוֹל נָתְנוּ בְּבֵית־יְהוָה כְּיוֹם מוֹעֵד

The SBH expression מוֹעֵד continued to occur alongside LBH זְמָן in post-exilic books, as the following examples demonstrate:

---

38. BDB, p. 273b: 'late'; KB, p. 259b: 'aram. LW'; *HALAT*, p. 262b: 'bestimmte Zeit, Stunde'.

39. For a fuller discussion see also Polzin, *Late Biblical Hebrew*, p. 136; Bergey, 'The Book of Esther', pp. 150–51.

40. BDB, p. 1091b: 'prob. loan-word from OPers. *zrvan, zarvâna, time, age*'; KB, p. 1072: 'jamāna, mpe. zamān'; HALAT, p. 262b.

41. BDB, p. 417b: 'appointed time, season'; KB, p. 503b; *HALAT*, p. 528b.

42. See Even-Shoshan, *A New Concordance of the Old Testament*, pp. 631–32.

Dan. 8.19 et passim[43]

הנני מודיעך את אשר־יהיה באחרית
הזעם כי למועד קץ

Even though the word appears to be of Persian origin (see above, p. 113), it displays the $q^e t\bar{a}l$ pattern displayed by other nouns which came from Aramaic.[44] The above evidence suggests that LBH זְמָן entered Hebrew from Persian (probably through Aramaic influence) and began to replace SBH מועד in similar contexts.

The late nature of LBH זְמָן is confirmed by its frequent appearance in post-biblical literature. It occurs most commonly in Tannaitic writings,[45] usually with the meaning (i) 'appointed time', but sometimes (ii) a festival season. Note the following illustrations:

(i) M. Berakhot 2.1   היה קורא בתורה והגיע זמן המקרא
    T. Berakhot 1.2   והגיע זמן קרית שמע
    Sifre Numbers 66 (62)   את הפסח בזמנו נמצאו מועדות בזמנו
(ii) M. Zebaḥim 1.1   הפסח בזמנו והחטאת בכל זמן
    M. Baba Meṣi'a 19(10).4   נתנו לו זמן...
    ונפלו בתוך זמן פטור לאחר זמן חייב

It also occurs 4 times in the Bar Kokhba texts:

Bar Kokhba 45 et passim[46]   עד זמן שילשלם זמן ההנות של עין־גדי

The earlier expression מועד continued to appear in post-biblical texts,[47] primarily in Ben Sira and the DSS, and usually with the meaning 'season, time of festival'. Note the following:

Ben Sira 50.8   וכירח מלא בימי מועד
11QT 43.8–9[48]   עד השנה השנית | מועד התירוש עד השנה השנית
    עד יום מועד | התירוש והיצהר מים מועדו
    עד השנה השנית | למועד וים הקרב שמן חדש
1QS 10.5   לראשי | מועדים בכול קץ נהיה...ברשית ירחים
    למועדיהם וימי קודש בתונם לזכרון במועדיהם
1QS 10.6   מועד קציר לקיץ ומועד זרע למועד דשא
1QM 1.8   קצוות תבל הלוך ואור עד תום כול מועדי חושך
    ובמועד אל יא?י?ר רום גודלו לכול קצי | [...]

---

43. See also Dan. 11.27, 11.35, 12.7; Ezra 3.5; Neh. 10.34; 1 Chron. 23.31; 2 Chron. 2.3, 8.13, 31.3. The Targumim consistently render BH מועד with זמן.

44. See the discussion of יקר above, pp. 90–92.

45. See *HDHL*, plates 8001–30; Bergey, 'The Book of Esther', p. 151. The example of זמן in Ben Sira 43.7 (|| מועד) is doubtful; Bergey, ibid., p. 151, n. 1; *contra* Polzin, *Late Biblical Hebrew*, p. 136.

46. There are 2 more examples in Bar Kokhba 45, and one in Bar Kokhba 46.

47. See *HDHL*, plates 9731–38.

48. For the understanding of מועד as 'festival', see Y. Yadin, *The Temple Scroll*, II (Jerusalem: Israel Exploration Society, 1983), p. 182.

Masada ShirShabb 1.3–4[49] עושה ראישונות |]ל[מעודן]ח[תיהם
ואחרונות למועדיהם

Hebrew מוֹעֵד occurs frequently in TH, where it most often means 'feast, festival', as the following examples illustrate:

M. Pesaḥim 1.3 לא בדק בארבעה־עשׂר יבדוק בתוך מועד
M. Megillah 3.5 בפסח קוראים בפרשת מועדות שבתורת־כהנים

Although LBH זְמָן and SBH מוֹעֵד both continued to appear in post-biblical texts, the above examples suggest that SBH מוֹעֵד was gradually restricted in meaning to 'feast, festival', while LBH זְמָן was used to express 'appointed time', as well as 'season, festival'.

The LBH lexeme זְמָן occurs nowhere in the 'J' source, which instead uses only SBH מוֹעֵד, as the following example demonstrates:

Gen. 18.14 למועד אשוב אליך כעת חיה ולשׂרה בן
(Note Tg. Onq.: לזמן איתוב לותך כעידן דאתון קיימין ולשׂרה
בר
and Tg. Yer. I: לזמן חנא איתוב לוותך בעידנא הדין ואתון
קיימין לשׂרה בר)

That 'J' uses only SBH מוֹעֵד 'appointed time' in preference to LBH זְמָן is further indication of the pre-exilic linguistic background of 'J'.

3. פִּתְגָם ('Word, Decree')

The lexeme פִּתְגָם 'word, decree' occurs twice in the Bible,[50] both times in post-exilic books:[51]

Esth. 1.20 ונשמע פתגם המלך אשר־יעשׂה בכל־מלכותו
Qoh. 8.11 אשר אין־נעשׂה פתגם

Both in Esth. 1.20 and Qoh. 8.11 the term פִּתְגָם is used in the sense of a judicial or government decree. The Aramaic equivalent פִּתְגָמָא occurs also in Biblical Aramaic.[52] Note the following examples:

Ezra 4.17 et passim[53] פתגמא שלח מלכא

---

49. See Newsom, *Songs of the Sabbath Sacrifice*, pp. 168–70: 'He makes the former things [in] their [seasons] and the latter things in their due time [ולמעודיהם]'.

50. BDB, p. 834b: 'Pers. loan-wd., OPers. *patigāma (patigam, come to, arrive)*'; KB, p. 786a; *HALAT*, p. 925a. See also Paton, *Esther*, p. 60; Driver, *An Introduction to the Literature of the Old Testament*, pp. 446, 455, 469n, 470n.

51. For a fuller discussion, see Bergey, 'The Book of Esther', p. 102.

52. BDB, p. 1109a; KB, p. 114b: 'LW *patgām'*.

53. See also Dan. 3.16, 4.14; Ezra 5.7, 5.11, 6.11.

Hebrew פתגם occurs nowhere in the early books of the Bible, which employ דבר (noun)/דבר (verb) or צוה/מצוה in similar contexts.[54] Note the following illustrations:[55]

Gen. 44.2	ויעש כדבר יוסף אשר דבר
2 Sam. 24.4	ויחזק דבר־המלך אל־יואב ועל שרי החיל
(Compare Tg. Onq.:	...ותקיף פתגמא דמלכא)
1 Kgs 2.43	...ואת־המצוה אשר־צויתי עליך
2 Kgs 18.36	כי־מצות המלך היא לאמר לא תענהו
(Compare Tg. Onq.:	...פתגם ארי תפקידת מלכא היא)

The above evidence makes clear that Hebrew פתגם 'word, decree' is a Persian loan-word which entered post-exilic Hebrew through an Aramaic intermediary פתגמא.

The LBH lexeme occurs occasionally in post-biblical texts.[56] It occurs twice in Ben Sira, for example:

Ben Sira 5.11 (A)	...ובארך רוח השב פתגם
Ben Sira 8.9 (A)	בעת צ<רד> להשיב פתגם

And it occurs once at Qumran:

4QpIsa[a]5.9	פתגם לאחרית הימים לביא

Thus פתגם is a post-exilic lexeme in Hebrew which continued to be used in post-biblical literature.

LBH פתגם does not occur in 'J' source verses, which employ only SBH דבר, for example:

Gen. 44.2	ויעש כדבר יוסף אשר דבר
(Compare Tg. Onq:	ועבד כפתגמא דיוסף דמליל
and Tg. Yer. I:	ועבד כפתגמא דיוסף דמליל)

Here דבר describes a decree by Joseph, a high official in the Egyptian government. Note also that the Targumim render Hebrew דבר with פתגמא, reflecting post-exilic usage. If 'J' were composed during the Persian period, the LBH lexeme פתגם would have been available to the author(s) of 'J', but the 'J' source displays only the SBH usage דבר 'word, decree'.

---

54. For דבר (noun) and דבר (verb), see BDB, p. 180b, 182a; KB, p. 200a, 201a. For מצוה and צוה, see BDB, p. 845b, 846a; KB, p. 556a, 797a.

55. Hebrew verses cited also in Bergey, 'The Book of Esther', p. 102.

56. *HDHL*, plate 15611.

Chapter 7

DISPUTED 'J' SOURCE VERSES

This chapter will discuss those verses attributed to the 'J' source by some but not all of the scholars that I have chosen to follow (see above, pp. 19–21). In several cases, the feature of LBH which is being compared to 'J' already has been discussed at length in earlier chapters. In these sections, I make note of the fact and direct the reader to the relevant pages above, and then briefly discuss the disputed 'J' source verses. In other cases, the feature of LBH being compared applies only to disputed 'J' source verses. In those sections, I provide a full discussion of the LBH characteristic. The following items are discussed in this chapter:

	Late Biblical Hebrew	*Standard Biblical Hebrew*
1)	שתיה	שתות, שתה
2)	Reduced use of את plus suffix	Predominant use of את plus suffix
3)	Infinitive construct with כ/ב-	Infinitive construct with כ/ב- with והיה/ויהי
4)	בין X ל-Y	בין X ובין Y
5)	נשא אשה	לקח אשה
6)	אני	אנכי
7)	בהל	חפז, מהר
8)	בכן	אז
9)	זקף	קום, נשא, נצב, רום
10)	כול עולמים	עולם
11)	כנס	קבץ, אסף
12)	מהלך	ארך, רחב, דרך
13)	סוף	אחרית, קצה, קץ
14)	שלט	משל
15)	Persian loan words	No Persian loan words
16)	דרמשק	דמשק
17)	בזה	שלל, בז
18)	מלכות	יהוה
19)	חנון ורחום	רחום וחנון
20)	רחם על	רחם
21)	שרביט	שבט

The following verses are attributed to 'J' by some but not all of the scholars I have used for this study. Following each verse or group of verses in parentheses are abbreviations for the name(s) of the scholar(s) which attribute to 'J' the verse or verses listed (CHB = Carpenter and Harford-Battersby; Dr = Driver; N = Noth; VR = Von Rad; Ei = Eissfeldt). Verses attributed to the combined 'JE' source are included in the list and are so noted.

Genesis
4.26 (N, Dr, Ei, VR)
5.29 (N, Dr, Ei, CHB)
7.17a (Dr, Ei), 23 (N, Dr, Ei, VR)
8.7 (Dr, Ei)
9.28–29 (VR)
10.1b (VR, CHB), 24 (Dr, Ei, CHB)
12.4b-5 (VR), 9 (N, Dr, VR, CHB)
13.1–2 (N, Dr, Ei, VR, CHB), 3–4 (Dr, VR, CHB), 5 (Dr, Ei, VR, CHB), 6b (CHB), 12b (Dr, Ei, VR, CHB), 12a (CHB)
15.1a, 1bß-2 (N, Ei), 3a (Ei, CHB), 3b (N, Ei, CHB), 4 (N, Ei), 6–12 (N, Ei, CHB), 13–15 (Ei, CHB), 17a-18 (N, CHB), 19–21 (N, Ei) (VR. ch. 15 = JE)
16.9–10 (N, Dr, Ei, VR)
19.36–38 (N, Ei, VR, CHB)
20.1a (N), 18 (CHB)
21.1a (Dr, Ei, CHB), 1b (Ei), 2a (Dr, CHB), 6 (Ei), 7 (N, Ei, CHB), 22–27 (Ei), 28–30 (Ei, CHB), 31–32 (Ei), 33 (Dr, CHB), 34 (Ei)
22.15–18 (Dr, Ei, CHB)
24.7–10, 12–17, 19–20 (N, Dr, VR, CHB)
25.6 (N, Dr, Ei, VR), 11a, 18 (Dr, Ei, CHB), 25b, 29–34 (N, Dr, Ei, VR)
26.3b-5 (N, Dr, VR), 15 (N, Ei, VR) (Dr. 15, 18 = JE)
27.1b, 3–4a, 5a, 7b-14, 16–18a, 21–33, 28, 31a, 35–45 (N, Dr, Ei, VR)
28.10 (N, Dr, CHB), 21b (CHB)
29.1, 15–23 (N, VR), 24 (N), 25, 27–28 (N, VR), 29 (N), 30 (N, VR), 31–35 (N, Dr, CHB)
30.2b-3a (Dr), 3b (Dr, CHB), 4–5, 7 (N, Dr, CHB), 8 (N, CHB), 9–16 (N, Dr, CHB), 20a (N), 20b (N, Dr), 21 (N), 22b-23a (CHB), 24 (N, Dr, CHB), 25–26, 28a (N, Dr, Ei), 28b (N, Dr), 29–30 (N, Dr, CHB), 31b-33, 38b (N, Dr, Ei)
31.1 (N, Ei, VR), 10, 12b, 17 (N, CHB), 18a (CHB), 19a (N, Ei), 19b (Ei), 20–23 (N, Ei), 24–25a (Ei, VR, CHB), 25b (N, Ei, VR, CHB), 26 (Ei), 27 (N, Ei, VR, CHB), 28–29 (Ei), 30a (N, Ei, VR), 30b (Ei), 31 (N, Ei, CHB), 32–37 (Ei), 38–40 (N, Ei), 41–42 (Ei), 43 (Ei, CHB), 44–45 (Ei), 47 (N, VR), 49 (N, Dr, Ei, VR), 50a (Dr, Ei, VR, CHB),

50b (Dr, Ei, VR),51 (N, Ei, VR, CHB), 52 (N, Ei, VR), 53a (N, Ei), 53b-54 (Ei) (VR. 1–24 = JE)

32.7b-13a (N, Dr, Ei, VR), 13b–21 (Ei, CHB), 22b (N, Dr, Ei, VR), 23a (N, Ei, VR), 30 (N, Dr, Ei, VR), 33 (Ei)

34.1–2a (N, Dr, CHB), 4 (Dr, CHB), 6 (N, Dr, CHB), 8–10 (Dr, CHB), 12–17 (N, Dr, CHB), 18a (Ei), 18b (N, Ei), 19 (Ei) (VR. 1–4, 6–10, 12–18a, 19 = JE)

35.5 (Ei), 14 (Dr, CHB), 16–20 (CHB), 22b (Dr, Ei, VR)

36.2b-5, 9–31 (Ei), 32–39 (Ei, CHB)

37.2b (CHB), 3a (N, Ei, CHB), 3b (Ei, CHB), 4 (N, CHB), 5–11 (N), 13b (N, Dr), 15–18a, 19–20 (N, Dr, Ei), 28a (N), 31 (Dr), 32a (Dr, CHB), 32b-33a (Dr), 33b (Dr, CHB), 34 (Dr), 35 (Dr, CHB)

39.6a, 7a (N, Dr, Ei)

40.3a, 5, 15a (CHB), 15b (Dr, CHB)

41.14a (Dr), 14b (Dr, CHB), 31 (CHB), 34a (N, CHB), 34 (CHB), 35a (N), 35b, 36b (CHB), 41–45a (N, CHB), 45b (N), 46b, 49 (N, CHB), 55 (N), 56a (N, CHB), 56b (N), 57 (N, CHB)

42.1b (N), 2 (CHB), 4 (N, CHB), 5 (N), 7 (CHB), 8–11a, 12 (N), 27–28a (Dr, CHB), 28b (Dr), 38 (Dr, CHB)

43.14 (N, Ei), 23b (N, Ei, CHB)

45.1a (N, CHB), 1b (N), 2b (CHB), 5a (N, CHB), 5b, 9–11, 13 (CHB), 16–18 (N), 19–21a (N, CHB), 21b-27 (N)

46.1a (CHB), 1b (Dr), 5b (N)

47.5a (N), 12 (Dr, CHB), 27a (Dr, CHB)

48.2b, 9b-10a, 13, 19 (CHB)

49.1b-24a (Dr, CHB), 24b-27, 28a (Dr), 33b (CHB)

50.10b (Dr, CHB), 18, 21, 24 (CHB)

Exodus

1.6 (Ei, CHB), 8–12 (N, Ei, CHB), 14a, 20b (CHB), 22 (N, CHB)

2.1–10 (N, Ei), 11–22 (N, Ei, CHB), 23a (N, CHB)

3.1 (N), 2–4a, 5 (N, CHB), 9a, 14 (CHB), 19–20 (N, Dr), 21–22 (N)

4.10–16 (N, Dr, CHB), 18, 20b (Ei), 21 (N, Ei, CHB), 27–28 (N, Dr), 30a (N, Dr, CHB)

5.1–2, 4 (N, Dr, Ei)

7.15, 17b (N, Dr), 21a (N, CHB), 23 (N, Dr), 24 (N, CHB)

8.11b (Eng. 15b) (Dr)

9.1–7 (N, CHB), 19–21 (N, Dr), 22–23a (N), 24a (N, Dr), 25a (N), 25b-30 (N, CHB), 31–32 (N), 33–34 (N, CHB), 35 (N)

10.8–11 (N, CHB), 12–13a (N), 14a (N, Dr), 20–23 (N), 24–27 (N, CHB)

11.1–3 (N)

12.21–23 (N, Ei, CHB), 24 (Ei), 25–27b (N, Ei, CHB), 28 (CHB), 31 (N, CHB), 32–34 (N, Ei, CHB), 35 (N), 36 (N, Ei), 37–39 (N, Ei, CHB) (Dr. 21–27 = JE)

13.3a (Ei, CHB), 3b (Ei), 4–7 (Ei, CHB), 8–9 (Ei), 10–13 (Ei, CHB), 14–16 (Ei), 20 (N, Ei)

14.5a (Dr, CHB), 7 (Dr), 10a, 11–12 (Dr, CHB), 20a (N, Dr), 21b, 25a (Dr, CHB), 27a (N), 27b (Dr, CHB), 28b (CHB), 31 (N, Dr)

15.1 (CHB), 20–21, 25b-26 (N, Ei), 27 (Dr, Ei, CHB)

16.4–5 (N, Dr, Ei), 25–28, 30 (Dr, Ei), 31, 35b, 36 (N, Ei)

17.1a (Ei), 1b (Dr, Ei), 2a (N, Dr, Ei), 3 (Ei, CHB), 4–7a (N, Ei, CHB), 8–16 (N, Ei)

18.2–4, 7, 9–11 (CHB)

19.2b (N), 3b-6 (CHB), 7–9 (N), 11b-13, 18 (N, CHB), 23 (N, Dr)

20.22–26 (Dr)

21.1–37 (Dr)

22.1–21a (Dr), 21b-22 (Dr, CHB), 23 (Dr), 24 (Dr, CHB)

23.1–13 (Dr, CHB), 14–15a (Dr), 15b (Dr, CHB), 16 (Dr), 17 (Dr, CHB), 18 (Dr), 19 (Dr, CHB), 20–22 (Dr, Ei), 23–25a (Dr, Ei, CHB), 25b-26 (Dr, Ei), 27 (Dr, Ei, CHB), 28–31a (Dr, Ei), 31b-33 (Dr, Ei, CHB)

24.1–2 (Ei, CHB), 3–8 (Dr), 9–11 (Ei, CHB), 12 (N), 13–15a (N, Ei)

32.1a, 4b-6 (N), 7–14 (CHB) (Dr. 9–14 = JE), 15–16 (N), 17–18 (N, Ei), 19–20 (N), 25–29 (N, Ei, CHB), 30–35 (N)

33.1 (N, Ei, CHB), 2 (N, Ei), 3a-4 (N, Ei, CHB), 5–11 (N), 12–23 (N, CHB) (Dr. 12–23 = JE)

34.1–23 (N, Ei, CHB), 24 (N, Ei), 25–28 (N, Ei, CHB), 29–35 (N) (Dr. 1–25 = JE)

Numbers

10.29–33 (N, Ei, CHB), 34 (N, Ei), 35–36 (N, CHB) (Dr. 29–36 = JE)

11.4–13, 15 (CHB), 16–17 (N), 18–24a (CHB), 24b-25 (N), 30–35 (CHB) (Dr. ch. 11 = JE)

12.1–15 (N), 16 (N, CHB) (Dr. ch. 12 = JE, probably E)

13.17b (N, CHB), 18a (N), 18b-19 (N, CHB), 20 (N), 22 (N, CHB), 23–24 (N), 27a (N, CHB), 27b (N), 28 (N, CHB), 29 (N), 30–31 (N, CHB) (Dr. 17b-20, 22–24, 26b-31, 32b-33 = JE)

14.1b (N, CHB), 3 (CHB), 4 (N), 8 (CHB), 11–24 (N, CHB), 25 (N), 31 (CHB), 39–40 (N), 41–45 (N, CHB) (Dr. 3–4, 8–9, 11–25, 39–45 = JE)

16.1b (N, CHB), 12 (N), 13–14a (N, CHB), 14b (N), 15 (N, CHB), 25–26 (N), 27b-31 (N, CHB), 32 (N), 33a (N, CHB), 32b-34 (N) (Dr. 1b-2a, 12–15, 25–26, 27b-34 = JE)

20.3a, 5, 8b (CHB), 19–20 (N, CHB), 21b (CHB), 22a (N) (Dr. 1b, 3a, 4–5, 7–11, 14–21 = JE)

21.1–3 (N, CHB), 4–9 (N), 10–15 (Ei), 16–20 (Ei, CHB), 21–24a (Ei), 24b-25 (Ei, CHB), 26–31 (Ei), 32 (Ei, CHB), 33–35 (Ei)

22.3b-7 (N, CHB), 8 (N), 11 (CHB), 13–16 (N), 17–18 (N, CHB), 19,

21 (N), 22–35 (N, CHB), 36–37a (N), 37b (CHB), 39 (N, CHB), 40 (N) (Dr. 2–40 = JE)
23.22–23 (CHB), 28 (N, CHB)
24.1–25 (N, CHB) (Dr. 1–25 = JE)
25.1b-2 (N, Ei, CHB), 3a (N, Ei), 3b-4 (N, Ei, CHB), 5 (N, Ei) (Dr. 1–5 = JE)
32.1, 16, 39–42 (N) (Dr. 1–17, 20–27, 34–42 = JE)
Deuteronomy
34.1b, 4 (CHB) (N. portions of ch. 34 are JE)

1. שתיה

The LBH expression שתיה, and its use in place of the SBH forms שתה and שתות, has been discussed earlier (see above, pp. 35–36). There are several verses which some scholars attribute to 'J' which employ SBH שתות in preference to the LBH equivalent שתיה as the following examples demonstrate:

Exod. 7.21a	ולא יכלו מצרים לשתות מים מן־היאר
Exod. 7.24b	כי לא יכלו לשתת
Exod. 17.1b	ואין מים לשתת העם
Numb. 20.5	ומים אין לשתות

Thus even in verses which not all scholars agree belong to the 'J,' we see a consistent preference for the SBH form as against the LBH expression שתיה which we encounter in post-exilic and post-biblical Hebrew

2. *(Reduced use of* את *plus pronominal suffix)*

As discussed above (pp. 37–41), we can observe a significant reduction in the use of את with suffix as opposed to the finite verb with suffix to express the direct object in LBH. The construction את plus pronominal suffix occurs frequently in disputed 'J' source verses. Note the following:

Gen. 15.10, 15.11, 15.13, 24.14, 27.9, 29.23, 30.9, 30.14, 30.20, 30.26, 30.30, 31.23, 31.27, 32.12, 32.30, 34.8, 34.9, 37.4 (2x), 37.9, 37.35, 40.3, 40.15, 41.41, 41.42 (2x), 41.43 (2x), 45.11, 50.21, 50.24 (2x)
Exod. 1.12, 2.2, 3.19, 3.20, 4.15, 9.28, 10.10, 10.11, 11.1 (2x), 12.32, 13.3, 18.10, 19.4 (2x), 22.22, 22.23, 23.33, 32.10, 32.19, 34.4
Numb. 10.29, 10.31, 11.8, 11.16, 11.24, 13.30, 14.8, 14.22, 16.30, 16.32, 21.3, 21.8 (2x), 21.34 (2x), 21.35, 22.8, 22.11, 22.33 (2x), 22.35, 24.13, 32.23, 32.41.

Compare this to the number of time disputed verses display the finite verb with suffix:

Gen. 5.29 (2x), 15.4 (2x), 15.7, 15.8, 15.13, 22.17, 24.7, 24.16, 24.17, 25.30, 27.10, 27.12, 27.23, 27.37 (2x), 27.38, 27.41, 27.45, 29.15, 29.18, 29.25, 29.32, 30.13, 30.16, 30.20 (2x), 30.25, 30.26, 31.18, 31.28, 31.32, 31.39 (2x), 31.40, 31.41, 32.9, 32.12, 32.18 (2x), 34.10, 35.12, 37.20 (3x), 37.33, 42.4, 42.8, 42.38, 45.5, 45.9, 48.9, 49.7, 49.8, 49.9, 49.19, 49.25 (2x)

Exod. 1.22, 2.9, 2.10, 2.14, 2.19, 3.14, 4.12, 4.14, 4.21, 4.28 (2x), 9.1, 9.8, 13.5, 13.9, 13.11 (2x), 13.13, 13.14 (2x), 13.16, 14.11, 16.25 (2x), 16.26, 17.3, 17.4, 18.9, 19.7, 19.23, 20.24, 21.6 (3x), 21.8 (2x), 21.9, 21.14, 21.16, 21.26 (2x), 21.27, 21.29, 21.33, 21.36, 21.37 (2x), 22.12, 22.15, 22.20, 23.4, 23.11 (2x), 23.15, 23.23 (2x), 23.24 (2x), 23.29, 23.30, 23.31, 24.20, 31.1, 32.8, 32.12, 32.25, 32.33, 33.5, 33.12 (2x), 33.13, 33.15, 33.20, 33.22, 34.9, 34.18

Numb. 11.4, 11.12 (2x), 11.15, 11.18, 11.23, 13.27, 14.8, 14.11, 14.12 (2x), 14.23, 14.24 (2x), 16.13, 16.14, 16.28, 16.29, 16.34, 20.5, 20.14, 21.5, 21.18 (2x), 22.11, 22.17, 22.28, 22.29, 24.9, 24.10, 24.11, 24.14, 24.17 (2x), 24.22

Deut. 34.4

The verses cited above represent a total of 77 examples of אֵת with suffix versus 171 instances of the finite verb with suffix, a ratio of 1:2.22. Although this is still higher than we find elsewhere in earlier books of the Hebrew Bible, it is significantly less than the adjusted ratio of 1:11.1 we find in post-exilic prose. In this instance, verses which not all scholars agree are 'J' conform more closely than undisputed 'J' verses to what we find in classical Hebrew.

3. (Infinitive construct plus ־בְּ/־כְּ)

That post-exilic writings demonstrate a strong preference for the introductory infinitive construction without preceding וְהָיָה/וַיְהִי has been discussed earlier at length (see above, pp. 42–45). There are several examples of the introductory infinitive construct plus ־בְּ/־כְּ in disputed 'J' verses, most of them with preceding וְהָיָה/וַיְהִי. Note the following:

(a) Gen. 35.17   וַיְהִי בְהַקְשֹׁתָהּ בְּלִדְתָּהּ

     Gen. 35.18   וַיְהִי בְּצֵאת נַפְשָׁהּ

     Numb. 10.35   וַיְהִי בִּנְסֹעַ הָאָרֹן

(b) Exod. 33.8   וַיְהִי כְּצֵאת מֹשֶׁה אֶל־הָאֹהֶל

     Exod. 33.9   וְהָיָה כְּבֹא מֹשֶׁה הָאֹהֱלָה

     Numb. 16.31   וַיְהִי כְּכַלֹּתוֹ לְדַבֵּר אֵת כָּל־הַדְּבָרִים הָאֵלֶּה

There are two examples of the infinite construct without preceding וַיְהִי/וְהָיָה:

(a) Numb. 10.36   ובנוחה

      Numb. 11.9   וברדת הטל על־המחנה לילה

Although the preferred LBH syntagma occurs slightly more frequently in disputed 'J' verses than in verses which are undisputed – a ratio of 2:6 as opposed to 1:12 – the contrast is still apparent. Verses which not all scholars agree belong to 'J' still display a preference for the infinitive construct plus כ/־ב with preceding ויהי/והיה. Such a preference more closely resembles the linguistic situation of the pre-exilic period.

4. Y ל ־ X בין (*'Between X and Y'*)

The construction Y ל ־ X בין is the predominant means of expressing 'between X and Y' in LBH, as discussed above (pp. 45–48). This syntagma is absent from disputed 'J' source verses, where instead we find only the preferred SBH construction X ובין Y בין. Note the following:

Gen. 13.3   בין בית־אל ובין העי

Exod. 9.4   בין מקנה ישראל ובין מקנה מצרים

Exod. 14.20b   ויבא בין מחנה מצרים ובין מחנה ישראל

Numb. 21.13   בין מואב ובין האמרי

That disputed verses use only the predominant SBH construction בין X ובין Y and never the preferred LBH expression בין X ל ־ Y indicates strongly a pre-exilic date of composition.

5. נשא אשה (*'Take as Wife'*)

As discussed above (pp. 71–74), the LBH expression נשא אשה 'take as wife' replaced SBH לקח אשה in similar contexts during the post-exilic period. Verses which not all scholars attribute to 'J' display 4 examples of the SBH construction. See the following:

Gen. 34.9   ואת־בנתינו תקחו־לכם

Gen. 34.16   את־בנתיכם נקח־לנו

Exod. 21.10   אם־אחרת [אשה] יקח־לו

Numb. 12.1 (2x)   על ־אדות האשה הכשית אשר לקח כי ־אשה כשית לקח

The absence of LBH נשא אשה in contexts where disputed 'J' verses employ only SBH לקח אשה is further evidence of a date of composition prior to the post-exilic period.

6. אֲנִי *(First Person Singular Pronoun)*

The predominant use of אֲנִי, as opposed to אָנֹכִי, in exilic and post-exilic texts has been discussed in an earlier chapter (above, pp. 79–82). In disputed 'J' source verses, there are 17 examples of אֲנִי. Note the following:

> Gen. 15.7, 27.8, 27.38, 31.44, 31.52, 37.10
> Exod. 2.9, 3.19, 4.21, 9.27, 15.26, 33.16 (2x), 33.19, 34.10
> Numb. 14.21, 20.19

Compare this to the 35 instances in which disputed 'J' verses employ אָנֹכִי:

> Gen. 15.1, 15.2, 15.14, 21.24, 21.26, 24.3, 24.13, 25.30, 25.32, 29.33, 30.2, 30.3, 30.30, 31.38, 31.39, 32.11, 37.16, 50.5, 50.21, 50.24
> Exod. 4.10, 4.11, 4.12, 4.15, 17.9, 19.9, 23.20, 32.18, 34.10, 34.11
> Numb. 11.12 (2x), 14.21, 22.30, 22.32

The ratio of אָנֹכִי to אֲנִי in disputed verses is 1:0.5, almost identical to the ratio we find elsewhere in the Pentateuch. That אָנֹכִי is the predominant form of the 1st common singular pronoun in verses which not all scholars assign to 'J' is further evidence of a pre-exilic linguistic background.

7. בהל *('Hasten')*

The verb בהל with the meaning 'hasten' occurs primarily in post-exilic texts, as discussed earlier (see above, pp. 82–84). Exilic and pre-exilic texts instead employ SBH מִהַר or חָפַז in similar contexts. In light of this contrast, we can note that LBH בהל 'hasten' never occurs in disputed 'J' source verses, which instead employ only the classical expression מִהַר. Note the following illustrations:

Gen. 45.13	וּמִהַרְתֶּם וְהוֹרַדְתֶּם אֶת־אָבִי הֵנָּה
Exod. 34.8	וַיְמַהֵר מֹשֶׁה

The consistent use of the SBH term מִהַר in contrast to the LBH equivalent בהל 'hasten' is further evidence of a date of composition before the post-exilic period.

8. בְּכֵן *('Thereupon, Then')*

The LBH expression בְּכֵן 'thereupon, then' occurs twice in post-exilic texts, appearing alongside the classical equivalent אָז 'then,' as seen in an earlier discussion (above, pp. 84–85). There is one instance of SBH אָז in a verse which not all scholars agree represents the 'J' source:

Gen. 49.4   אז חללת יצועי עלה
(Compare Tg. Onq.   (בכין אחילתא לשיויי ברי סליקתא

Note that the Targum renders אז in this verse with בכין, the Aramaic
equivalent of LBH בכן. That a disputed 'J' verse displays the classical
expression אז instead of the LBH equivalent is further evidence of an
earlier date of composition.

9. זקף *('Raise')*

The LBH lexeme זקף, and its use in place of SBH expressions such as
נשא, קום, רום, and נצב, has been discussed in an earlier chapter (above,
pp. 88–90). There is one instance of a disputed verse in which 'J' employs
SBH רום in preference to LBH זקף:

Gen. 31.45   ויקח יעקב אבן וירימה מצבה
(Note Tg. Onq.:   (ונסיב יעקב אבנא שזקפה קומא

Note that this verse, which not all scholars agree belongs to 'J', still
employs the SBH lexeme רום in contrast to the post-exilic equivalent זקף.
Furthermore, Tg. Onqelos renders רום with Aramaic זקף in accordance
with post-exilic usage.

10. כל עולמים *('Everlastingness, All Eternity')*

The late character of כל עולמים, and possibly of עולמים, has been
discussed earlier (see above, pp. 68–71). There are several disputed verses
of 'J' in which עולם is employed in preference to עולמים or the
equivalent. Note the following:

Gen 21.33   ויקרא־שם בשם יהוה אל עולם
(Compare 1QapGen 21.2:   (וקרית תמן בשם מרה עלמיא
Gen 49.26   תאות גבעת עולם
Exod 12.24   לחק־לך ולבניך עד־עולם
Exod 19.9[1]   וגם־בך יאמינו לעולם
Exod 21.6   ועבדו לעלם
Exod 32.13   ונחלו לעלם
(Compare 1QapGen 21.12:   (וירחונה לכול עלמים

Even verses which not all scholars agree belong to 'J' employ the SBH
expression עולם.

---

1. See Noth, *A History of Pentateuchal Traditions*, p. 31, n. 112: 'Ex. 19.3b-9a(9b) is
again a supplement in Deuteronomistic style'.

11. כנס ('Gather')

As demonstrated in a previous chapter (see above, pp. 92–95), the Piel of
the verb כנס 'assemble, gather' occurs exclusively in exilic and post-exilic
texts, although twice it occurs in other conjugations in earlier texts. It is
used in contexts where pre-exilic texts use instead the classical expressions
(a) אסף and (b) קבץ. In light of this diachronic contrast, it is noteworthy
that LBH כנס 'gather, assemble' never appears in disputed 'J' source
verses, which instead employ only SBH אסף or קבץ. Note the following
illustrations:

(a)	Numb. 11.24	ויאסף שבעים איש מזקני העם
	Numb. 11.32	ויאספו את־השלו הממציט אסף עשרה חמרים
	Numb. 21.23	ויאסף סיחן את־כל־עמו
(b)	Gen. 49.2[2]	הקבצו ושמעו בני יעקב

Even verses which not all scholars agree belong to 'J' consistently use only
the SBH terms אסף and קבץ as opposed to LBH כנס, reflecting a pre-
exilic linguistic background.

12. מהלך ('Journey, Distance')

The LBH term מהלך 'journey, distance' is used in exilic and post-exilic
texts in place of SBH דרך in similar contexts, as discussed previously (see
above, pp. 95–97). There are 3 examples of SBH דרך with the meaning
'journey, distance' in verses which not all scholars attribute to 'J'. See the
following:

Gen. 31.23	וירדף אחריו דרך שבעת ימים
(Compare Tg. Onq.	ורדף...מהלך שבעה יומין
and Tg. Yer. I	(ורדף...מהלך שובאא יומין)
Numb. 10.33	ויסעו מהר יהוה דרך שלשת ימים
(Compare Tg. Onq. and Tg. Yer. I	ונטלו...מהלך תלתא (יומין)
Numb. 11.31	ויטש על־המחנה כדרך יום כה וכדרך יום כה
(Compare Tg. Onq.	...כמהלך יומא לכא וכמהלך יומא לכא
and Tg. Yer. I	(כמהלך יומא כציפונא וכמהלך יומא לדרומא)

Note that the Targumim consistently translate דרך as מהלך, reflecting
the later usage. That disputed 'J' source verses consistently use the SBH
term דרך 'journey, distance' instead of the LBH equivalent מדלך
suggests strongly a pre-exilic linguistic background.

---

2. Genesis 49 is not truly 'J', notwithstanding those scholars that attribute it to the
Yahwist, since it is a poem embedded into a 'J' narrative.

13. סוֹף *('End')*

The LBH lexeme סוֹף 'end' as a post-exilic equivalent of SBH קֵץ, קָצָה, and אַחֲרִית has been discussed in an earlier chapter (see above, pp. 101–103). We can see this diachronic contrast in verses which not all scholars attribute to the 'J' source. Note the following examples where SBH (a) קָצָה and (b) אַחֲרִית are employed instead of LBH סוֹף:

(a)	Exod. 19.12	השמרו לכם עלות בהר ונגע בקצהו
	Numb. 11.1	ותאכל בקצה המחנה
	Numb. 23.13	לך־נא אתי אל מקום...אפס קצהו תראה
(b)	Numb. 24.14	לכה איעצך אשר יעשה העם הזה לעמך
		באחרית הימים

If the 'J' source were composed during the post-exilic period, we could expect instances of the LBH term סוֹף to express 'end, limit', but such is not the case. Even disputed 'J' verses consistently reflect the pre-exilic linguistic situation.

14. שׁלט *('Rule, Have Mastery [over]')*

The use of the verb שׁלט in post-exilic writings has been discussed earlier (see above, pp. 108–110). This feature of LBH does not occur anywhere in disputed 'J' source verses, where instead we find the equivalent SBH verb משׁל:

Gen. 37.8   ויאמרו לו...המלך תמלך עלינו אם־משׁול תמשׁל בנו

That a disputed 'J' verse employs a classical expression instead of LBH שׁלט reflects the linguistic situation prior to the post-exilic period.

15. *(Persian loan-words)*

The presence, location, and significance of words in Biblical Hebrew of Persian origin have already been discussed in chapter 6. There is one such Persian loan-word where a contrast can be demonstrated between LBH and disputed 'J' source verses.

זמן *('Season, Appointed Time')*
As discussed (pp. 117–119), the LBH lexeme זמן 'season, appointed time' entered Hebrew during the post-exilic period and began to replace SBH מועד 'appointed time, season' in similar contexts. There are several disputed verses in which SBH מועד is employed instead of LBH זמן. Note the following examples:

Gen. 21.2	ותלד שרה לאברהם בן לזקניו למועד
(Note Tg. Onq.:	ועדיאת ויל ידת שרה לאברהם בר
	לסיבתוהי לזמנא
and Tg. Yer. I:	וילידת שרה לאברהם בר דדמי
	(ליה לסיבתוי לזימנא
Exod. 9.5	וישם יהוה מועד
(Note Tg. Onq.:	ושוי יוי זמנא
and Tg. Yer. I:	(וקבע ייי זימנא
Exod. 13.10	ושמרת את־החקה הזאת למועדה מימים ימימה
(Note Tg. Onq.:	ותיטר ית קיימא הדין בזמניה מזמן לזמן
and Tg. Yer. I:	(ותינטור ית קיימא הדא דתפילי לזמנא
Exod. 23.15, 34.18	את־חג המצות תשמר...למועד חדש האביב
(Note Tg. Onq.:	...לזמנא ירחא דאביבא
and Tg. Yer. I:	(...לזמן ירחא דאביבא

Thus even in verses which not all scholars attribute to 'J,' the consistent use of SBH מועד in place of LBH זמן demonstrates the pre-exilic linguistic character of 'J'.

16. דרמשׂק *('Damascus')*

Just as Hebrew displays an alternation between SBH שבט 'scepter' and LBH שרביט (see below, pp. 141–142), it also displays an alternation between SBH דמשׂק 'Damascus' and LBH דרשׂמק.[3] For the form דרשׂמק in post-exilic texts, note the following examples:

2 Chron. 28.23	ויזבח לאלהי דרשׂמק
2 Chron. 28.5 et passim[4]	ויביאו דרמשׂק

Elsewhere in the Hebrew Bible, only the form דשׂמק is attested, for example:

1 Kgs 11.24	וילכו דמשׂק
Jer. 49.24	רפתה דמשׂק הפנתה לנוס
Jer. 49.27	והצתי אש בחומת דמשׂק

The form דמשׂק displays the dissimilation of geminate consonants which occurs sometimes in Aramaic.[5] The frequent appearance of דרמשׂק and similar spellings in post-biblical literature confirms the lateness of the

---

3. דמשׂק, BDB, p. 199b; KB, p. 214b; *HALAT*, p. 218b. For דרשׂמק, see BDB, p. 199b: 'late'; KB, p. 219a; *HALAT*, p. 223b.

4. See also 2 Chron. 16.2, 18.5, 24.3, 28.5, 28.23.

5. Rosenthal, *GBA*, pp. 16–17. See also Hurvitz, *Beyn Lashon le-Lashon*, p. 19, n. 12. Bergsträsser cited other examples of such dissimilation in Biblical Hebrew: נלבע from בלע, and כרסם from כסם; Bergsträsser, *HG*, I, p. 110, §20b.

form דרמשק. All seven appearances of דמשק in the MT of Isaiah are replaced by דרמשק in the Isaiah scroll from Qumran.[6] Kutscher noted:

> Rabbinic Literature contains the forms דרמסקינא, דרמשק, דרמסקוס as well as the adjective דורמסקית... and in Syriac the form is דרמסוק. However, the form דמשק continued to be found... side by side with the form דרמשק. In short: the form דרמשק *et sim.* is no earlier than the last centuries BCE.[7]

The above evidence demonstrates that the form דרמשק is characteristic of LBH.

The term דמשק occurs once in a verse which not all scholars agree belongs to 'J':

Gen. 15.2	וּבֶן־מֶשֶׁק בֵּיתִי הוּא דַמֶּשֶׂק אֱלִיעֶזֶר
(Compare Tg. Yer. I:	אליעזר בר פרנסת ביתי...
	(איתעבידו לי ניסין בדרמשק

Although some scholars have raised questions about the presence and meaning of דמשק in this passage,[8] it has the same form as דמשק elsewhere in the Bible, and reflects the SBH spelling of the term. Note also that Tg. Yerushalmi I rendered Hebrew דמשק with the late spelling דרמשק.[9] The constrast between SBH דמשק and LBH דרמשק represents another instance in which a feature of post-exilic Hebrew does not appear in the 'J' source.

17. בזה *('Spoil, Booty')*

The lexeme בזה 'spoil, booty' occurs 10 times in the Hebrew Bible,[10] always in clearly late books.[11] See the following examples:

Esth. 9.10	הָרְגוּ וּבַבִּזָּה לֹא שָׁלְחוּ אֶת־יָדָם
Esth. 9.15, 9.16	וּבַבִּזָּה לֹא שָׁלְחוּ אֶת־יָדָם
Dan. 11.24	בִזָּה וְשָׁלָל וּרְכוּשׁ לָהֶם יִבְזוֹר
Dan. 11.33	וְנִכְשְׁלוּ בְּחֶרֶב וּבְלֶהָבָה בִּשְׁבִי וּבְבִזָּה יָמִים
Ezra 9.7	נִתְּנוּ אֲנַחְנוּ... בַּחֶרֶב בַּשְּׁבִי וּבַבִּזָּה וּבְבֹשֶׁת
Neh. 3.36	וּתְנֵם לְבִזָּה בְּאֶרֶץ שִׁבְיָה
2 Chron. 14.13	וַיָּבֹזּוּ אֶת־כָּל־הֶעָרִים כִּי־בִזָּה רַבָּה הָיְתָה בָהֶם

---

6. Kutscher, *The Language and Linguistic Background of the Isaiah Scoll (1QIsa)*, pp. 3–5.

7. Kutscher, *The Language and Linguistic Background of the Isaiah Scoll (1QIsa)*, p. 3.

8. Note *BHS* critical apparatus for this verse: 'prb gl aram ad בֶן־מֶשֶׁק'.

9. Tg. Yerushalmi could have translated דמשק differently: Tg. Onqelos to Gen. 15.2 has דמסקאה.

10. BDB, p. 103a: 'late'; KB, p. 116a: 'Plünderung, Plündergut'; *HALAT*, p. 113b

11. For a fuller discussion, see Polzin, *Late Biblical Hebrew*, p. 130.

2 Chron. 25.13   ויבזו בזה רבה

2 Chron. 28.14   ויעזב החלוץ את־השביה ואת־הבזה

This expression does not occur anywhere in exilic or pre-exilic texts. Instead, the terms (a) שלל[12] and (b) בז[13] are employed to express the same meaning of 'spoil, booty'. Note the following illustrations:[14]

(a) Exod. 15.9   אמר אויב ארדף אשיג אחלק שלל

     Josh. 11.14   וכל שלל הערים האלה והבהמה בזזו להם בני ישראל

     Isa. 10.2, 10.6   להיות אלמנות שללם ואת יתומים יבזו

(b) Deut. 1.39   וטפכם אשר אמרתם לבז יהיה

     2 Kgs 21.14   ונתתים ביד איביהם והיו לבז ולמשסה

     Isa. 10.6   לשלל שלל ולבז בז

Note however that שלל continued to appear in exilic and post-exilic books. Note the following:

     Ezek. 38.13   הלשלל שלל אתה בא הלבז בז

     1 Chron. 26.27   מן־המלחמות ומן־השלל הקדישו

     Esth. 3.13, 8.11   ונשלוח ספרים...ושללם לבוז

Whereas SBH בז occurs in exilic but not in post-exilic texts:

     Jer. 2.14   העבד ישראל אם־יליד בית הוא מדוע היה לבז

     Isa. 42.22   והוא עם־בזוז ושסוי...היו לבז ואין מציל

     Ezek. 29.19   ונשא המנה ושלל שללה ובזז בזה

The above evidence suggests בזה 'spoil, booty' is a form that developed within the Hebrew language during the post-exilic period and replaced the earlier expression בז (but not שלל). Exactly how and why this form developed is uncertain, but it does not appear to be due to external influence (such as Aramaic).

The late character of בזה is confirmed by its frequent attestation in post-biblical literature. It is common in Tannaitic Hebrew, as the following examples demonstrate:[15]

     T. Soṭah 4.7   מלמד שכל העם היו עסוקין בביזה והוא עוסק

                                              במצוה

     Sifre Numbers 131   אבל משנתמלא ישר' ביזה התחולה

                                     מבזבזין את הביזה

     Mekhilta Pesḥa 13 (47)   ומנין שביזה הים גדולה מביזת מצר'

---

12. BDB, p. 1021b; KB, p. 979a; *HALAT*, p. 1417b.

13. BDB, p. 103a; KB, p. 115b: 'Plünderung, Plündergut'; *HALAT*, p. 113a.

14. See Even-Shoshan, *A New Concordance of the Old Testament*, p. 1155, s.v. שלל; ibid., pp. 161–62, s.v. בז.

15. See *HDHL*, plates 5698–99.

Interestingly, LBH בזה does not occur in the DSS, which instead display four examples of SBH בז. Note the following:[16]

TS 59.8[17]   ואסתיר פני מהמה והיו לאוכלה | ולבז ולמשוסה
4Q169 2.5 (Pesher Nahum)   לא ימוש מקרב עדתם חרב גוים שבי ובז
וחרחור בינותם וגל?ו?ת

On the other hand, שלל remains common throughout post-exilic literature, including the DSS. Note the following examples:[18]

Ben Sira 37.6	ואל תעזבהו בשללך
TS 55.8	ואת כול שללה בקבוץ אל תיך	רבובה
1QM 7.2	וכול מפשוטי החללים ושוללו השלל
M. Sanhedrin 6.1	שללה לא שלל שמים
Mekhilta Shirah 7 (140)	מחולק הוא שללי וממוני להם

We may conclude that בזה is an expression for 'spoil, booty' that was in use throughout much of the history of Hebrew – pre-exilic, exilic, post-exilic, and post-biblical (DSS and TH). When we look at the equivalent expressions בז and שלל there is a clear chronological divide: SBH בז is the earlier term, absent in post-exilic books, and surviving only in four instances in the DSS; LBH בזה is the later form, absent in pre-exilic and exilic books, and common in rabbinic literature.

The post-exilic expression בזה 'spoil, booty' occurs nowhere in disputed 'J' source verses, which instead employ the SBH form בז, as the following demonstrate:

Numb. 14.3	נשינו וטפנו יהיו לבז
Numb. 14.31	וטפכם אשר אמרתם לבז יהיה

Even verses which not all scholars ascribe to 'J' consistently prefer the earlier formulation, thus reflecting a pre-exilic linguistic situation.

18. *מלכות* ('Kingdom [of Yhwh]')

The Hebrew Bible sometimes employs alternative expressions in place of the divine name יהוה; such circumlocutions for יהוה occur most commonly in later texts of the Bible, and reflect a trend in post-exilic Judaism in which the biblical authors sought to avoid direct reference to the proper name יהוה. J. Loader commented:

> With the absolute monotheism that began to take shape since the exile
> (cf. Deutero-Isaiah) a new aspect came to the fore. A proper name is

---

16. See *HDHL*, plate 5698.
17. See also TS 60.5, 60.8.
18. See *HDHL*, plate 17725.

only needed by a god who finds himself between other gods – in order to be distinguished from them.... More and more circumlocutions [for Yahweh] came into use, e.g. 'Heaven', 'the High', 'the Majesty', 'the Great Majesty', 'the Glory'.... In this way the transcendence of God is emphasized.[19]

Examples of such circumlocutions are כבוד, שם, and הדר. Although occasionally these terms were used in early texts before the name יהוה, in late texts circumlocutions are used to avoid יהוה altogether. The term מלכות, itself a LBH lexeme,[20] is often used in conjuction with such terms as כבוד or הדר (of God); such compound expressions appear chiefly in late texts:

Ps. 103.19	יהוה: :הכון כסאו ומלכותו בכל משלה
Ps. 145.11	כבוד מלכותך יאמרו וגבורתך ידברו
Ps. 145.12	להודיע...גבורתיו וכבוד הדר מלכותו

Note that in each of these instances the Hebrew Bible employs מלכות (or a similar expression) where the reader would expect to see God's name. Such circumlocutions resemble, and may even be based upon, the similar use of מלכות to refer to a human king. Note the following examples from the Persian period (the first is Hebrew, the second is Aramaic):

Esth. 1.4	בהראתו את עשר כבוד מלכותו ואת יקר תפארת גדולתו
Dan. 4.33	מנדעי יתוב עלי וליקר מלכותי הדרי וזוי יתוב עלי

Note that both Esther and Daniel refer not to glory of the king but to the glory of his kingdom.

Exilic and pre-exilic works, however, do not emply this circumlocution for the divine name, but rather refer directly to the הדר or כבוד of God. Note the following diverse examples:

Numb. 14.21	כבוד יהוה את כל הארץ
1 Kgs 8.11	כבוד יהוה את בית יהוה
Isa. 35.2	כבוד יהוה הדר אלהינו

---

19. J. Loader, *Polar Structures in the Book of Qohelet*, (BZAW, 152; Berlin: Walter de Gruyter, 1979), pp. 124–125.

20. See Hurvitz, *Beyn Lashon le-Lashon*, pp. 79–82. See also מלכות, BDB, p. 574: 'chiefly late'; KB, p. 531b; *HALAT*, p. 561a. The term מלכות occurs occasionally in early texts such as Numb. 24.7; Jer. 10.7, 49.34; Ps. 45.7. Numb. 24.7 is part of the Balaam oracles which evidence style switching; see Rendsburg, *Linguistic Evidence for the Northern Origin of Selected Psalms*, p. 11, and p. 11, nn. 44–45. Jer. 10.7 occurs in an oracle addressed to the northern kingdom of Israel and may be an example of address switching (compare Jer 10.11, which is in Aramaic). Jer. 49.34 occurs in an oracle addressed to the Ammonites. On addressee switching, see G.A. Rendsburg, 'The Strata of Biblical Hebrew', *JNSL* 17 (1991), pp. 96–97. Psalm 45 is clearly a northern text; see above, p. 48, n. 47; Rendsburg, *Linguistic Evidence for the Northern Origin of Selected Psalms*, pp. 45–50. Could מלכות be another example of a feature of IH that becomes more common in LBH during the post-exilic period?

In addition, SBH attributes certain characteristics to God, including his glory and his splendor:

Deut. 5.24	הן הראנו יהוה...את כבדו ואת גדלו
Isa. 2.10	בוא בצור...מפני פחד יהוה ומהדר גאנו
Ps. 24.10	מי הוא זה מלך הכברד יהוה צבאות הוא מלך הכבוד
Ps. 29.2	הבו ליהוה כבד שמו
Ps. 96.6	הוד והדר לפניו

It appears that during the pre-exilic period, Israelite authors refered directly to the attributes of God, or ascribed those same attributes to God. In the late contexts quoted earlier, it appears that the biblical writers, in order to emphasize the remoteness and transcendence of God,[21] began to use those attributes to refer to the deity in order to avoid direct use of his name.

Further examples demonstrate that this late usage persisted in post-biblical literature. Note the following examples from Qumran:

1QM 12.6	ואתה אל נ[ורא]בכבוד מלכותכה...לעזר עולמי[ם]
4Q400 2 1.3	וספרו הוד מלכותו כדעתם
4Q403 1 1.25	[מה]ללי מלכות כבודו [...] נאה
4Q403 1 1.32	תשבחות כבוד מלכותו בה

The above evidence indicates that this shift – from the SBH practice of referring directly to God or his attributes to the LBH practice of using מלכות as a circumlocution – is a stylistic and/or linguistic practice of the writers of post-exilic biblical books and post-biblical literature.

It is significant in light of the above evidence that disputed 'J' source verses never employ the later circumlocutions for God. In an instance where such verses could substitute מלכות (or the earlier equivalent ממלכה) for יהוה or employ it in conjunction with reference to an attribute of God, they exhibit only the earlier practice:

Exod. 33.18	ויאמר הראני נא את־כבדך
Numb. 14.21	וימלא כבוד יהוה את כל הארץ

In Exod. 33.18, Moses asks God to show him 'your glory,' rather than the later expression, 'the glory of your kingdom'. And in Numb. 14.21, the verse reads 'the glory of YHWH' instead of 'the glory of his kingdom'. This is one more example of how, given a difference in language usage between SBH and LBH, verses which not all scholars agree belong to 'J' use the SBH expression in preference to the later formulation.

---

21. Loader began his discussion of religio-historical developments in Judaism during the exile thus: 'Here I wish to show that (a) God became remote and far from believers of the post-exilic period, and (b) that Judaism filled the vacuum thus created by a series of intermediaries'; Loader, *Polar Structures in the Book of Qohelet*, p. 124.

19. חנון ורחום ('Gracious And Loving')

The lexical pair חנון ורחום 'gracious and loving' occurs several times in the Hebrew Bible,[22] 5 times in texts which are clearly late:

Jonah 4.2	כי אתה אל חנון ורחום ארך אפים
Ps. 145.8	חנון ורחום יהוה
Neh. 9.17	חנון ורחום ארך אפים
Neh. 9.31	כי אל חנון ורחום אתה
2 Chron. 30.9	חנון ורחום יהוה

And thrice in texts of uncertain date:[23]

Joel 2.13	חנון ורחום הוא ארך אפים
Ps. 111.4	חנון ורחום יהוה
Ps. 112.4	חנון ורחום וצדיק

The same pair occurs in the reverse order, twice in early texts:

Exod. 34.6	רחום וחנון ארך אפים
Ps. 86.15	רחום וחנון ארך אפים

And only once in a clearly late text:

Ps. 103.8[24]	רחום וחנון יהוה ארך אפים

The distribution of חנון ורחום versus רחום וחנון in the Hebrew Bible suggests that רחום וחנון was the order of the word-pair in SBH;[25] in the post-biblical period, the earlier order was reversed to חנון ורחום.[26] Although the earlier form still appeared in one late text, it is the later form חנון ורחום which predominated. Although the SBH form רחום וחנון did not completely disappear, the LBH expression continued to dominate in post-biblical literature.[27] Note the following:

M. Shavu'ot 4.13	וחנון וברחום
Mekhilta Shira 3 (117)	חנון ורחום אף אתה
Mekhilta Baḥodesh 6 (226)	חנון ורחום
Mekhilta Kaspa 20 (332)	חנון ורחום ארך אפים

---

22. For a fuller discussion, see Hurvitz, *Beyn Lashon le-Lashon*, pp. 104–07.

23. Both Psalm 111 and 112 contain two features of LBH. See Hurvitz, *Beyn Lashon le-Lashon*, p. 174.

24. Briggs and Briggs point out that verses 3–5 of Psalm 103 refer to events in the book of Exodus ('cf. Ex. 34.7... cf. Ex. 15.26'), and suggest that Ps. 103.8 is a gloss based on Exod, 34.6, intended to balance verse 9. See Briggs and Briggs, *Psalms*, pp. 324–26.

25. See BDB, p. 337a: 'רחום וחנון... the earlier phrase'; KB, p. 315a; *HALAT*, p. 319b.

26. See BDB, p. 337a: '...the later וחנון ורחום'.

27. The examples below are from *HDHL*, plate 17053. The word-pair is so far unattested at Qumran.

But note also examples where SBH רחום וחנון continued to be employed:

Sifre Deuteronomy 49 (114)[28]   אלא נקרא המקום רחום וחנון
שנ' ''חנון ורחום''

Mekhilta Shirah 3 (117)   חנון ורחום אף אתה תהא רחום וחנון

Note that in both of the above examples, the rabbinic text notes that the SBH phrase רחום וחנון is equivalent to the LBH and post-biblical phrase חנון ורחום. It is possible that in Mekhilta Shira 3, both the SBH and LBH expressions are employed for poetic variation.

In light of the evidence, it is significant that in a disputed 'J' verse, it is the SBH expression which is employed in preference to the LBH form. Note the example:

Exod. 34.6   רחום וחנון ארך אפים

Even this verse which some scholars exclude from 'J' reflects the pre-exilic linguistic background of 'J'.

20. רחם על ('Have Compassion Upon')

There is one example in late Hebrew in which Piel רחם takes the preposition על before its object:[29]

Ps. 103.13   כרחם אב על בנים רחם יהוה על יראיו

Compare this to the normal pattern in BH, in which Piel רחם takes a direct object without intervening על. Note the following examples:[30]

Exod. 33.19 et passim[31]   ורחמתי את־אשר ארחם
Deut. 13.18 et passim[32]   ונתן־לך רחמים ורחמך
Isa. 13.18 et passim[33]   ופרי־בטן לא ירחמו

The single occurrence of רחם על in Psalm 103 reflects a development which took place in post-exilic Hebrew. The vitality of the expression רחם על is reflected by its frequent occurrence in post-exilic literature.[34] For

---

28. Note that the text quotes a GN רחום וחנון but renders it with the later expression TH חנון ורחום.

29. BDB, p. 933a; KB, p. 885b; *HALAT*, p. 1135a. For a fuller discussion, see Hurvitz, *Beyn Lashon le-Lashon*, pp. 107–09.

30. See Even-Shoshan, *A New Concordance of the Old Testament*, p. 1072.

31. For other examples of רחם taking the direct object indicator, see 2 Kgs 13.23; Isa. 14.1; Jer. 42.12; Hos. 1.6, 7; 2.6, 25; Zech. 1.12.

32. For other examples if רחם with attached pronominal suffix, see Deut. 30.3; Isa. 27.11; 30.18; 49.10; 54.8, 10; 55.7; 60.10; Jer. 12.15; 31.20; 33.26; Zech. 10.6.

33. For other examples of רחם taking a direct object without intervening את, see also Isa. 49.13, 15; Jer. 30.18; Ezek. 39.25; Ps. 102.14.

34. See *HDHL*, plates 17052–53.

example, it appears in apocryphal literature such as Ben Sira. Note the following:[35]

Ben Sira (B) 36.17	רחם על עם נקרא בשמך
Ben Sira (B) 36.18	רחם על קרית קדשך
Ben Sira (B) 15.20	ולא מרחם על עושה שוא

The verb רחם occurs frequently with על in texts from Qumran. Note these examples:

1QS 20.10	ולוא ארחם על כול סוררי דרך
CD 9.13	וירחם עליהם
4Q509 16.3	ור]חמהם על תעניתם
1QH 9.36	כמרחמת על עולה

Note especially how the Isaiah Scroll from Qumran renders רחם with על...רחם:[36]

1QIsa[a] 13.18	ועל פרי בטן לוא ירחמו
(Note MT:	(ופרי־בטן לא ירחמו

Finally, רחם occurs commonly with the preposition על in rabbinic writings. Note the following:

M. Soṭah 8.1	וירחמו עליכם
M. Taʿanit 2.4	ייי המרחם על הארץ
T. Berakhot 4.16	מרחמין עליהם

In Aramaic, as well, the verb רחם usually takes the preposition על. Note the following examples from the Targumim:

Tg. Hosea 1.6	לרחמא על בית ישראל
(Note MT:	(ארחם את־בית ישראל
Tg. Jer 31.20	רחמא ארחים עליהון
(Note MT:	(רחם ארחמנו

The evidence clearly indicates that in SBH, the verb רחם 'have compassion for' took either the prominal suffix, or a direct object with or without את. In LBH, however, רחם began to take the preposition על before its object. Although there is only one such example in the MT, examples of רחם with על in post-biblical literature are common.

Compare LBH רחם על to the use of the SBH formulation רחם with את in a verse which some scholars attribute to 'J' or to 'JE':

Exod. 33.19	ורחמתי את אשר ארחם
(Compare Tg. Onq. and Tg. Yer. I:	(וארחים על מן דארחים

---

35. Also cited in Hurvitz, *Beyn Lashon le-Lashon*, p. 108.
36. Also cited in Hurvitz, *Beyn Lashon le-Lashon*, p. 109.

Even those verses whose attribution to the 'J' source is uncertain display the SBH usage of רחם without the preposition על; Exod. 33.19 does not reflect Late Biblical Hebrew.

21. שׁרבִיט ('Scepter')

The lexeme שׁרבִיט[37] 'scepter' is a dissimilated form from *שׁבִיט[38] which occurs only in the clearly post-exilic book of Esther:[39]

Esth. 4.11   לבד מאשר יושיט לו המלך את־השרביט הזהב וחיה
Esth. 5.2   ויושיט המלך לאסתר את־השרביט הזהב אשר בידו
Esth. 8.4   ויושט המלך לאסתר את שרבט הזהב

In each of these three instances שׁרבִיט occurs in a royal context: the king extends his sceptre. This expression does not occur in earlier books of the Bible, which employ the term שׁבט 'scepter, mark of authority'.[40] In early as well as later poetic texts, שׁבט occurs in royal contexts. Note the following examples:[41]

Judg. 5.14   ומזבולין משכים בשבט ספר
Ezek. 19.11   ויהיו־לה מטות עז אל־שבטי משלים
Zech. 10.11   ושבט מרצים יסור

In some instances, however, שׁבט has the sense 'rod, staff; chastisement' but not in association with royalty, as the following examples illustrate:

Exod. 21.20   וכי־יכה איש... בשבט
2 Sam. 7.14[42] והכחתיו בשבט אנשים

---

37.   KB, p. 1010b: '(=שׁבט)'; BDB, p. 987a; *HALAT*, p. 1523a.

38.   We can reasonably postulate the form *שׁבִיט on the basis of Akkadian *šabbiu*; *CAD*, Š1, p. 10. For the dissimilation of *שׁבִיט > שׁרבִיט, see Bergsträsser, *HG*, I, p. 110, §20b, who also cites גבע > גלבע, כסם > כרסם, and דמשׁק > דרשׁמק (see above, pp. 132–133); and Joüon-Muraoka, p. 255, §88K. See also Hurvitz, *Beyn Lashon le-Lashon*, p. 18, n. 12; Kutscher, *The Language and Linguistic Background of the Isaiah Scroll (1QIsa)*, pp. 4, 5, 77. On the dissimilation of geminate consonants in BA, see Rosenthal, *A Grammar of Biblical Aramaic*, pp. 16–17. Although Rosenthal discusses only the substitution of nasalization (נ) for gemination in BA, the substitution of ר for gemination in Aramaic is also attested (דרמשׁק in Imperial Aramaic; BA כרסא for BH כסא and Akk. *kissû*).

39.   For a fuller discussion, see Bergey, 'The Book of Esther', pp. 50–51.

40.   KB, p. 941a; BDB, p. 986b, s.v. שׁבט, §1d: 'truncheon, sceptre'; *HALAT*, p. 1291a. The expression שׁבט can also have the meaning 'tribe', but examples of such do not enter into this discussion of שׁרבִיט.

41.   Bergey commented that the meaning is not entirely clear in these passages, citing J. Skinner, *Genesis*, (ICC; Edinburgh: T. and T. Clark, 1930), pp. 519–20; E.A. Speiser, *Genesis*, (AB; Garden City, NY: Doubleday, 1964), pp. 361, 365: 'Both commentators render this word "scepter" and state that authority is implied by its possessor'; ibid., p. 50, n. 2.

42.   Though its use here probably is related to the context of the royal theology central to this chapter.

Lam. 3.1   אני הגבר ראה עני בשבט עברתו

The distribution of שרביט 'scepter' in a post-exilic book and its contrast with שבט 'scepter, mark of authority' clearly suggest that שרביט is a dissimilated form that penetrated the Hebrew language during the post-exilic period.

The late character of שרביט '(royal) scepter' is confirmed by its attestation in post-exilic literature, where it occurs in rabbinic texts:[43]

M. Sanhedrin 2.8(5) et passim[44]   ואין משתמשין בשרביטו

It is significant in light of the above evidence that verses which some scholars ascribe to 'J' use only SBH שבט 'scepter'. Note the following examples:

Gen. 49.10[45]   לא־יסור שבט מיהודה
Numb. 24.17   וקם שבט מישראל

If the 'J' source were composed during the post-exilic period, we could expect it to employ LBH שרביט in place of SBH שבט 'scepter, mark of authority', but such is not the case.

---

43. *HDHL*, plates 18298–99. Several examples of שרביט in TH have the sense 'branch, stalk, rod'; see Bergey, 'The Book of Esther', p. 51, n. 1.

44. See also T. Sanhedrin 4.2; Sifre Deuteronomy 157 (209).

45. As note earlier, Genesis 49 is not truly 'J' because it is a poem embedded into a 'J' narrative.

Chapter 8

CONCLUSIONS

This study discussed 40 linguistic features which, because of distribution, contrast, and post-biblical attestation, can with confidence be regarded as characteristic of Late Biblical Hebrew. It can be argued that there are more than 40 features of LBH discussed in this study.[1] In several instances, more than one late feature is present in a given item. For example, the LBH terms יקר and שאר also display the late phonological pattern $q^etāl$.[2] The LBH lexemes דת, פתגם, and possibly זמן are also considered late because they represent Persian influence on Biblical Hebrew during the later post-exilic period.[3] Not only is the expression כול עולמים itself late, occuring only in clearly post-exilic texts, but the term עולמים, which is part of that expression, can also be considered late, even though it occurs sporadically in early texts.[4]

We may speak nevertheless of 40 features discussed in this study which entered Biblical Hebrew during the exilic or post-exilic period, occuring alongside or eventually replacing earlier features of equivalent meaning. The items discussed in this study were chosen not simply because they characterize later Hebrew, but because they are features where a contrast or a similarity can be demonstrated between Late Biblical Hebrew and what we find in 'J' or disputed 'J' source verses. Many features of Late Biblical Hebrew where no such contrast or similarity can be shown were not included in this analysis. For example, LBH כתר 'crown' competes with SBH נזר and עטרה 'crown' in post-exilic texts.[5] But since SBH נזר and עטרה nor LBH כתר occur nowhere in 'J' or disputed 'J' verses, it cannot be shown in this instance that 'J' reflects the earlier usage. Therefore LBH כתר was excluded from this study.

Of those items where a useful comparison could be made between LBH and 'J' or disputed 'J' source verses, two were phonological in nature. Both examples display the dissimilation of geminate consonants which

---

1. Note similar comments made by Bergey, 'The Book of Esther', p. 168, n. 1.
2. See above, pp. 90–92.
3. See above, pp. 115–200, 131–132.
4. See above, pp. 68–71, 129
5. Bergey, 'The Book of Esther', pp. 98–99.

occurs sporadically in post-biblical texts: LBH דרמשׁק versus SBH דמשׂק, which occurs in 'J'; LBH שׁרבים versus SBH שׁבט, which occurs once in a disputed 'J' verse.

Several of the items discussed above reflect morphological developments in LBH. Some of the items are forms which occurred rarely in the pre-exilic period but became much more productive in LBH: the first person prefixed preterite form (also known as the *waw*-consecutive) in SBH is nearly always ואקטל, whereas in LBH ואקטלה becomes much more common; the third masculine plural pronominal suffix after the feminine plural ending ־ות in LBH is predominantly ־ותיהם, versus the predominant SBH construction ־ותם; the third singular masculine perfect of היה in SBH is חי, compared to the regular LBH form חיה; Some items are forms which appear only in exilic and post-exilic texts: LBH חיה versus SBH חי; the LBH form שׁתיה versus the equivalent expressions שׁתה and שׁתות; the LBH form בזה versus SBH בז (and we may compare also LBH בזה to SBH שׁלל which is used in similar contexts). In all these cases, morphological developments associated with LBH do not appear in 'J' or disputed 'J' source verses.

A large number of items discussed in this study concern styntax. In several instances a particular syntagma or expression occurs in pre-exilic texts, but becomes more productive in LBH: the relatively high use of את plus pronominal suffix to express the direct object in SBH compared to the predominant use of the pronominal suffix attached to the finite verb in LBH; introductory infinitive construct clauses in SBH are regularly preceded by ויהי/והיה, whereas in LBH such clauses generally omit ויהי/ והיה; the predominant SBH syntagma בין X ובין Y 'between X and Y' versus the LBH expression בין X ל־Y; the SBH expressions X X or X X־ו 'each, every X' versus the LBH syntagma כל X ו X־; the LBH syntagma לולי...שׁ־...אז/אזי which does not appear in SBH, where instead we find לולי/לולא...כי; LBH למען לא compared to פן and לבלתי which are employed in SBH to express a negative wish or purpose. In all of the above examples, 'J' and disputed 'J' verses do not display the characteristic features of LBH.

Several items discussed constitute expressions or phrases which occur exclusively or predominantly in LBH. In a few cases, the LBH phrase occurs sporadically in early texts but is rare and unproductive. These include the SBH phrase לקח אשׁה 'take, obtain a wife' which is frequently replaced in LBH by נשׂא אשׁה; the LBH phrase כל עולמים compared to equivalent SBH expressions which employ עולם, עד, נצח. In several instances the LBH phrase or syntagma occurs only in exilic and post-exilic books: the LBH calender formulae בחדשׁ X ב־Y בו and ביום X לחדשׁ Y compared to equivalent expressions in SBH; the LBH expression ברך אתה יהוה versus the SBH equivalent ברך יהוה; the LBH phrase ברך שׁם יהוה לעולם/עד עולם which never occurs in early texts; the LBH expression (חוקים/פקודים/מצות (יהוה, whereas in SBH we find דרש יהוה or (יהוה) דרש דבר; although the word מלכות occurs occasionally in early texts, only in LBH is it employed as a circumlocution for deity; the LBH phrase עשה (כ)רצון 'do, act (according to) the will (of someone)' compared to SBH expressions such as עשה הטוב בעינים and עשה הישר בעינים 'do what is good or right in the eyes (of someone)'; the LBH construction שלום על compared to SBH שולם ל־ which is identical in meaning; the use of על to express the direct object of רחם in LBH, whereas in SBH רחם is used without על; the words חנון and רחום occur together in LBH as חנון ורחום, whereas in SBH we find only the word order רחום וחנון.

There are numerous LBH items of a lexical nature for which a contrast can be made with 'J' or disputed 'J' verses. In one case, a term is employed much more frequently in LBH than in SBH: the first person singular pronoun אני occurs alongside אנכי in SBH, but in LBH it becomes far more predominant. There are several examples of lexemes which are rare and unproductive in pre-exilic texts, but are used regularly in LBH: LBH בהל versus SBH מהר and חפז; LBH מערב 'west' compared to SBH which uses ים and מבוא to express the same meaning; the Piel of קבל 'to receive' in LBH compared to SBH which uses לקח in similar contexts; LBH שבח compared to SBH ברך, הלל, הודה, and הגיד which are used in similar contexts. Other lexemes appear not to have entered Biblical Hebrew until the exilic or post-exilic periods: SBH אז 'then' versus LBH כבן, which occurs only in Esther; the Niphal of בעת 'be terrified, frightened' in LBH compared to the similar use of פחד and ירא in SBH; the expression גזר על in LBH compared to the similar use of צוה in SBH; the Piel of כנס in LBH to mean 'gather' versus SBH אסף and קבץ;[6] the LBH lexeme מהלך to mean 'distance' as opposed to the similar use of SBH ארך, רחב, דרך; LBH סוף versus the equivalent SBH terms קץ, קצה, אחרית; LBH שלט compared to the use of SBH מלך and משל in similar contexts; LBH תאב versus the use of SBH אוה, כסף, or תשוקה in similar contexts; LBH יקר versus כבוד in SBH; LBH זקף which is often used in place of such verbs as נשא, קום, רום, and נצב in SBH. In none of the above examples do 'J' or disputed 'J' source verses employ the LBH feature.

It is particularly worth noting the absence of Persian loan-words in 'J' or disputed 'J' source verses. Since such words do not appear to have entered Biblical Hebrew until at least the second half of the fifth century BCE, we can with confidence conclude that the Yahwist source could not have been composed any later than that. Moreover, there were three Persian loan-words for which we could demonstrate a contrast with 'J' or disputed 'J' source verses: LBH דת 'law, decree' versus the similar use of

6. For problems with כנס as an example of LBH, see above, p. 94–95 and references.

חק in 'J'; LBH זמן 'appointed time, (period of) time' compared to SBH מועד in 'J' and disputed 'J' verses; LBH פתגם 'word, decree' as opposed to the use of SBH דבר in a similar context in 'J'. Not only are Persian loan-words absent from 'J' and disputed 'J' verses, but there are a few cases where 'J' and disputed 'J' source verses employ the SBH equivalent(s) of a Persianism.

The analysis presented in this study confirms that Late Biblical Hebrew is itself a language in transition. Although it is still useful to divide the language of the Hebrew Bible into three main chronological stages – Archaic Biblical Hebrew (ABH), Standard Biblical Hebrew (SBH), and Late Biblical Hebrew (LBH) – we must recognize that the precise boundaries between these stages – particularly between SBH and LBH – are not always clear. It is perhaps preferable to regard these stages as regions on a spectrum of chronological development. The transition from Standard to Late Biblical Hebrew is not sudden but gradual. Subtle distinctions can be drawn even within the broad category called Late Biblical Hebrew. The most obvious of these is between Late Biblical Hebrew before and after the second wave of returnees from Exile in the latter half the fifth century BCE; although Persian loan-words are indeed a feature of LBH, they do not appear in early post-exilic books such as Haggai, Zechariah, and Malachi.[7]

Several of the characteristically late linguistic features discussed in this study occur sporadically in earlier texts, as can be seen in Tables 1a, 1b, 1c, and 1d (pp. 147–150). In some cases, this reflects different usages in prose and poetic texts. For example, the use of the finite verb with pronominal suffix predominates in several pre-exilic books, including Isaiah 1–39, Hosea, Amos, Obadiah, Micah, Nahum, Habakkuk, Psalms, Proverbs. But it is in prose texts that we discern a sharp reduction in the use of את plus pronominal suffix. The economy of language which characterizes Hebrew poetry of all time periods means that these poetic books naturally would prefer the verb with suffix over את with suffix. That pre-exilic poetry makes little use of את with suffix does not necessarily indicate late usage, nor does it imply that the sharp increase in

---

7. The majority of characteristic features of LBH are concentrated in books which date to the time of Ezra-Nehemiah and thereafter: Qohelet, Esther, Daniel, Ezra, Nehemiah, and Chronicles. Further research is required to determine the character and boundaries of different sub-stages within Late Biblical Hebrew. Compare the effort to establish a precise diachronic grammar of Egyptian texts from the 20th Dynasty, based on irregularities in verbal orthography; Israelit-Groll, 'Diachronic Grammar as a Means of Dating Undated Texts', pp. 10–104.

8. The same argument applies to the introductory infinitive construct plus ־ב/־כ in exilic and pre-exilic poetry. It is in prose texts that we can discern a sharp contrast between the predominant use of the infinitive plus ־ב/־כ with ויהי/והיה in early books and the predominant use of the infinitive plus ־ב/־כ only in later writings.

the use of the finite verb with suffix in late prose is any less characteristic of the post-exilic period.[8]

Table 1a. Late features discussed in this study in 'J', disputed 'J' verses, pre-exilic, and exilic books[9]

	J	J[disp]	Gen.	Exod.	Lev.	Numb.	Deut.
אני							
(disuse) suffix + את							x
בהל							
ביום X לחדש Y							
בין X ל־ Y			x		x	x	x
infinitive + כ/ב־					x	x	
ואקטלה			x				
־ותיהם							
חיה							
כול X ו X־							
כל עולמים							
כנס							
מערב							
מלכות							
משא אשה							
עשה (מ)רצון							
קבל							
קים							
תשבחה, שבח							
שלט							

9.   This table indicates the diffusion (x) of late linguistic features discussed in this study that appear in pre-exilic and exilic texts. For those items where the frequency of a given feature indicates late usage, the following conventions were used to determine if a text displays the LBH trait: if the ratio of אנכי to אני is at least 1:2; if the ratio of את plus suffix to the finite verb with suffix is at least 1:3; if the ratio of the infinitive plus כ/ב־ with ויהי/ והיה to the infinitive plus כ/ב־ only is at least 1:1; if the ratio of ־ותם to ־ותיהם is at least 1:1.

Table 1b. Late features discussed in this study in 'J', disputed 'J' verses, pre-exilic and exilic books

	Josh.	Judg.	Sam.	Kgs	Isa.$^{1-39}$	Isa.$^{40-66}$	Jer.	Ezek.
אני				X		X		X
(disuse) suffix + את					X	X		
בהל								
ביום X לחדש Y								
בין X ל־Y								
infinitive + כ/ב־					X	X	X	X
ואקטלה	X	X						
־ותיהם								
חיה								
כול X ו־X								
כל עולמים								
כנס								
מערב								
מלכות								
נשא אשה								
עשה (כ)רצון								
קבל								
קים								
תשבחה, שבח								
שלט								

Table 1c. Late features discussed in this study in 'J', disputed 'J' verses, pre-exilic and exilic books

	Hos.	Amos	Obad.	Micah	Nah.	Hab.	Zeph.
אני						x	x
(disuse) suffix + את	x	x	x	x	x	x	
בהל							
ביום X לחדש Y							
בין X ל־Y							
infinitive + ־כ/ב	x						
ואקטלה							
ותיהם־							
חיה							
כול X ו־X							
כל עולמים							
כנס							
מערב							
מלכות							
נשא אשה							
עשה (כ)רצון							
קבל							
קים							
תשבחה, שבח							
שלט							

Table 1d. Late features discussed in this study in 'J', disputed 'J' verses, pre-exilic, and exilic books

	Pss.[10]	Prov.	Ruth	Song	Lam.
אני	X	X		X	X
(disuse) suffix + את	X	X	X	X	
בהל	X	X			
ביום X לחדש Y					
בין X ל־Y					
infinitive + כ/ב־	X	X			
ואקטל ה	X				
־ותיהם					
חיה					
כול X ו־X	X				
כל עולמים					
כנס					
מערב	X				
מלכות					
נשא אשה			X		
עשה (ב)רצון	X				
קבל		X			
קים			X		
תשבחה, שבח	X				
שלט					

Many of those late features that appear occasionally in early texts can be attributed to dialectal variation within pre-exilic Hebrew.[11] Although the LBH expression כול עולמים occurs once in a post-exilic text, the term עולמים occurs occasionally in pre-exilic texts, most of which display other northern features: 1 Kgs 8.13; Isa. 26.4; Ps. 77.6, 77.8.[12]

10. This includes those Psalms which are not clearly post-exilic; see above, Introduction, p. 13. Late features in post-exilic Psalms are indicated in Table 2b.

11. This paragraph has recently been expanded and published as a separate article; see Wright, 'Further Evidence for North Israelite Contributions to Late Biblical Hebrew', pp. 129–48.

12. See above, p. 68, n. 54. Rendsburg, *Linguistic Evidence for the Northern Origin of Selected Psalms*, pp. 73–81. Although he does not discuss specifically עולמים in Isa. 26.4, see Noegel, 'Dialect and Politics in Isaiah 24–27', pp. 177–92. The use of עולמים in Ps. 61.5 cannot be explained currently as dialect variation.

The LBH syntagma X ו X כול occurs in Ps. 45.18, clearly a northern Psalm.[13] Although the Hithpael form of כוס is not characteristic of LBH, the use of the root כוס in Isa. 28.20 (התכנס) might represent addressee switching in a text addressed to the tribe of Ephraim.[14] The Piel of קבל occurs in the pre-exilic book of Proverbs (19.20), which displays other features of Israelean Hebrew.[15] The LBH expression מערב 'west' appears in Psalm 75 (75.7), a clearly northern text.[16] The verb בהל with the meaning 'hasten' occurs in two texts that contain other features of IH, Ps. 48.6 and Prov. 20.21.[17] Although some of the examples discussed in this paragraph may represent style- or addressee-switching and thus do not reflect necessarily a regional dialect of the writer(s),[18] it would appear that in some cases IH expressions penetrated the literary idiom in the post-exilic period.[19] Such evidence would support the hypothesis by C. Gordon that Israelian Hebrew

13. See above, 78, n. 227; Rendsburg, *Linguistic Evidence for the Northern Origin of Selected Psalms*, pp. 45–50. Evidence for the dialectal nature of this expression comes from an Eteocretan inscription from the 6th century BCE, where we read κλ ες υ ες (compare BH כל איש ואיש); Rendsburg, 'Late Biblical Hebrew and the Date of "P"', p. 69; C.H. Gordon, *Evidence for the Minoan Language* (Ventnor, NJ: 1966), p. 10.

14. See above, p. 93, n. 63; Hurvitz, *A Linguistic Study of the Relationship between the Priestly Source and the Book of Ezekiel*, p. 124; Rendsburg, 'The Strata of Biblical Hebrew', pp. 96–97. Although התכנס in Isa. 28.20 is not discussed specifically, on dialectal features in Isaiah 28 as a whole, see Noegel, 'Dialect and Politics in Isaiah 24–27', pp. 189–91. (Despite the title of the article, in these pages Noegel discusses Isaiah 28.) The Qal of כוס in Ps. 33.7 presently cannot be explained as dialectal variation. (For possible evidence against כוס as a feature of LBH, see Naveh, 'Hebrew and Aramaic Inscriptions', pp. 1–14, especially pp. 2–3; and above, p. 94–95 and references.)

15. See above, p. 104, n. 109; Albright, 'Some Canaanite Sources of Hebrew Wisdom', pp. 1–15; Ginsberg, *The Israelian Heritage of Judaism*, p. 36; Rendsburg, *Linguistic Evidence for the Northern Origin of Selected Psalms*, p. 10 and nn. 39–40.

16. See above, p. 98, n. 64; Rendsburg, *Linguistic Evidence for the Northern Origin of Selected Psalms*, pp. 73–81.

17. See above, p. 83, nn. 17–18; Rendsburg, *Linguistic Evidence for the Northern Origin of Selected Psalms*, pp. 10, 51–60.

18. For example, נשׂא אשׁה in Judg. 21.23 and התכנס in Isa. 28.20.

19. For the view that something similar happened in Ancient Egyptian – that is, that earlier dialects affected later literary style – see Joseph H. Greenberg, 'Were There Egyptian Koines?' in *The Fergusonian Impact*, I, *From Phonology to Society* (ed. Joshua A. Fishman et al.; Berlin: de Gruyter, 1986), pp. 271–90.

influenced post-exilic Hebrew when refugees from the Northern kingdom (re)encountered their Judean counterparts in exile.[20]

Not all examples of late linguistic features in pre-exilic texts can be explained as poetic usage or dialectal variation. But such examples do not force us to conclude that those texts are late or that the feature does not represent late usage. A given text should not be considered late unless there is an accumulation of late features, particularly if that text in most other respects reflects a pre-exilic linguistic background.[21] For example, one of only two features of LBH discussed in this study which appear in Deuteronomy is the reduced use of את plus suffix.[22] Given that Deuteronomy normally employs SBH as opposed to LBH, we can conclude safely that the aversion to את plus pronominal suffix in Deuteronomy is a stylistic peculiarity of the writer(s).

In many cases late linguistic features which occur sporadically in an early book are not characteristic of the text in question. For example, the other late feature which occurs in Deuteronomy is the syntagma X בין Y־ל, occuring twice in one verse (17.8). But the normal SBH construction בין X ובין Y occurs three times elsewhere in the book, in Deut. 1.1, 1.16, 5.5. Although the LBH construction occurs in Deuteronomy, the earlier expression predominates.

We must also recognize that some synchronic variation existed during

---

20.   Gordon argued:

> Such northernisms (alien to pre-exilic Judean Hebrew) can only have reached the postexilic authors in Babylonia and Persia via the North Israelite tribes who had been in exile since the eighth century in the Assyrian Empire, and had retained their identity so that they survived to join the Judean exiles in Neo-Babylonian times.... We have therefore an answer to much of the problem posed by the sharp break between pre-exilic and postexilic Hebrew prose. The break was largely due to the impact of the Northern Israelite tribes.

See Cyrus Gordon, 'North Israelite Influence on Postexilic Hebrew', *IEJ* 5 (1955), pp. 85–88, especially pp. 86–87. Note that some scholars have expressed doubt concerning this scenario; see Gevirtz, 'Of Syntax and Style in the "Late Biblical Hebrew"–"Old Canaanite" Connection', pp. 25–26; and Wright, 'Further Evidence for North Israelite Contributions to Late Biblical Hebrew', pp. 146–48 and references.

21.   See Hurvitz, 'Linguistic Criteria for Dating Problematic Biblical Texts', p. 76. Granted, how much accumulation of late features is required to indicate that a text is late is probably subjective. Hurvitz commented, 'This accumulation is relative. It is very doubtful whether we can mechanically apply statistical criteria to linguistic issues like these'; idem., 'Linguistic Criteria for Dating Problematic Biblical Texts', p. 76. However, if the text is question consistently employs early language over late equivalents, this increases our confidence that the occasional late feature is either a late gloss or is part of the idiolect of the biblical writer(s).

22.   The ratio of את plus suffix to the finite verb with suffix in Deuteronomy is 1:3.74, closer to the post-exilic prose ratio of 1:5.83 than to the ratio of 1:1.30 we find elsewhere in the Pentateuch; see above, p. 38.

the pre-exilic period. For example, although the long *waw*-consecutive
וְאָקְטֵל ה characterizes post-exilic prose, it occurs occasionally in pre-exilic
texts. Both the long and the short *waw*-consecutive apparently were
available in the pre-exilic period.[23] But it was precisely this sort of
synchronic variation that led to the predominant use of וְאָקְטֵל ה in the
post-exilic period. As T. Bynon commented:

> It is precisely this variation within a speech community which provides
> the key to the mechanism of language change. By acting as a living
> vehicle or medium for the retraction and promotion of competing
> forms, which will show themselves in retrospect as members of the
> successive grammars of the language, it makes change possible. This
> does not mean that all linguistic variation is necessarily associated with
> ongoing change but simply that any change which does take place
> assumes the presence of linguistic variation.[24]

Although many of the late linguistic features discussed in this study
appear first in exilic or post-exilic writings, several such features appear in
pre-exilic texts as alternative expressions that competed with their earlier
counterparts. It was not until the post-exilic period that such competing
forms were used increasingly at the expense of the earlier expression or
replaced the earlier form altogether.[25] In such cases it is the increased or
predominant use of the language element in post-exilic texts which marks
that element as characteristically late.[26]

Further evidence that LBH was a language in transition is the
chronological differences that can be discerned even among late books.
As can be seen in Tables 2a 2b, and 2c (below, pp. 156–160), some LBH
sources display more than others the late linguistic features discussed in
this study. The diffusion of such late elements in ascending order is:
Malachi 1, Isaiah 40–66 2, Joel 2, Lamentations 2, Jeremiah 3, Haggai 3,
prose Job 3, Jonah 4, Zechariah 4, Ezekiel 9, Qohelet 10, Daniel 11, Ezra
11, Nehemiah 14, Chronicles 19, late Psalms 20, Esther 23, Qumran

---

23. See above, pp. 22–26.

24. T. Bynon, *Historical Linguistics* (Cambridge: Cambridge University Press, 1979), pp.
198–99.

25. See discussion in Bergey, 'The Book of Esther', pp. 173–74; Bergey, 'Post-exilic
Hebrew Linguistic Developments in Esther', pp. 167–68.

26. For example, see comments by Hurvitz concerning the intensification of the use of
יוֹתֵיהֶם in the late period; *A Linguistic Study of the Relationship between the Priestly Source
and the Book of Ezekiel*, pp. 24–27, especially p. 25, n. 9; and concerning the increased use of
בֵּין X לְ־Y; ibid., pp. 113–15, especially p. 114, n. 179.

Hebrew 34, Tannaitic Hebrew 34.[27] Most characteristics of LBH are to be found in late post-exilic works, that is, texts which date to the time of Ezra and Nehemiah or later; comparitively fewer features of LBH are to be found in exilic and early post-exilic works. This would appear to support the contention of Driver that 'the great turning-point in Hebrew style falls in the age of *Nehemiah*' (emphasis in original),[28] although we must not ignore that undisputably late features do occur in early post-exilic texts such as Haggai, Zechariah, and Malachi.[29]

27. Compare these results to the diffusion of 58 late features in Esther which were analyzed by Bergey: Jeremiah 11, Ezekiel 13, Daniel 15, Ezra 17, Nehemiah 20, Chronicles 26, the DSS 29, the Mishnah 41, Esther 58; Bergey, 'The Book of Esther', pp. 175–178. Note that Bergey included only undisputed late prose texts in his analysis, excluding such works as Isaiah 40–66, Joel, Jonah, Haggai, Zechariah, Malachi, late Psalms, Qohelet, Lamentations. For a recent and excellent examination of the relationship between LBH, QH, and MH, see David Talshir, 'The Habitat and History of Hebrew During the Second Temple Period', in Ian Young (ed.), *Biblical Hebrew: Studies in Chronology and Typology* (London: T. and T. Clark, 2003), pp. 251–275.

28. Driver, *An Introduction to the Literature of the Old Testament*, pp. 504–05. Driver divided the chronological development of Biblical Hebrew roughly into four stages: the classical Hebrew of 'JE', Deuteronomy, and Judges through Kings; Jeremiah, the latter part of Kings, Ezekiel, Second Isaiah, and Haggai, all of which show '*slight* signs of being later than the writings first mentioned'; the 'memoirs' of Ezra and Nehemiah, and Malachi, where 'a more marked change is beginning to show itself'; and the Hebrew of Qohelet, Daniel, Esther, and Chronicles, where the changes of the previous stage are 'more palpable' (emphasis in original); pp. 505–06. Driver did not specify into which stage other books belong, nor did he elaborate on the 'slight signs of being later' which we might find in Jeremiah, the latter part of Kings, Ezekiel, Second Isaiah, or Haggai. Although Driver was correct to recognize the contrast between early and late post-exilic writings, some of his views have since been challenged, as seen below; see Hurvitz, *A Linguistic Study of the Relationship between the Priestly Source and the Book of Ezekiel*, p. 153, n. 36.

29. See Hill, 'Dating Second Zechariah: A Linguistic Reexamination', pp. 105–34; Hill, 'Dating the Book of Malachi: A Linguistic Reexamination'; Hurvitz, 'The Evidence of Language in Dating the Priestly Code', p. 55, n. 57.

Table 2a. Late features discussed in this study in exilic and post-exilic books[30]

	Isa.⁴⁰⁻⁶⁶	Jer.	Ezek.	Joel	Jonah	Hag.	Zech.	Mal.
Persian loan-words								
אני	X		X			X		X
(disuse) suffix + את					X			
בהל								
בזה								
בחדש X ב־ Y בו								
ביום X לחדש Y						X	X	
בין X ל־ Y			X	X				
infinitive + כ/ב־			X	X				
בכן								
ברוך אתה יהוה								
יהוה שם יהוה לעולם								
גזר על								
דרמשק								
/דרש + מצות								
חוקים/פקודים								
וְאֶקְטְלָה	X	X				X		
־ותיהם	X		X					
זקף								
חיה		X	X					
חנון ורחום					X			
יקר								
כול X ו־ X								
כל עולמים								
כנס			X					
לולי...ש־...אזי								
למען לא			X					

30.   This table indicates the diffusion (x) of late linguistic features discussed in this study that appear in exilic and post-exilic texts, as well as post-biblical sources. DSS includes post-biblical materials other than rabbinic literature, such as texts from Genizah and Murabba'at. For those items where the frequency of a given feature indicates late usage, the following conventions were used to determine if a text displays the LBH trait: if the ratio of אנכי to אני is at least 1:2; if the ratio of את plus suffix to the finite verb with suffix is at least 1:3; if the ratio of the infinitive plus ב־/כ with והיה/ויהי to the infinitive plus ב־/כ only is at least 1:1; if the ratio of ־ותם to ־ותיהם is at least 1:1.

Table 2a (continued). Late features discussed in this study in exilic and post-exilic books, post-biblical Hebrew

	Isa.$^{40-66}$	Jer.	Ezek.	Joel	Jonah	Hag.	Zech.	Mal.
מהלך			x		x		x	
מערב	x							
מלכות								
נבעת								
נשׂא אשׁה								
סוף				x				
עשׂה (ב)רצון								
קבל								
קים			x					
רחם על								
שׁבח, תשׁבחה								
שׁלום על								
שׁלט								
שׁרביט								
שׁתיה								
תאב								

Table 2b. Late features discussed in this study in exilic, post-exilic books, and post-biblical Hebrew

	Ps.[late]	Job[31]	Qoh.	Lam.	Esth.	Dan.
Persian loan-words			X		X	X
אני		X	X	X	X	X
(disuse) suffix + את	X			X	X	X
בהל					X	
בזה					X	X
בחדש X ב־ Y בו					X	
ביום X לחדש Y					X	X
בין X ל־Y						X
infinitive + כ/ב־			X		X	X
בכן			X		X	
ברוך אתה יהוה	X					
בוך שם יהוה לעולם	X					X
גזר על					X	
דרמשק						
חוקים/פקודים/מצות + דרש	X					
ואקטלה	X					X
־ותיהם		X				
זקף	X					
חיה				X		
חנון וחרום	X					
יקר					X	
כול X ו־ X	X				X	

31. Job here refers to those prose portions of Job which are demonstrably post-exilic; see above, Introduction, p. 13, n. 63.

Table 2b (continued). Late features discussed in this study in exilic, post-exilic books, and post-biblical Hebrew

	Ps.[late]	Job[32]	Qoh.	Lam.	Esth.	Dan.
כל עולמים	X					
כנס			X		X	
לולי...ש־...אזי	X					
למען לא	X					
מהלך						
מערב	X					
מלכות	X				X	X
נבעת					X	X
נשא אשה						
סוף			X			
עשה (ב)רצון	X				X	X
קבל		X			X	
קים	X				X	
רחם על	X					
שבח, תשבחה	X		X			
שלום על	X					
שלט	X		X		X	
שרביט					X	
שתיה					X	
תאב	X					

32. Job here refers to those prose portions of Job which are demonstrably post-exilic; see above, Introduction, p. 13, n. 63.

Table 2c. Late features discussed in this study in exilic, post-exilic books, and post-biblical Hebrew

	Ezra	Neh.	Chron.	DSS	TH
Persian loan-words	X	X	X	X	X
אני	X	X	X	X	X
(disuse) suffix + את	X	X	X	X	X
בהל			X		X
בזה	X	X		X	
בחדש X ב־Y בו					X
ביום X לחדש Y	X	X	X	X	
בין X ל־Y		X	X	X	X
infinitive + כ־/ב־	X		X	X	
בכן				X	
ברוך אתה יהוה			X		X
יהוה שם יהוה לעולם				X	X
גזר על					X
דרמשק			X	X	
חוקים/פקודים/מצות + דרש	X		X	X	X
וְאִקְטְלָה	X	X		X	
־ותיהם	X	X		X	X
זקף				X	X
חיה				X	X
חנון וחרום		X	X		X
יקר		X		X	X
כול X ו־X				X	X
כל עולמים				X	X
כנס		X	X	X	X
לולי...שׁ־...אזי				X	X
למען לא				X	X

Table 2c (continued). Late features discussed in this study in exilic, post-exilic books, and post-biblical Hebrew

	Ezra	Neh.	Chron.	DSS	TH
מהלך		X		X	X
מערב			X	X	X
מלכות				X	X
נבעת			X	X	X
נשא אשה	X	X	X	X	X
סוף			X	X	X
עשה (כ)רצון	X	X		X	X
קבל			X	X	X
קים				X	X
רחם על				X	X
שבח, תשבחה				X	X
שלום על			X	X	X
שלט		X			X
שרביט				X	
שתיה				X	X
תאב					X

Exilic writings represent an important transitional period in the development from classical to post-classical Hebrew.[33] That is, texts which can be dated to the time of the exile display some of the features which become characteristic of post-exilic Hebrew.[34] This is particularly evident in the case of Ezekiel, which Hurvitz demonstrated displays numerous late linguistic features that do not appear in pre-exilic writings or the 'P' source. He concluded:

> The *exilic* period, which is a transitional period between *pre-exilic* (classical) and *post-exilic* (post-classical) Hebrew, naturally cannot be expected to possess yet all the typical peculiarities exhibited in LBH proper. By definition, the term 'transitional period' implies that while it no longer includes all the linguistic elements which typified the earlier period, at the same time it is still lacking some of the characteristic

33. For a different point of view see especially Jacobus Naudé, 'The Transitions of Biblical Hebrew in the Perspective of Language Change and Diffusion', in Ian Young (ed.), *Biblical Hebrew: Studies in Chronology and Typology* (London: T. & T. Clark, 2003), pp. 188–214.

34. Granted, other exilic compositions do not display as many LBH traits as Ezekiel. But note that Jeremiah, which represents both the late pre-exilic and early exilic periods, displays more late characteristics than have been discussed in this study; see Bergey, 'The Book of Esther', especially pp. 175–77.

features of subsequent periods. To be sure, a few of the post-classical linguistic traits which occur in Ez. do not appear even in the latest biblical compositions. However, on the whole there are far fewer late elements in Ez. than in the distinctly post-classical compositions (such as Ezr., Neh., or Ch.). Furthermore, the Book of Ez. occupies a position midway between classical BH and late BH not only as regards the *nature* of these elements which have found their way into this composition, but also (in certain instances) as regards the *nature* of these elements. ... *The language of the Book of Ezekiel is therefore, both typologically and chronologically, a forerunner of LBH – i.e.,* it already displays rudiments of linguistic processes which reached full maturity only later on in the literature of the post-exilic period (emphasis in original).[35]

Because Ezekiel frequently exhibits late language in contexts where the 'P' source employs only the classical expression, Hurvitz concluded that 'P' must antedate Ezekiel; and since Ezekiel is widely held to date to the exilic period (593–571 BCE),[36] the Priestly source must likewise be pre-exilic.[37]

In light of the above observations, we can attempt to place the 'J' source within the chronological development of Hebrew. Of the 40 late language elements discussed in this study, never does 'J' appear to reflect late usage. In 37 instances, late expressions which appear only in late post-exilic writings do not appear in 'J' source verses, which instead employ only the SBH equivalent.[38] There are 8 features of LBH that appear in early post-exilic works but not in the 'J' source of the Pentateuch.[39] And there are 5 features which occur in exilic texts which 'J' avoids in favour of the earlier usage.[40] Although the strongest contrast is between the language background of 'J' and that of the late post-exilic period, we can still see several instances where 'J' does not display characteristics of LBH that occur in exilic and early post-exilic texts. *With one possible exception, what we find in 'J' is early, and what is missing is late.*[41] Given the finding of Hurvitz that LBH elements begin to appear in exilic texts, and that a diachronic contast can be seen between exilic and pre-exilic texts, it is significant that this study found a contrast between 'J' and exilic period texts. The 'J' source reflects substantially a pre-exilic linguistic back-

---

35. Hurvitz, *A Linguistic Study of the Relationship between the Priestly Source and the Book of Ezekiel*, pp. 161–62.

36. See above, p. 12, n. 59.

37. Hurvitz, *A Linguistic Study of the Relationship between the Priestly Source and the Book of Ezekiel*, pp. 151–55.

38. See Tables 2a, 2b above, pp. 155–158.

39. See Table 2a, 2b, 2c above, pp. 155–160.

40. See Tables 1b, 1c above, pp. 148–149.

41. Because in every other instance 'J' displays early rather than late usage, it appears likely that the low use of אֵת with suffix in 'J' source verses is either a coincidence or a stylistic peculiarity of the Yahwist writer(s).

ground. *We may therefore conclude that 'J' is (most likely) a product of the pre-exilic period.*

Verses which not all scholars assign to 'J' yielded similar results. Disputed 'J' verses do not display any clearly late characteristics. It was not possible in every instance to find the same contrast between disputed verses and late Hebrew as could be seen between the 'J' source and late texts. For example, the late expression שלום על does not occur in 'J' verses, which instead employ only the SBH construction שלום ל־. But neither שלום על nor שלום ל־ occur in disputed 'J' verses, so with respect to this language feature no constrast can be shown. There were some cases, however, where a contrast could be demonstrated between late texts and only disputed 'J' verses. For example, disputed 'J' source verses employ only the early lexeme בז 'booty, spoil,' and never the later alternative בזה. This contrast cannot be seen with respect to the 'J' source which never uses SBH בז or שלל. Except for the reduced use of את plus suffix, disputed 'J' source verses reflect the same pre-exilic linguistic background as texts which belong to 'J' by scholarly consensus.

How do these conclusions affect scholarly arguments for a relatively late date of composition for the Yahwist source? Perlitt and Schmid both detected strong similarities between 'J' and Deuteronomistic texts, dating the work of the Yahwist historian(s) to the late 7th century BCE;[42] the conclusions of this study do not appear to pose a strong challenge to their proposed date for 'J'.[43]

Rose and Van Seters went a step further, concluding that 'J' was composed as a prologue to DtrG, and thus should be dated to the late exilic period.[44] Although Rendtorff challenged the longstanding assumption that 'J' is a continuous literary strand in the Pentateuch, by arguing that the 'major (independent) units' which comprise the 'J' narrative were united by a Deuteronomistic redactor he effectively suggested that the materials which traditionally were attributed to 'J' did not achieve their final form until the Exile.[45] Hans-Christoff Schmitt analyzed the 'non-

42. Perlitt, *Bundestheologie im Alten Testament*; Schmid, *Der sogenannte Jahwist*.

43. Although this is not the place to go into details, Jeremiah shows seeds of LBH which are lacking in 'J' and disputed 'J' source verses. It is noteworthy that 'J', which the above scholar would date to the late pre-exilic period, lacks LBH features which occur in Jeremiah, most of which was composed at that time.

44. Rose, *Deuteronomist und Jahwist*; Rose, 'La croissance du corpus historiographique de la Bible – une proposition', pp. 217–26; van Seters, *Abraham in History and Tradition*; van Seters, 'The Yahwist as Historian'; van Seters, *In Search of History: Historiography in the Ancient World and the Origins of Biblical History*; van Seters, *Prologue to History: The Yahwist as Historian in Genesis*; van Seters, *The Life of Moses: The Yahwist as Historian in Exodus-Numbers*.

45. Rolf Rendtorff, *Das überlieferungsgeschichtliche Problem des Pentateuch*, (BZAW, 147; Berlin: Walter de Gruyter, 1977).

Priestly' Joseph Story (Genesis 37–50) and isolated three distinct layers: a Judah-Israel strand from the Davidic-Solomonoic period, a Reuben-Jacob strand from the last years of the monarchy, and finally a late Yahwistic strand dating to the exilic or post-exilic periods.[46]

Although in many instances these scholars made significant contributions to the literary-critical and form-critical study of the so-called 'J' source, their analyses have not considered the linguistic evidence. We know that exilic compositions reflect the transition from SBH to LBH; late linguistic features begin to appear in such works as Jeremiah, Isaiah 40–55, and especially Ezekiel. The complete absence of late linguistic items in 'J' casts doubt on attempts to date 'J' to the exilic period.

The same can be said with respect to those who attribute 'J' to the post-exilic period, such as Alonso-Schökel, Mendenhall, de Catanzaro, Wagner, and particularly Winnett.[47] And of course the position of those scholars who have attempted a radical redating of 'J', placing its composition in the late Persian or even the Hellenistic period – here I have in mind P.R. Davies, Niels P. Lemche, Frederick H. Cryer, and T.L. Thompson – is even more perilous.[48] Texts dating to the Persian period, particularly the period after Ezra and Nehemiah, exhibit even more of the late features which distinguish LBH from SBH. Such traits are absent from 'J', a finding which should cause us to question a post-exilic date for 'J' on linguistic grounds.

---

46. Hans-Christoff Schmitt, *Die nichtpriesterliche Josephsgeschichte*, (BZAW, 154; Berlin: Walter de Gruyter, 1980).

47. Alonso-Schökel, 'Motivos sapienciales y de aliana en Gn 2–3', pp. 295–316; Mendenhall, 'The Shady Side of Wisdom: The Date and Purpose of Genesis 3', pp. 319–34; de Catanzaro, 'A Literary Analysis of Genesis 1–11'; Wagner, 'A Literary Analysis of Genesis 12–36'; Wagner, 'Abraham and David?', pp. 117–40; Winnett, 'Re-examining the Foundations', pp. 1–19; Winnett, 'The Arabian Geneologies in the Book of Genesis', pp. 171–96.

48. P.R. Davies, *In Search of 'Ancient Israel*, (JSOTSup, 148; Sheffield: JSOT Press, 1992); Niels P. Lemche, 'The Old Testament – A Hellenistic Book?' *SJOT* 7 (1994), pp. 163–93; Frederick H. Cryer, 'The Hebrew 3rd Masc. Sg. Suffix -JW on Dual and Plural Nouns', *SJOT* 6 (1992), pp. 205–12; Frederick H. Cryer, 'The Problem of Dating Biblical Hebrew and the Hebrew of Daniel', in Knud Jeppsen, Kisten Nielsen, and Bent Rosendal (eds.), *In The Last Days: On Jewish and Christian Apocalyptic and its Period*, (Aarhus: Aarhus University Press, 1994), pp. 185–198; T.L. Thompson, *Early History of the Israelite People from the Written and Archeological Sources* (Leiden: E.J. Brill, 1992). See the recent critique of this position by A. Hurvitz, 'Continuity and Innovation in Biblical Hebrew – The Case of "Semantic Change" in Post-Exilic Writings', in T. Muraoka (ed.), *Studies in Ancient Hebrew Semantics*, (Abr-Nahrain Supplement Series, 4; Louvain: Peeters, 1995), p. 10, and p. 10, nn. 26–29. The arguments presented by Cryer are so without foundation that a detailed rebuttal is unnecessary.

The only conclusion which the linguistic evidence permits is a pre-exilic date for 'J'. Indeed, given the total absence of late features in 'J', one should look to a period antedating the late pre-exilic period.[49]

49. Several of the articles that appeared recently in Ian Young (ed.), *Biblical Hebrew: Studies in Chronology and Typology* (T. and T. Clark: London, 2002) – especially those by Philip Davies, Martin Ehrensvärd, Robert Rezetko, and Ian Young – challenged the basic approach employed in this study. In some cases those scholars who challenged the 'chronological approach' questioned whether particular items can be identified as early or late Hebrew. In some cases – especially Philip Davies and Ian Young – those scholars challenged the notion that post-exilic scribes could not have written in early Hebrew (or SBH) without at some point employing their own (dialect of) late Hebrew (or LBH). Several years after completing my doctoral dissertation I have reached the conclusion that in both cases *these scholars are at least partly correct*.

On the one hand, I concede that scholars who take the 'chronological approach' need to refine their methodology and reexamine some of their evidence. It may well be that some items identified herein as LBH are not – just as the Rendsburg, Gevirtz, and others have found when reexamining the work of Robert Polzin and scholars who based their research on the pattern set by him. But we should note that several purported features of LBH have withstood the test of reexamination.

On the other hand, I must admit that it is possible – it is *possible* – that post-exilic scribes could have written biblical texts in early Hebrew (or SBH). But is it probable? Is such a scenario persuasive? Thus I must agree with Ian Young who recently stated, 'Linguistic evidence is just that: evidence'. The fact remains that, even if some of the items identified as LBH in this study are later found not to be distinctively late, there is still *no late language in 'J'*. Perhaps the findings of this study do not constitute 'proof' of a pre-exilic date for the Yahwist source of the Pentateuch. Perhaps they constitute nothing more than 'evidence'. But it is evidence that may be sufficiently persuasive for the reader.

BIBLIOGRAPHY

Academy of the Hebrew Language, *Historical Dictionary of the Hebrew Language* (Jerusalem: Academy of the Hebrew Language, 1988; microfiche).

Ackroyd, P., review of D. Hillers, *Lamentations, Int* 27 (1973), pp. 223–26.

Aharoni, Y., 'Hebrew Ostraca from Tel Arad', *IEJ* 16 (1966), pp.1–7.

—*Arad Inscriptions* (Jerusalem: Israel Exploration Society, 1981).

Ahlström, G.W., *Joel and the Temple Cult of Jerusalem* (VTSup, 21; Leiden: E.J. Brill, 1971).

Albright, W.F., 'A New Hebrew Word for "Glaze" in Proverbs 26.23', *BASOR* 98 (1945), pp. 24–25.

—'Some Canaanite-Phoenician Sources of Hebrew Wisdom', in M. Noth and D.W. Thomas (eds.), *Wisdom in Israel and in the Ancient Near East* (VTSup, 3; Leiden: E.J. Brill, 1960), pp. 1–15.

Albright, W.F. and William L. Moran, 'A Re-interpretation of an Amarna Letter', *JCS* 2 (1948), pp. 239–48.

Alexander, P., 'Targum, Targumim', *ABD*, VI (New York: Doubleday, 1992), pp. 320–31.

Allegro, John M., *Qumrân Cave 4*, I (DJD, 5; Oxford: Clarendon Press, 1968)

Allen, L., *The Books of Joel, Obadiah, Jonah, and Micah*, (NICOT; Grand Rapids, MI: Eerdmans, 1976).

Alonso-Schökel, L., 'Motivos sapienciales y de alianza en Gn 2–3'. *Biblica* 43 (1962), pp. 295–316.

Alter, Robert, *The Art of Biblical Narrative* (New York: Basic Books, 1981).

—*World of Biblical Literature* (New York: Basic Books, 1992).

Anderson, Bernhard, *Understanding the Old Testament* (Englewood Cliffs, NJ: Prentice-Hall, 1966; 2nd edn).

Anderson, George W., *A Critical Introduction to the Old Testament* (London: Gerald Duckworth, 1959).

Avigad, N. and Y. Yadin, *A Genesis Apocryphon: A Scroll from the Wilderness of Judea* (Jerusalem: Magnes Press, 1956).

Baillet, Maurice. *Qumrân Grotte 4*, III (DJD, 7; Oxford: Clarendon Press, 1982).

Baillet, M., J.T. Milik, and R. de Vaux, *Les "Petites Grottes" de Qumrân: Textes* (DJD, 3; Oxford: Clarendon Press, 1962).

Bar-Asher, M., 'The Study of Mishnaic Hebrew Grammar - Achievements, Problems, and Goals', in M. Bar-Asher (ed.), *Proceedings of the Ninth World Congress of Jewish Studies 1985: Panel Sessions: Hebrew and Aramaic* (Jerusalem: World Union of Jewish Studies; Hebrew), pp. 3–37.

Barkay, G., 'The Priestly Benediction on Silver Plaques from Ketef Hinnom in Jerusalem', *Tel Aviv* 19 (1992), pp.139–92.

Barr, James. 'A New Look at Kethibh-Qere', *Remembering All the Way....* (Oudtestamentlischer Studien, 21; 1981), pp.19–37.

Barthélemy, D., and J.T. Milik, *Qumran Cave I* (DJD, 1; Oxford: Clarendon Press, 1955).

Barton, G., *A Critical and Exegetical Commentary on the Book of Ecclesiastes* (ICC; Edinburgh: T. & T. Clark, 1908).

Batten, L., *An Exegetical and Critical Commentary on the Books of Ezra and Nehemiah* (ICC; Edinburgh: T. & T. Clark, 1913).

Becker, J., review of A. Hurvitz, *A Linguistic Study of the Relationship Between the Priestly Source and the Book of Ezekiel, Biblica* 64 (1983), pp.583–586.

Beer, Georg (ed.), *Faksimile-Ausgabe des Mischnacodex Kaufmann A. 50* (The Hague: Nijhoff, 1929).

Benoit, P., J.T. Milik, and R. de Vaux, *Les Grottes de Murabbàât: Textes* (DJD, 2; Oxford: Clarendon Press, 1961).

Berg, S., *The Book of Esther: Motifs, Themes, and Structures* (SBLDS, 44; Missoula, MT: Scholars Press, 1979).

Bergey, Ronald L., 'The Historical Periods of the Hebrew Language', in Herbert Paper (ed.), *Jewish Languages: Themes and Variations. Proceedings of Regional Conferences of the Association for Jewish Studies Held at The University of Michigan and New York University in March-April 1975* (Cambridge, MA: Association for Jewish Studies, 1978), pp. 1–14.

—'The Book of Esther - Its Place in the Linguistic Milieu of Post-Exilic Biblical Hebrew Prose. A Study in Late Biblical Hebrew' (unpublished doctoral dissertation; Dropsie College for Hebrew and Cognate Learning, 1983).

—'Late Linguistic Features in Esther', *JQR* 75 (1984), pp. 66–78.

—'Post-exilic Features in Esther', *JETS* 31 (1988), pp. 161–68.

Bernal, Martin, *Black Athena*, II (New Brunswick, NJ: Rutgers University Press, 1991).

Biblia Hebraica Stuttgartensia (eds. K. Elliger and W. Rudolph; Stuttgart: Deutsche Bibelgesellschaft, 1967/1977).

Blenkinsopp, Joseph, *The Pentateuch* (New York: Doubleday, 1993).

Boadt, L., 'Ezekiel, Book of', *ABD*, II (New York: Doubleday, 1992), pp. 711–22.

Boling, R., *Judges* (AB; Garden City, NY: Doubleday, 1985).

Boling, Robert, 'Joshua, Book of', *ABD*, III (New York: Doubleday, 1992), pp. 1002–15.

—'Judges, Book of', *ABD*, III (New York: Doubleday, 1992), pp. 1107–27.

—review of J. van Seters, *Prologue to History, Int* 48 (1994), pp.289–91.

Böttcher, F., *Ausführliches Lehrbuch des hebräischen Sprache* II (ed. F. Mühlau; Leipzig: Johann Ambrosius Barth, 1868).

Briggs, Charles, *A Critical and Exegetical Commentary on the Book of Psalms* (ICC; Edinburgh: T. & T. Clark, 1906–1907).

Bright, J., *Jeremiah* (AB; Garden City, NY: Doubleday, 1965).

Broshi, Magen, *et al.*, *Qumran Cave 4*, XIV, *Parabiblical Texts, Part 2* (DJD, 19; Oxford: Clarendon Press, 1995).

Brown, Francis, S.R. Driver, and Charles Briggs (eds.), *A Hebrew and English Lexicon of the Old Testament* (Oxford: Clarendon Press, 1974).

Burney, C.F., *Notes on the Hebrew Text of the Book of Kings* (Oxford: Clarendon Press, 1903).

Bynon, T., *Historical Linguistics* (Cambridge: Cambridge University Press, 1979).

Caine, Ivan, 'Numbers, Book of', *EncJud*, XII (Jerusalem: Keter, 1972), columns 1249–54.

Campbell, A., *Of Prophets and Kings* (CBQMS, 17; Washington, DC: Catholic Biblical Association of America, 1986).

Campbell, A. and M. O'Brien, *Sources of the Pentateuch: Texts, Introduction, Annotations* (Minneapolis, MN: Fortress Press, 1993).

Campbell, E.F., *Ruth* (AB; Garden City, NY: Doubleday, 1975).

Carpenter, J. and G. Harford-Battersby, *The Hexateuch According to the Revised Version.* (vol. 1; London: Longmans, Green, and Company, 1900).

Catanzaro, C.J. de, 'A Literary Analysis of Genesis 1–11' (unpublished doctoral dissertation; University of Toronto, 1957).

Charlesworth, James H. and R.E. Whitaker, *Grapahic Concordance to the Dead Sea Scrolls* (Tübingen: J.C.B. Mohr, 1991).

Chomsky, William, *Hebrew: The Eternal Language* (Philadelphia: Jewish Publication Society, 1957).

Clarke, E. (ed.), *Targum Pseudo-Jonathan of the Pentateuch: Text and Concordance* (Hoboken, NJ: Ktav, 1984).

Cohen, A., 'Makotkha', *Bet Mikra* 61 (1975), pp. 303–05.

Cohen, H., 'Ha-Shimush be-Kinuy ha-Mu_a' ha-Davuq le-'Umat ha-Shimush 'et + Kinuy' ('ot-) be-Lashon ha-Mishna', *Leš* 47 (1983), pp. 208–18.

Collins, J., 'Daniel, Book of', *ABD*, II (New York: Doubleday, 1992), pp. 29–37.

—'Dead Sea Scrolls', *ABD*, II (New York: Doubleday, 1992), pp. 85–101.

Corwin, R., 'The Verb and the Sentence in Chronicles, Ezra and Nehemiah' (unpublished doctoral dissertation; University of Chicago, 1909).

Crenshaw, J., 'Ecclesiastes, Book of', *ABD*, II (New York: Doubleday, 1992), pp. 271–80.

—'Job, Book of', *ABD*, III (New York: Doubleday, 1992), pp. 858–68.

—'Proverbs, Book of', *ABD*, V (New York: Doubleday, 1992), pp. 513–20.

Cross, Frank Moore, *The Ancient Library of Qumran* (Garden City, NY: Doubleday, 1961).

—*Canaanite Myth and Hebrew Epic* (Cambridge, MA: Harvard University Press, 1973).

—'A Reconstruction of the Judean Restoration', *JBL* 94 (1975), pp. 4–18.

Cross, Frank Moore. and David Noel Freedman, *Studies in Ancient Yahwistic Poetry* (SBLDS, 21; Missoula, MT: Scholars Press, 1975).

Cryer, Frederick H. 'The Hebrew 3rd Masc. Sg. Suffix -JW on Dual and Plural Nouns', *SJOT* 6 (1992), pp. 205–12.

—'The Problem of Dating Biblical Hebrew and the Hebrew of Daniel', in Knud Jeppsen, Kirsten Niesen, and Bent Rosendal (eds.), *In The Last Days: On Jewish and Christian Apocalyptic and its Period* (Aarhus: Aarhus University Press, 1994), pp. 185–98.

Curtis, Edward L. and A. Madsen, *A Critical and Exegetical Commentary on the Books of Chronicles* (ICC; Edinburgh, T. & T. Clark, 1910).

Davies, G., review of A. Hurvitz, *A Linguistic Study of the Relationship Between the Priestly Source and the Book of Ezekiel*, *VT* 37 (1987), pp. 117–118.

—*Ancient Hebrew Inscriptions* (Cambridge: Cambridge University Press, 1991).

Davies, P.R. *In Search of Ancient Israel* (JSOTSup, 148; Sheffield: JSOT Press, 1992).

Den Blaauwen, Ewald, 'Object Suffixation in Classical Hebrew', *Acta Orientalia Academiae Scientiarum Hungaricae* 41 (1987), pp.125–28.

Donner, H. and W. Röllig, *Kanaanäische und aramöische Inschiften*, (3 vols.; Wiesbaden: Otto Harrassowitz, 1962–1964).

Driver, S.R., *A Treatise on the Use of the Tenses in Hebrew* (Oxford: Clarendon Press, 1892).

—*An Introduction to the Literature of the Old Testament* (repr., New York: Meridian Books, 1957)

Duhm, B., *Die Theologie der Propheten als Grundlage für die innere Entwicklungsgeschichte der israelitischen Religion* (Bonn: Adolph Marcus, 1875).

Ehrensvärd, Martin, 'Linguistic Dating of Biblical Texts', in Ian Young (ed.), *Biblical Hebrew: Studies in Chronology and Typology* (London: T. & T. Clark, 2003), pp. 164–188.

Eissfeldt, Otto, *The Old Testament: An Introduction* (trans. P. Ackroyd; New York: Harper and Row, 1965).

Elliger, K., *Die Einheit des Tritojesaiah (Jesaiah 56–66)* (Stuttgart: W. Kohlhammer, 1928).

Eskhult, Mats, 'The Importance of Loanwords for Dating Biblical Hebrew Texts', in Ian Young (ed.), *Biblical Hebrew: Studies in Chronology and Typology* (London: T. & T. Clark, 2003), pp. 8–23.

Even-Shoshan, A., *A New Concordance of the Old Testament* (Jerusalem: Kiryat Sefer, 1990).

Fellman, Jack, 'The Linguistic Status of Mishnaic Hebrew', *JNSL* 5 (1979), pp. 21–22.

Fitzmeyer, J., *The Genesis Apocryphon of Qumran Cave I: A Commentary* (BibOr, 18; Rome: Pontifical Biblical Institute, 1966).

Flanagan, J., 'Samuel, Book of 1–2', *ABD*, V (New York: Doubleday, 1992), pp. 957–65.

Fohrer, G., 'Die Glossen im Buche Ezekiel', *ZAW* 63 (1950), pp.33–53.

Fredericks, D., *Qoheleth's Language: Re-evaluating its Nature and Date* (Ancient Near Eastern Texts and Studies, 3; Lewiston, NY: Edwin Mellen, 1988).

Garr, W. Randall, *Dialect Geography of Syria-Palestine, 1000–586 BCE* (Philadelphia, PA: University of Pennsylvania, 1985).

Gertner, M., 'Terms of Scriptural Interpretation: A Study in Hebrew Semantics', *BSO(A)S* 25 (1962), pp.1–27.

Gesenius, Wilhelm, E. Kautzsch and G. Bergsträsser, *Hebräische Grammatik* (Hildesheim: G. Olms, 28th edn, 1962).

Gevirtz, Stanley. 'Of Syntax and Style in the "Late Biblical Hebrew" - "Old Canaanite" Connection', *JANESCU* 18 (1986), pp.25–29.

Gibson, J., *Textbook of Syrian Semitic Inscriptions*, I, *Hebrew and Moabite Inscriptions* (3 vols.; Oxford: Clarendon Press, 1971).

Ginsberg, H.L., 'The North-Canaanite Myth of Anat and Aqht', *BASOR* 98 (1945), pp.15–23.

—'Ugaritic Studies and the Bible', *BA* 8 (1945), pp.57–58.

—*The Israelian Heritage of Judaism* (New York: Jewish Theological Seminary, 1982).

Ginzberg, L., *An Unknown Jewish Sect* (New York: Jewish Theological Seminary, 1970).

Goerwitz, R., 'The Accentuation of the Hebrew Jussive and Preterite', *JAOS* 112 (1992), pp.198–203.

Gordis, Robert, 'Studies in the Relationship of Biblical and Rabbinic Hebrew' in *Louis Ginzberg Jubilee Volume* (New York: American Academy for Jewish Research, 1945), pp. 173–99.

—*The Book of God and Man: A Study of Job* (Chicago: University of Chicago Press, 1965).

Gordon, C.H., 'North Israelite Influence on Post-exilic Hebrew', *IEJ* 5 (1955), pp.85–88.

—*Ugaritic Textbook* (Analecta Orientalia, 38; 3 vols.; Rome: Pontificium Institutum Biblicum, 1965).

—*Evidence for the Minoan Language* (Ventnor, NJ: Ventnor, 1966).

Greenberg, Joseph H., 'Were there Egyptian Koines?' in Joshua A. Fishman *et al.* (ed.), *The*

Fergusonian Impact: In Honor of Charles A. Ferguson on the Occasion of His 65th Birthday, I, *From Phonology to Society* (Berlin: de Gruyter, 1986), pp. 271–90.

Greenberg, Moshe, 'Exodus, Book of', *EncJud*, VI (Jerusalem: Keter, 1972), columns 1050–67.

—*Ezekiel 1–20* (AB; Garden City, NY: Doubleday, 1983).

Greenstein, Edward, 'On the Prefixed Preterite in Biblical Hebrew', *Hebrew Studies* 29 (1988), pp.7–17.

Guenther, A.R., 'A Diachronic Study of Biblical Hebrew Prose Syntax. An Analysis of the Verbal Clause in Jeremiah 37–45 and Esther 1–10' (unpublished doctoral dissertation; University of Toronto, 1977).

Hannemann, G., "Al Millat-ha-Yaḥas "Beyn" ba-Mishna u-va-Mikra', *Leš* 40 (1975–1976), pp.33–53 (Hebrew).

Hanson, P., *The Dawn of Apocalyptic* (Philadelphia: Fortress Press, 1975).

Haran, Menahem, *Temples and Temple-Service in Ancient Israel: An Inquiry into the Character of Cult Phenomena and the Historical Setting of the Priestly School* (Oxford: Clarendon Press, 1978).

Harrelson, H., *Interpreting the Old Testament* (New York: Holt, Rinehart and Winston, 1964).

Harrison, R.K., *Introduction to the Old Testament* (Grand Rapids, MI: Eerdmans, 1969).

Hartman, L. and Alexander di Lella, *The Book of Daniel* (AB; Garden City, NY: Doubleday, 1978).

Hendel, R., 'Genesis, Book of', *ABD*, II (New York: Doubleday, 1992), pp. 932–41.

Hiebert, T., 'Joel, Book of', *ABD*, III (New York: Doubleday, 1992), pp. 873–80.

Hill, Andrew, 'The Book of Malachi: Its Place in Post-Exilic Chronology Linguistically Reconsidered' (unpublished doctoral dissertation; University of Michigan, 1981).

—'Dating Second Zechariah: A Linguistic Reexamination', *HAR* 6 (1982), pp.105–134.

—'Dating the Book of Malachi: A Linguistic Reexamination', in Carol Meyers and M. O'Conner (eds.), *The Word of the Lord Shall Go Forth: Essays in Honor of David Noel Freedman in Celebration of His Sixtieth Birthday* (Winona Lake, IN: Eisenbrauns, 1983), pp. 77–89.

—'Malachi, Book of' *ABD*, IV (New York: Doubleday, 1992).

Hillers, Delbert R., *Lamentations* (AB; Garden City, NY: Doubleday, 1972).

—'Lamentations, Book of', *ABD*, IV (New York: Doubleday, 1992), pp. 137–41.

Hillers, Delbert R., and Eleonora Cussini, *Palmyrene Aramaic Texts* (Baltimore, MD: Johns Hopkins University Press, 1996).

Holloway, S., 'Kings, Book of 1–2', *ABD*, IV (New York: Doubleday, 1992), pp. 69–83.

Holm-Nielsen, S., *Hodayot Psalms from Qumran* (Acta Theologica Danica, 2; Aarhus, Denmark: Universitetsforlaget, 1960).

Howie, C., *The Date and Composition of Ezekiel* (Society for Biblical Literature Monograph Series, 4; Philadelphia: Scholars Press, 1950).

Huehnergard, John, 'The Early Hebrew Prefix-Conjugations', *Hebrew Studies* 29 (1988), pp.19–23.

Hurvitz, Avi, 'Observations on the Language of the Third Apocryphal Psalm from Qumrân', *Revue de Qumrân* 5 (1965), pp.225–32.

—'The Usage of *šēš* and *bûṣ* in the Bible and its Implications for the Date of P', *HTR* 60 (1967), pp.117–21.

—'The Chronological Significance of "Aramaisms"', *IEJ* 18 (1968), pp.234–40.

—*Beyn Lashon le-Lashon* (Jerusalem: Mosad Byalik, 1972) (Hebrew).
—'Linguistic Criteria for Dating Problematic Biblical Texts', *Hebrew Abstracts* 14 (1973), pp.74–79.
—'The Date of the Prose-Tale of Job Linguistically Reconsidered', *HTR* 67 (1974), pp.17–34.
—'The Evidence of Language in Dating the Priestly Code - A Linguistic Study in Technical Idioms and Terminology', *RB* 81 (1974), pp.24–56.
—'Sheliphat ha-Na'al', *Shnaton* 1 (1975), pp.xiii-xiv, 45–49 (Hebrew).
—'History of a Legal Formula', *VT* 32 (1982), pp.257–67.
—*A Linguistic Study of the Relationship between the Priestly Source and the Book of Ezekiel: A New Approach to an Old Problem* (Cahiers de la Revue Biblique, 20; Paris: J. Gabalda, 1982.
—'Ruth 2.7 - "A Midrashic Gloss"?', *ZAW* 95 (1983), pp.121–23.
—Review of D. Fredericks, *Qoheleth's Language, Hebrew Studies* 31 (1990), pp.144–52.
—בית־קברות and בית־עולם: Two Funerary Terms in Biblical Literature and Their Linguistic Background', *Maarav* 8 (1992), pp.59–68.
—'Continuity and Innovation in Biblical Hebrew – The Case of "Semantic Change" in Post-Exilic Writings', in T. Muraoka (ed.), *Studies in Ancient Hebrew Semantics* (Abr-Nahrain Supplement Series, 4; Louvain: Peeters, 1995), pp. 1–10.
—'Hebrew and Aramaic in the Biblical Period', in Ian Young (ed.), *Biblical Hebrew: Studies in Chronology and Typology* (London: T. & T. Clark, 2003), pp. 24–27.
Israelit-Groll, Sarah. 'Diachronic Grammar as a Means of Dating Undated Texts', in S. Israelite-Groll, *Egyptological Studies* (*Scripta Hierosolymitana*, 28; Jerusalem: Magnes Press, 1982), pp. 10–104.
Japhet, Sara, 'Sheshbazzar und Zerubbabel - Against the Background of the Historical and Religious Tendencies of Ezra-Nehemiah', *ZAW* 95 (1982), pp.66–98.
—'Interchanges of Verbal Roots in Parallel Texts in Chronicles', *Hebrew Studies* 28 (1987), pp. 9–50.
Jastrow, Marcus, *A Dictionary of the Targumim, Talmud Babli Yerushalmi, and Midrashic Literature* (New York: Judaica Press, 1971).
Jean, C.-F. and J. Hoftijzer, *Dictionnaire des Inscriptions Sémitiques de l'Ouest* (Leiden: E.J. Brill, 1965).
Joüon, Paul, and Takamitsu Muraoka, *A Grammar of Biblical Hebrew* (Subsidia Biblica, 14; 2 vols.; Rome: Pontifical Biblical Institute, 1993).
Kaufmann, Y., *The Religion of Israel: From its Beginnings to the Babylonian Exile* (trans. M. Greenberg; Chicago: Chicago University Press, 1960; rev. edn).
Kautzsch, E., *Aramaismen im alten Testament* (Halle: Niemeyer, 1902).
Kautzsch, E. (ed.), *Gesenius' Hebrew Grammar* (revised and trans. A.E. Cowley; Oxford: Clarendon Press, 1910).
Keet, C., *A Study of the Psalms of Ascents: A Critical and Exegetical Commentary Upon Psalms CXX to CXXIV* (Greenwood: Attic, 1969).
Kissane, E., *The Book of Isaiah* (Dublin: Brown and Nolan, 1960; rev. edn).
Kittel, Bonnie, *The Hymns of Qumran* (SBLDS, 50; Missoula, MT: Scholars Press, 1981).
Klein, R., 'Chronicles, Book of 1–2', *ABD*, I (New York: Doubleday, 1992), pp. 992–1002.
—'Ezra-Nehemiah, Books of', *ABD*, II (New York: Doubleday, 1992), pp. 731–42.
Koehler, Ludwig and Walter Baumgartner, *Hebräische und Armamäische Lexikon zum Alten Testament* (6 vols.; Leiden: E.J. Brill, 1967-).
—*Lexicon in Veteris Testamenti Libros*, Leiden: E.J. Brill, 1985).

Kraus, H.-J., *Geschichte der historisch-kritischen Erforschung des Alten Testaments* (Neukirchen-Vluyn: Neukirchener Verlag, 1969).

Kropat, Arno, *Die Syntax des Autors der Chronik* (BZAW, 16; Gießen: Alfred Töpelman, 1909).

Kutscher, E.Y. 'Hebrew Language, DSS', *EncJud*, XVI (Jerusalem: Keter, 1972), columns 1584–90.

—'Hebrew Language, Mishnaic Hebrew', *EncJud*, XVI (Jerusalem: Keter, 1972), columns 1590–1607.

—*The Language and Linguistic Background of the Isaiah Scoll (1QIs^a)* (Studies on the Texts of the Desert of Judah, 6; Leiden: E.J. Brill, 1974).

—*Hebrew and Aramaic Studies* (ed. Z. Ben-Hayyim *et al.*; Jerusalem: Magnes Press, 1977).

—*A History of the Hebrew Language* (ed. Raphael Kutscher; Jerusalem, 1982).

Lamarches, P., *Zacharies IX-XIV. Structure Lettéraire et Messianisme* (Paris: Gabalda, 1961).

LaSor, W., *Handbook of Biblical Hebrew* (2 vols.; Grand Rapids, MI: Eerdmans, 1979).

Lemche, Niels P., 'The Old Testament – A Hellenistic Book?' *SJOT* 7 (1994) pp. 163–93.

Lemke, Werner, 'The Synoptic Problem in the Chronicler's History', *HTR* (1965), pp.349–63.

Lieberman, Stephen, 'Response', in Herbert Paper (ed.), *Jewish Languages: Theme and Variations* (Cambridge, MA: Association for Jewish Studies, 1978), pp. 21–28.

Lindenberger, J., *Ancient Aramaic and Hebrew Letters* (Society for Biblical Literature Writings from the Ancient World Series, 4; Atlanta, GA: Scholars Press, 1994).

Loader, J.A. *Polar Structures in the Book of Qohelet* (BZAW, 152; Berlin: De Gruyter, 1979).

Löhr, M., 'Der Sprachgebrauch des Buches der Klagelieder', *ZAW* 14 (1894), pp.31–50.

Lundbom, J., 'Jeremiah, Book of', *ABD*, II (New York: Doubleday, 1992), pp. 706–21.

Magonet, J., 'Jonah, Book of', *ABD*, III (New York: Doubleday, 1992), pp. 936–42.

McCarter, P. Kyle, *1 Samuel* (AB; Garden City, NY: Doubleday, 1980).

—*2 Samuel* (AB; Garden City, NY: Doubleday, 1984).

McKenzie, S., *The Chronicler's Use of the Deuteronomistic History* (HSM; Cambridge, MA: Harvard University, 1985).

—'Deuteronomistic History', *ABD*, II (New York: Doubleday, 1992), pp. 160–68.

Meinhold, A., 'Die Gattung der Josephgeschichte und des Estherbuches: Diasporanovelle', *ZAW* 88 (1975/76), pp. 306–24.

Mendenhall, George, 'The Shady Side of Wisdom: The Date and Purpose of Genesis 3', in H.N. Bream *et al.* (eds.), *A Light Unto My Path. Studies in Honor of Jacob M. Myers* (Philadelphia: Temple University Press, 1974), pp. 319–34.

Meyers, C. and E. Meyers, 'Haggai, Book of', *ABD*, III (New York: Doubleday, 1992), pp. 20–23.

Meyers, J., *Ezra, Nehemiah* (AB; Garden City, NY: Doubleday, 1965).

Milgrom, Jacob, *Studies in Levitical Terminology* (Berkeley: University of California, 1970).

—Review of A. Hurvitz, *A Linguistic Study of the Relationship Between the Priestly Source and the Book of Ezekiel*, *CBQ* 46 (1984), pp.118–19.

Millar, William. 'Isaiah, Book of (Chaps. 24–27)', *ABD*, III (New York: Doubleday, 1992), pp. 488–90.

—*Isaiah 24–27 and the Origin of the Apocalyptic* (HSM, 11; Missoula, MT: Scholars Press, 1976).

Mitchell, Hinckley G.T., John M.O. Smith, and Julius A. Bewer, *A Critical and Exegetical*

Commentary on Haggai, Zechariah, Malachi and Jonah (ICC; Edinburgh: T. & T. Clark, 1912).

Montgomery, J., *A Critical and Exegetical Commentary on the Book of Daniel* (ICC; Edinburgh: T. & T. Clark, 1927).

Moore, C., *Esther* (AB; Garden City, NY: Doubleday, 1971).

—'Esther, Book of', *ABD*, II (New York: Doubleday, 1992. 633–43.

Morag, S., 'Qumran Hebrew: Some Typological Observations', *VT* 38 (1988), pp.148–64.

Morgenstern, J., 'The Mythological Background of Psalm 82', *HUCA* 14 (1939), pp.93–94.

Mowinckel, S., 'Some Remarks on Hodayot 39.5–20 1QH5', *JBL* 75 (1956), p. 266.

Murphy, R. 'Song of Songs, Book of', *ABD*, VI (New York: Doubleday, 1992), pp. 150–55.

Myers, L.M. *The Roots and Modern English* (Boston: Little Brown and Company, 1966).

Naudé, Jacobus, 'The Transitions of Biblical Hebrew in the Perspective of Language Change and Diffusion', in Ian Young (ed.), *Biblical Hebrew: Studies in Chronology and Typology* (London: T. & T. Clark, 2003), pp. 189–214.

Naveh, J. 'Hebrew and Aramaic Inscriptions', in D.T. Ariel (ed.) *Excavations at the City of David 1978–1985 Directed by Yigal Shiloh*, VI, *Inscriptions* (Qedem, 41; Jerusalem: Hebrew University, 2000).

Naveh, J., and J. Greenfield. 'Hebrew and Aramaic in the Persian Period' in W.D. Davies and Louis Finkelstein (eds.) *The Cambridge History of Judaism*, I, *Introduction to the Persian Period* (ed. W.D. Davies and Louis Finkelstein; Cambridge: Cambridge University Press, 1984), pp. 115–29.

Newsom, Carol, *Songs of the Sabbath Sacrifice: A Critical Edition* (Harvard Semitic Studies, 27; Atlanta, GA: Scholars Press, 1985).

Nicholson, R., *Deuteronomy and Tradition* (Philadelphia: Fortress Press, 1967).

Noegel, S.B., 'Dialect and Politics in Isaiah 24–27', *Aula Orientalis* 12 (1994), pp.177–92.

Noth, Martin, *A History of Pentateuchal Traditions* (trans. B. Anderson; repr., Chico, CA: Scholars Press, 1981).

—*The Deuteronistic History* (JSOTSup, 15; Sheffield, England: JSOT press, 1981).

Ólaffson, S., 'Late Biblical Hebrew: Fact or Fiction?' in Z. Kapera (ed.), *Intertestamental Essays in Honour of Józof Tadeusz Milik* (Krakow: Enigma Press, 1992), pp. 135–47.

Orlinsky, Harry. 'The Origin of the Kethib-Qere System: A New Approach', *Congress Volume: Oxford, 1959* (VTSup, 7; Leiden: E.J. Brill, 1960), pp. 184–209.

Oswalt, John, *The Book of Isaiah Chapters 1–39* (NICOT; Grand Rapids, MI: Eerdmans, 1986).

Otzen, B., *Studien über Deuterosacharja* (Acta Theologica Danica, 6; Copenhagen: Prostant apud Munksgaard, 1964).

Pardee, D., *Handbook of Ancient Hebrew Letters* (SBLSBS, 15; Chico, CA: Scholars Press, 1982).

Paton, L., *A Critical and Exegetical Commentary on the Book of Esther* (ICC; Edinburgh: T. & T. Clark, 1908).

Paul, S., *Amos* (Hermeneia; Minneapolis, MN: Frotress Press, 1991).

Perlitt, L., *Bundestheologie im Alten Testament* (Neukirchen-Vluyn: Neukirchener Verlag, 1969).

Peterson, D., *Zechariah 9–14 and Malachi. A Commentary* (OTL; Lousville, KY: Westminster/John Knox Press, 1990).

—'Zechariah, Book of', *ABD*, VI (New York: Doubleday, 1992), pp. 1061–68.

Polzin, Robert, *Late Biblical Hebrew: Toward an Historical Typology of Biblical Hebrew Prose* (HSM, 12; Missoula, MT: Scholars Press, 1976).

Pope, Marvin, *Job* (AB; Garden City, NY: Doubleday, 1973).

—*Song of Songs* (AB; Garden City, NY: Doubleday, 1977).

Preuss, R., 'Der zeitgeschichtliche Hintergrund der Wallfahrtpsalmen', *Theologische Zeitschrift* 14 (1958), pp. 401–15.

Pury, Albert de, 'Yahwist ("J") Source', *ABD*, VI (New York: Doubleday, 1992), pp. 1012–20.

Qimron, Elisha, 'Li-Lshon Bayit Sheni be-Sefer Tehillim', *Bet Mikra* 23 (1978), pp.139–150 (Hebrew).

—'Leshono shel Sefer Yonah ke-Madad li-Qviat Zemen Hibburo', *Bet Mikra* 81 (1980), pp.181–182 (Hebrew).

—*The Hebrew of the Dead Sea Scrolls* (HSS; Atlanta, GA: Scholars Press, 1986).

—'Consecutive and Conjunctive Imperfect: the Form of the Imperfect with *Waw* in Biblical Hebrew', *JQR* 77 (1986–1987), pp.149–161.

—'Observations on the History of Early Hebrew (1000 BCE-200 CE) in the Light of the Dead Sea Documents', in D. Dimand and U. Rappaport (eds.), *The Dead Sea Scrolls: Forty Years of Research* (Leiden: E.J. Brill, 1992), pp. 349–61.

Rabin, Chaim, 'The Historical Background of Qumran Hebrew', *Scripta Hierosolymitana* 4 (1958), pp. 144–61.

—'Hebrew', *Current Trends in Linguistics,* VI (ed. T. Sebeok; The Hague: Moulton, 1970), pp. 304–346.

—'Hebrew and Aramaic in the First Century'. in S. Safrai and M. Stern (eds.), *The Jewish People in the First Century: Historical Geography, Political History, Social, Cultural and Religious Life and Institutions*, Compendia Rerum Iudicarum ad Novum Testamentum, II (Philadelphia: Fortress Press, 1976), pp. 1007–39.

Rad, Gerhard von, *Genesis: A Commentary* (trans. J. Marks; Philadelphia, PA: Westminster, 1972; rev. edn).

—*The Problem of the Hexateuch and Other Essays* (trans. E.W. Trueman Dicken; London: SCM Press, 1966).

Rainey, Anson, 'The Ancient Hebrew Prefix Conjugation in the Light of Amarnah Canaanite', *Hebrew Studies* 27 (1986), pp.4–19.

—'Further Remarks on the Hebrew Verbal System', *Hebrew Studies* 29 (1988), pp.35–42.

Ratner, R., 'Morphological Variation in Biblical Hebrew Rhetoric', *Maarav* 8 (1992), pp. 143–59.

Redford, Donald, *A Study of the Biblical Story of Joseph (Genesis 37–50)* (VTSup, 20. Leiden: E.J. Brill, 1970).

Rendsburg, Gary, 'Hebrew *'šdt* and Ugaritic *išdym*', *JNSL* 8 (1980), pp. 81–84.

—'Late Biblical Hebrew and the Date of "P" ', *JANESCU* 12 (1980), pp. 6 5–80.

—'Dual Personal Pronouns and Dual Verbs in Hebrew', *JQR* 73.1 (1982), pp. 38–58.

—'David and His Circle in Genesis XXXVIII', *VT* 36 (1986), pp. 438–46.

—*The Redaction of Genesis* (Winona Lake, IN: Eisenbrauns, 1986).

—'Eblaite *Ù-MA* and Hebrew *WM*-', in C.H. Gordon and G.A. Rendsburg (eds.), *Eblaitica*, I (Winona Lake, IN: Eisenbrauns, 1987), pp. 33–41.

—*Diglossia in Ancient Hebrew* (AOS, 72; New Haven, CT: American Oriental Society, 1990).

—*Linguistic Evidence for the Northern Origin of Selected Psalms* (SBLMS, 43. Atlanta, GA: Scholars Press, 1990).

174 Linguistic Evidence for the Pre-exilic Date of the Yahwistic Source

—'The Strata of Biblical Hebrew', *JNSL* 17 (1991), pp.81–99.

—'Israelian Hebrew Features in Genesis 49', *Maarav* 8 (1992), pp.161–170.

—'Morphological Evidence for Regional Dialects in Ancient Hebrew' in W. Bodine *Linguistics and Biblical Hebrew* (Winona Lake, IN: Eisenbrauns, 1992), pp. 65–88.

—'Biblical Literature as Politics: The Case of Genesis', in A. Berlin (ed.), *Religion and Politics in the Ancient Near East* (Bethesda, MD: University Press of Maryland, 1996), pp. 47–70.

—'Linguistic Variation and the "Foreign" Factor in the Hebrew Bible', in S. Izre'el and R. Drory (eds.), *Language and Culture in the Near East* (Israel Oriental Studies,15; Leiden: E.J. Brill, 1996), pp. 177–90.

—*Israelian Hebrew in the Book of Kings* (Occasional Publications of the Department of Near Eastern Studies and the Program of Jewish Studies, Cornell University, 5; Bethesda, Maryland: CDL Press, 2002).

Rendtorff, R., *Das überlieferungsgeschichtliche Problem des Pentateuch* (BZAW, 147; Berlin: Walter de Gruyter, 1977).

Revell, E., 'The Two Forms of First Person Singular Pronoun in Biblical Hebrew: Redundancy or Expressive Contrast?', *JSS* 40 (1955), pp.199–217.

—'Stress and the "*Waw* Consecutive" in Biblical Hebrew', *JAOS* 104 (1984), pp.437–44.

—'First Person Imperfect Forms with *Waw* Consecutive', *VT* 38 (1988), pp. 419–26.

Rezetko, Robert, 'Dating Biblical Hebrew: Evidence from Samuel-Kings and Chronicles', in Ian Young (ed.), *Biblical Hebrew: Studies in Chronology and Typology* (London: T. & T. Clark, 2003), pp. 214–50.

Rooker, Mark, 'The Diachronic Study of Biblical Hebrew', *JNSL* 14 (1988), pp. 199–214.

—*Biblical Hebrew in Transition: The Language of the Book of Ezekiel* (JSOTSup, 90. Sheffield, England: JSOT Press, 1990).

—'Ezekiel and the Typology of Biblical Hebrew', *HAR* 12 (1990), pp. 133–155.

—'Dating Isaiah 40–66: What Does the Linguistic Evidence Say?' *WTJ* (1996), 58 pp. 303–312.

Rose, M., *Deuteronomist und Jahwist* (ATANT, 67. Zürich: W. de Gruyter, 1981).

—'La croissance du corpus historiographique de la Bible - une proposition', *RTP* 118 (1986), pp. 217–26.

Rosenthal, F., *A Grammar of Biblical Aramaic*, (Wiesbaden: Otto Harrassowitz, 1995; 6th edn).

Rudolph, W. 'Der Text der Klagelieder', *ZAW* 56 (1938), pp. 101–22.

Sáenz-Badillos, A., *A History of the Hebrew Language* (trans. John Elwolde; Cambridge: Cambridge Univerty, 1993).

Sanders, J.A., *The Psalms Scroll of Qumrân Cave 11* (Oxford: Clarendon Press, 1965).

Sarna, Nahum, 'Genesis, Book of', *EncJud*, VII (Jerusalem: Keter, 1972), columns 386–98.

—Review of *In Search of History*, by J. van Seters, *BARev* 3 (1977), pp. 5–9.

—'Exodus, Book of', *ABD*, II (New York: Doubleday, 1992), pp. 689–700.

Sasson, J., *Jonah* (AB; Garden City, NY: Doubleday, 1990).

Schmid, H., *Der sogennante Jahwist* (Zürich: Theologischer Verlag, 1976).

Schmitt, Hans-Christoph, *Die nichtpriesterliche Josephsgeschichte* (BZAW, 154; Berlin: Walter de Gruyter, 1980).

Schoors, A., *The Preacher Sought to Find Pleasing Words: A Study of the Language of Qoheleth* (Orientalia Lovaniensa Analecta, 41; Leuven: Peeters, 1992).

Scott, R., *Proverbs, Ecclesiastes* (AB; Garden City, NY: Doubleday, 1965).

Scullion, J. 'Genesis, the Narrative of', *ABD*, IV (New York: Doubleday, 1992), pp. 1146–55.

Segal, M.H. 'Mishnaic Hebrew and its Relation to Biblical Hebrew and to Aramic', *JQR* 20 (1908), pp.647–737.

—*A Grammar of Mishnaic Hebrew* (Oxford: Clarendon Press, 1927).

Seitz, C. 'Isaiah, Book of (Third Isaiah)', *ABD*, III (New York: Doubleday, 1992), pp. 501– 507.

Seow, C.L. 'Linguistic Evidence and the Dating of Qohelet', *JBL* 115 (1996), pp. 643–66.

—*Ecclesiastes* (AB; New York: Doubleday, 1997).

Seybold, K., *Die Wallfahrtpsalms: Studien zu Entstehungsgeschichte von Psalm 120–134* (Neukirchen-Vluyn: Neukirchener Verlag, 1978).

Skinner, *Genesis* (ICC: Edinburgh: T & T. Clark, 1930).

Smend, R., 'Das Gesetz und die Völker. Ein Beitrag zur deuteronomistischen Redaktionsgeschichte' in H. Wolff (ed.), *Probleme biblischer Theologie* (G. von Rad Festschrift; Munich: Chron. Kaiser Verlag, 1971), pp. 494–509.

Smith, M., *The Origins and Development of the Waw-consecutive* (HSS, 39; Atlanta, GA: Scholars Press, 1991).

Speiser, *Genesis* (AB; Garden City, NY: Doubleday, 1964).

Sperber, Alexander, *The Bible in Aramaic*, I, *The Pentateuch According to Targum Onqelos* (Leiden: Brill, 1959).

—*A Historical Grammar of Biblical Hebrew* (Leiden, 1966).

Stade, B., 'Deuterosacharja: Eine kritische Studie', *ZAW* 2 (1882), pp. 275–309.

Sternberg, M., *The Poetics of Biblical Narrative: Ideological Literature and the Drama of Reading* (Bloomington, IN: Indiana University Press, 1985).

Striedl, H., 'Untersuchung zur Syntax und Stilistik des hebräischen Buches Esther', *ZAW* 55 (1937), pp. 73–108.

Talshir, David, 'The Habitat and History of Hebrew During the Second Temple Period', Ian Young (ed.), *Biblical Hebrew: Studies in Chronology and Typology* (London: T. & T. Clark, 2003), pp. 251–75.

Thompson, J.A., *The Book of Jeremiah* (NICOT; Grand Rapids, MI: Eerdmans, 1980).

Thompson, Thomas L., *The Historicity of the Patriarchal Narratives* (Berlin: de Gruyter, 1974).

—*Early History of the Israelite People from the Written and Archeological Sources* (Leiden: E.J. Brill, 1992).

Tigay, Jeffrey, 'An Empirical Basis for the Documentary Hypothesis', *JBL* 94 (1975), pp.329–41.

—*The Evolution of the Gilgamesh Epic* (Philadelphia: University of Pennsylvania Press, 1982).

Torczyner, H., *Lachish*, I, *Lachish Letters* (London: Oxford University Press, 1938).

Tov, Emmanuel (ed.), *Dead Sea Scrolls on Microfiche* (Leiden: E.J. Brill, 1993; Fiche).

Trible, P., 'Ruth, Book of', *ABD*, V (New York: Doubleday, 1992), pp. 842–47.

Van Seters, John, *Abraham in History and Tradition* (New Haven, CT: Yale University Press, 1975).

—*In Search of History* (New Haven, CT: Yale University Press, 1983).

—'The Yahwist as Historian' (SBLSP, 25; Atlanta: Scholars Press, 1986), pp. 37–55.

—*Prologue to History: The Yahwist as Historian in Genesis* (Lousiville, KY: Westminster/ John Knox Press, 1992).

—*The Life of Moses: The Yahwist as Historian in Exodus-Numbers* (Louisville, KY: Westminster/John Knox Press, 1994).

Verhoef, P., *The Books of Haggai and Malachi* (NICOT; Grand Rapids, MI: Eerdmans, 1987).

Vorländer, H., *Die Enstehengszeit des jehowistischen Geschichtswerkes* (Frankfurt: Peter Lang, 1978).

Wagner, N.E., 'A Literary Analysis of Genesis 12–36' (unpublished doctoral dissertation; University of Toronto, 1965).

—'Abraham and David?', in J.W. Wevers and D.B. Refford (eds.), *Studies on the Ancient Palestinian World Presented to Professor F.V. Winnett* (Toronto: University of Toronto, 1972), pp. 117–40.

Waltke, Bruce and M. O'Connor, *An Introduction to Biblical Hebrew Syntax* (Winona Lake, IN: Eisenbrauns, 1990).

Weinfeld, Moshe, *Deuteronomy and the Deuteronomic School* (Oxford: Clarendon Press, 1972).

—'Pentateuch', *EncJud*, XII (Jerusalem: Keter, 1972), columns 232–61.

—'Deuteronomy, Book of', *ABD*, II (New York: Doubleday, 1992), pp. 168–83.

Wellhausen, Julius, *Die Composition des Hexateuchs und der historischen Bücher des Alten Testaments* (Berlin: W. de Gruyter, 1899).

—*Prologomena to the History of Ancient Israel* (New York: Meridian Books, 1957; repr., Edinburgh: A. and C. Black, 1885).

Westermann, C., *Isaiah 40–66* (OTL; Philadelphia: Westminster Press, 1969).

Williamson, H. *Ezra, Nehemiah* (Word Biblical Commentary, 16; Waco, TX: Word Books, 1985).

Winnett, Frederick, 'Re-Examining the Foundations', *JBL* 84 (1965), pp.1–19.

—'The Arabian Genealogies in the Book of Genesis' in Harry Frank and William Reed (eds.), *Translating And Understanding the Old Testament: Essays in Honor of Herbert Gordon May* (Nashville, TN: Abingdon Press, 1970), pp. 171–96.

Wolff, H., *Dodekapropheten 3. Obadja und Jona* (BKAT, XIV/3; Neukirchen-Vluyn: Neukirchener Verlag, 1977).

—*Joel and Amos* (Hermeneia; Philadelphia: Fortress, Press, 1977).

Wright, Richard M., 'Further Evidence for North Israelite Contributions to Late Biblical Hebrew', in Ian Young (ed.), *Biblical Hebrew: Studies in Chronology and Typology* (London: T. & T. Clark, 2003), pp. 129–48.

Yadin, Y., *The Temple Scroll*, II (Jerusalem: Israel Exploration Society, 1983).

Young, G.D., 'The Origin of the Waw Conversive', *JNES* 12 (1953), pp. 248–52.

Young, Ian, *Diversity in Pre-Exilic Hebrew* (Forschungen zum Alten Testament; Tübingen: J.C.B. Mohr, 1993).

—'Late Biblical Hebrew in Hebrew Inscriptions', in Ian Young (ed.), *Biblical Hebrew: Studies in Chronology and Typology* (London: T. & T. Clark, 2003), pp. 276–311.

Zevit, Ziony, *Matres Lectionis In Ancient Hebrew Epigraphs* (American Schools of Oriental Research Monograph Series, 2; Cambridge, MA: American Schools of Oriental Research, 1980).

—'Converging Lines of Evidence Bearing on the Date of P', *ZAW* 94 (1982), pp. 481–511.

—'Clio, I Presume', review of *In Search of History* by J. van Seters, *BASOR* 260 (1985), pp. 71–82.

—'Review of Ian Young (ed.) *Biblical Hebrew*. (*http://www.bookreviews.org/pdf/4084_3967.pdf*), pp. 8–9.

Zimmerli, W., *Ezekiel*, I (Hermeneia; Philadelphia: Fortress Press, 1979), pp. 593–71.

Index of References

Genesis – continued

10.24	122
10.25–30	20
11.1–9	20
11.2	44
11.9	41
11.12	30
11.14	30
11.28–30	20
11.29	74, 106
12–36	163
12–26	2
12.1–4a	20
12.1	41
12.2	41
12.4b–5	122
12.6–8	20
12.8	100
12.9	122
12.15	108
13.1–2	122
13.3–4	122
13.3	46, 127
13.5	122
13.6b	122
13.7–11a	20
13.7	46
13.9	41
13.10	89
13.12a	122
13.12b	122
13.13–18	20
13.14	89, 100
13.15	41, 71
13.17	41, 71
15	122
15.1a	122
15.1b–2	122
15.1	128
15.2	128, 133
15.3a	122
15.3b	122
15.4	122, 126
15.6–12	122
15.7	126, 128
15.8	126
15.10	125

15.11	125
15.13–15	122
15.13	125, 126
15.14	128
15.17a–18	122
15.19–21	122
16.1b–2	20
16.4–8	20
16.5	82
16.9–10	122
16.11–14	20
17.21	117
18.1–33	20
18.2	89
18.5	41, 106
18.6	84
18.7	84, 106
18.8	107
18.9	77
18.13	82
18.14	119
18.15	86
18.16	29
18.17	82
18.19	41
18.21	41
18.27	82
19.1–28	20
19.4	103
19.5	41
19.8	41
19.14	106
19.15	55, 106
19.17	44, 55
19.19	41, 55, 82
19.21	55
19.30–35	20
19.30	86
19.34	41
19.36–38	122
20.1a	122
20.3	72
20.18	122
21.1a	122
21.1b	122
21.2	132
21.2a	122

Genesis – continued			
27.7b–14	122	29.3	95
27.8	128	29.6	78
27.9	106, 125	29.7	95
27.10	126	29.9	29
27.12	126	29.13	44
27.13	106	29.15–23	122
27.14	106	29.15	126
27.15	106	29.18	126
27.16–18a	122	29.23	125
27.18b–20	20	29.24	122
27.19	41, 82	29.25	122, 126
27.20	83, 84	29.26	20
27.21–33	122	29.27–28	122
27.23	126	29.29	122
27.24–27	20	29.30	20, 122
27.24	82	29.31–35	122
27.25	41	29.32	126
27.27	41	29.33	128
27.28	122	29.35	61, 64
27.29–30	20	30.2b–3a	122
27.29	41	30.2	128
27.31a	122	30.3	128
27.31b–34	20	30.3b	122
27.31	41	30.4–5	122
27.32	82	30.7	122
27.33	26	30.8	122
27.34	41, 45, 82	30.9–16	122
27.35	105, 106	30.9	125
27.35–45	122	30.13	126
27.36	106	30.14	125
27.37	126	30.16	126
27.38	126, 128	30.20	125, 126
27.41	126	30.20a	122
27.45	106, 126	30.20b	122
28.1	72	30.21	122
28.6	72, 87	30.22b–23a	122
28.10	122	30.24	122
28.13–16	20	30.25–26	122
28.13	41, 82	30.25	126
28.14	100	30.26	125
28.15	41, 82	30.27	20
28.16	82	30.28a	122
28.19a	20	30.28b	122
28.21b	122	30.29–30	122
29.1	122	30.30	125, 128
29.2–14	20	30.31a	20
		30.24–38a	20

Genesis – continued	
34.21	72
34.26	20
34.30–31	20
34.30	41, 82
34.34	123
34.35a	123
35.5	123
35.12	126
35.14	123
35.16–20	123
35.17	126
35.18	126
35.21–22a	20
35.22	44
35.22b	123
36.2b–5	123
36.2	72
36.9–31	123
36.32–39	123
37–50	3, 163
37.2b	123
37.3a	123
37.3b	123
37.4	123, 125
37.5–11	123
37.7	89
37.8	131
37.9	125
37.10	128
37.12–13a	20
37.13	41
37.13b	123
37.14b	20
37.14	41
37.15–18a	123
37.16	128
37.18	41
37.18b	20
37.19–20	123
37.20	126
37.21	20, 41
37.25b–27	20
37.25	89
37.27	41
37.28a	123
37.28b	20

37.28	44
37.31	123
37.32a	123
37.32b–33a	123
37.33	126
37.34	123
37.35	123, 125
38	8
38.1–30	20
38.2	106
38.6	106
38.8	41
38.10	41
38.17	82
38.20	106
38.22	41
38.23	41, 106
38.24	41
38.25	82
38.26	41
38.28	106
39.1–5	20
39.1	41
39.4	41
39.6a	123
39.6b	20
39.7a	123
39.7b–23	20
39.7	89
39.10	50, 51
39.9	41
39.10	44
39.13	44
39.14	26
39.15	26, 44
39.18	26, 44
39.19	44
39.20	41, 106
40.1	20
40.3	125
40.3a	123
40.5	123
40.15	125
40.15a	123
40.15b	123
41.11	24
41.14a	123

Genesis – continued	
48.9	126
48.9b–10a	123
48.13	123
48.19	123
49	93, 130, 142
49.1b–24a	123
49.2	130
49.4	129
49.6	75
49.7	126
48.8	126
49.9	126
49.10	142
49.19	126
49.24b–27	123
49.25	126
49.26	128
49.28a	123
49.33b	123
49.6	92
50.1–10a	20
50.10b	123
50.5	41, 128
50.6	41
50.14	20
50.18	123
50.21	123, 125, 128
50.24	123, 125, 128
Exodus	
1.6	123
1.8–12	123
1.12	125
1.14a	123
1.20b	123
1.22	123, 126
2.1–10	123
2.2	125
2.9	126
2.10	126
2.11–22	123
2.14	126
2.18	83, 84
2.19	126
2.23a	123
3.1	123

3.2–4a	123
3.5	123
3.7–8	20
3.8	26
3.9a	123
3.14	123, 126
3.15	49
3.16–18	20
3.16	41, 95
3.17	26, 41
3.18	97
3.19–20	123
3.19	125
3.20	125
3.21–22	123
4.1–9	20
4.3	41
4.5	26
4.9	106
4.10–16	123
4.10	128
4.11	128
4.12	128
4.12	126
4.14	126
4.15	125, 128
4.18	123
4.19–20a	20
4.20	106
4.20b	123
4.21	123, 126
4.22–26	20
4.23	26, 41, 82
4.25	106
4.26	85
4.27–28	123
4.28	126
4.29	20
4.30a	123
4.30b–31	20
5.1–2	123
5.3	20, 41, 55, 97
5.4	123
5.5–23	20
5.5	29, 41
5.11	106
5.13	52

Jeremiah – continued		25.10	53
39.2	56	26.1	57
42.12	139	26.20	53
44.10	116	29.1	57
46.17	117	29.13	102
49.24	132	29.17	57
49.27	132	29.19	134
49.34	136	30.20	57
51.31	101	31.1	57
52.4	56	32.1	57
52.6	56	32.17	57
52.31	57	33.21	57
		33.22	45
Ezekiel		34.17	45
1.2	57	38.13	134
3.3	24	39.25	139
5.7	116	39.28	92, 94
6.14	26	40.1	57
7.2	102	41.12	96
8.1	57	41.18	45
8.3	46	42.4	95, 96
8.16	46	42.20	45
9.8	24	44.22	73
11.17	93, 94	45.18	57
13.6	32	45.20	57
14.4	50	45.21	57
14.7	50	45.25	57
14.10–11	54	47.9	30
14.11	53	47.16	46
16.1	24	48.22	46
16.8	44		
16.30	109	*Hosea*	
18.13	30	1.6	139, 140
18.23	31	1.7	139
18.24	30	2.6	139
19.9	53, 54	2.25	139
19.11	141	9.5	117
20.1	57, 65	10.12	66
20.3	65		
20.11	30	*Joel*	
20.13	30	2.13	138
20.21	30	2.17	45
22.20	93	2.20	101
22.21	92	2.26	62
22.25	90		
22.26	45	*Amos*	
24.1	57	6.8	110

Psalms – continued

63.4	106	103.12	98
68.27	61	103.13	139
69.12	24	103.19	136
69.13	50	103.20	61
69.21	24	103.21	61, 75
69.31	61	103.22	61
72	13	104	13
72.3	78	104.1	61
72.17	63	104.19	99
72.18	59, 61	104.33	61
72.19	60	104.35	61
73.16	24	105.1	61
74.21	62	105.2	61
75	13, 98, 151	105.31	61
75.7	98, 151	106	13, 59
77	68	106.1	61
77.6	69, 150	106.23	53
77.8	69, 150	106.31	50
77.9	50	106.47	62
78.9	91	106.48	59, 61, 63
78.34	64	107	13, 98
79.13	107	107.1	61
84.3	111	107.3	98
85.6	50	107.8	61
86.12	62	107.15	61
86.15	138	108.4	61
87.5	50	109	13
89.2	50	109.30	61
89.5	50	110.7	88
89.53	59, 63	111	13, 138
90.10	24	111.1	61
92.2	61	111.4	138
96.1	61	112	13, 138
96.2	61, 63	112.1	61
96.6	137	112.4	138
98.1	61	113	13
98.5	61	113.1	61, 62
99.3	62	113.2	60
100.4	63	113.3	99
101.1	61	115.18	61
102.13	50	116.19	61
102.14	139	117	13
103	13, 139	117.1	61, 106
103.1	61, 62	117.2	61
103.3–5	138	118.29	61
103.8	138	119	13, 24
		119.11	54

Proverbs – continued	
26.23	14
27.13	52
27.24	50

Ruth	
2.7	13
4.5	14
4.7	13
4.14	59

Song of Songs	
6.11	114

Qohelet	
1.10	69
2.5	114
2.8	92
2.19	108, 109
2.26	92
3.1	113, 117
3.2–9	117
3.5	92
3.11	101
4.2	106, 108
4.8	102
4.13	114
5.18	109
6.2	109
6.6	31
6.11	113
7.2	101
7.19	109
8.4	109
8.8	109
8.9	108, 109
8.10	84
8.11	114, 119
8.15	35, 36, 106, 108
9.18	91
10.5	109
12.12	36
12.13	101, 102

Lamentations	
2.7	117
3.1	141

5.19	50

Esther	
1.3–4	90
1.3	114
1.4	90, 136
1.6	114
1.8	35, 50, 75, 113, 115
1.13	113, 115
1.15	113, 115
1.19	113, 115, 116
1.20	90, 91, 114, 119
1.22	50
2.1	87
2.3	93
2.8	93, 113, 115
2.9	83
2.10	87
2.11	50
2.12	113, 115
2.15	115
2.19	93
3.8	113, 115, 116
3.9	56, 113
3.11	76
3.12	50, 56, 57
3.13	134
3.14	113, 114, 115, 116, 117
3.15	113
3.17	113
4.3	113, 115
4.4	104
4.7	113
4.8	113, 114, 115
4.11	31, 113, 116, 141
4.16	84, 92, 113, 115
5.2	141
6.3	90
6.6	90, 115
6.7	90
6.9	90, 114, 115
6.11	90
6.13	115
6.14	83
6.16	115
7.6	85, 86
7.25	115

2 Chronicles – continued	
28.14	134
28.23	132
28.25	50
29.10	61
29.16	104
29.17	57
29.22	104
29.30	61
30.9	138
30.15	57
30.17	36
30.19	66
30.21	61
31.3	118
31.8	61
32.30	98
33.8	116
33.14	98
34.21	62
35.1	57
35.21	83

Deuterocanonicals and Apocypha

Daniel

3.52 (Greek)	70

Tobit

8.5 (B, A)	63
8.5 (S)	70
8.15 (B, A)	70
8.15 (S)	70
11.14	70
13.4	70
13.4 (B, A)	70
13.17	70
13.18 (B, A)	70

Ben Sira

5.11 (A)	120
5.22 (B)	76
7.23	73
8.9 (A)	120
8.18	102
15.2	105
15.20 (B)	140
36.17 (B)	140

36.18 (B)	140
37.6	135
38.8	55
42.4	47
43.7	118
43.27	103
44.(title) (B)	107
45.26	55
46.20	103
50.8	118
50.22 (B)	76
51.14 (B)	107
51.23 (B)	66
51.30 (B)	107

Extracanonical Psalms

150	47

Targums

1 Sam.

2.35	76

2 Sam.

22.50	107
24.4	120

Isa.

12.5	107
14.7	107
25.8	70

Jer.

31.20	140

Hosea

1.6	140

Micah

7.18	70

Pss.

20.9	88
27.13	53
41.14	63
44.5	70
84.3	111
110.7	88

Gezer Tablet
1	93

Masada ShirShabb
1.3–4	119

Murabba'at
24 2 14	102
24 B16	51
24 C18	51
42.5	53
45.9	102

Panammu
13	99

Palmyra inscriptions
C4002.1	63

Rabbinic Texts
Mishnah
'Avot
2.4	76
5.4	51
5.7	83
5.19	47
5.22(20)	76

Baba Batra
3.1	94
8.5	34
9.7	33

Baba Meṣi'a
19(10).4	118

Berakhot
1.2	47
2.1	118
2.2	105
4.4	59
6.6	51
8.1	74

'Eduyyot
1.3	33
2.9	101

Ketuvot
7.6	116
13.11	74

Kil'ayim
3.3	102

Ma'aser Sheni
1.7	35
3.5	99
5.2	96
5.13	88

Megillah
1.9	47
3.5	119
3.7(5)	58

Menaḥot
10.4	110

Middot
1.2	78
3.1	47

Nedarim
5.5	47

Nedarim
8.7	35

'Oholot
16.3	47

Pesaḥim
1.3	119
10.4	108
10.5	108
10.6	59

Rosh Hashanah
1.2(1)	58
1.9	96

Sanhedrin
2.8(5)	142
4.2	142
5.2	108
6.1	135

Shabbat
15.8	31

Shavu'ot
3.6	33, 34
4.8	94
4.13	138

Sheqalim
1.1	58
1.3	58
5.4	104
6.5	51
8.1	140

Soṭah
5.4	51

Ketuvot
7.6   116

Makkot
5.11   33

Ma'aserot
1.6   105

Pesaḥim
3(2).19   76
8.3   97

Rosh Hashanah
1.15   86

Shevi'it
3.10   88

Soṭah
4.7   134

Zebaḥm
1.11   104

Sifra Qedoshim
1.3 (4.87)   86

Talmud
Shabbat 62b   89

Peshitta
Isa.
42.10–12   107
Ps.
106.23   53

New Testament
Jude
1.25   70